HUMAN AGENCY
Language, Duty, and Value

HUMAN AGENCY
Language, Duty, and Value

Philosophical Essays in Honor of J. O. URMSON

Edited by JONATHAN DANCY,
J. M. E. MORAVCSIK, *and* C. C. W. TAYLOR

Stanford University Press   1988
Stanford, California

B
29
.H85
1988

Stanford University Press, Stanford, California
© 1988 by the Board of Trustees of the
Leland Stanford Junior University

Printed in the United States of America

CIP data appear at the end of the book

Preface

The fifty years of Jim Urmson's philosophical career, from pre-war undergraduate days in Oxford through the heyday of the post-war ordinary language movement to the present, have been a particularly eventful period in the history of philosophy, characterized by rapid and not always orderly developments in many directions and in many areas. Urmson has contributed seminally to many of these developments, notably in the philosophy of language, in ethics, where he has enlivened by his very personal style the Oxford tradition of historically based investigation of problems, and in aesthetics, where his pioneering application of philosophical techniques to musical theory has been particularly influential. The range of his contribution is attested by the bibliography of his writings included in this volume; its thematic unity is emphasized in the Introduction, while the depth of his influence is acknowledged by the contributors, who range from distinguished philosophers of his own generation to younger writers working in fields that he has helped to map out. All the essays, with the exception of Kendall Walton's paper, have been specially written for this volume.

One of the editors, Jonathan Dancy, was a pupil of Urmson's at Corpus Christi College, Oxford, and the others, C. C. W. Taylor and J. M. E. Moravcsik, were colleagues of many years' standing, respectively at Corpus Christi and at Stanford. All count it a privilege to have known and worked with him, and to offer this volume as a token, not merely of professional regard for an esteemed philosopher, but of personal affection for a dear friend.

The Editors

Contents

Contributors	ix
Introduction *J. M. E. Moravcsik*	1
Prichard and Knowledge *J. O. Urmson*	11

Part I: Theories of Language Use

Things Done with Words *Jennifer Hornsby*	27
Context-fixing Semantics for the Language of Action *Patrick Suppes and Colleen Crangle*	47
Mood and the Analysis of Non-declarative Sentences *Deirdre Wilson and Dan Sperber*	77

Part II: Duty and the Moral Life

Aristotle on Moral Luck *Anthony Kenny*	105
Urmson on Aristotle on Pleasure *C. C. W. Taylor*	120
The Perils of Friendship and Conceptions of the Self *J. M.E. Moravcsik*	133

Moral Subjects, Freedom, and Idiosyncrasy *David Heyd*	152
Supererogation and Moral Realism *Jonathan Dancy*	170
What Does Intuitionism Imply? *Bernard Williams*	189

Part III: Aesthetic Values and Valuations

Aesthetic Satisfaction *Bruce Vermazen*	201
Live Performances and Dead Composers: On the Ethics of Musical Interpretation *Peter Kivy*	219
The Presentation and Portrayal of Sound Patterns *Kendall L. Walton*	237
Sports and Art: Beginning Questions *Ted Cohen*	258
Philosophical Writings of J. O. Urmson	277
Notes	283
Index of Names	305

Contributors

Ted Cohen is Professor of Philosophy at the University of Chicago. He is the editor, with Paul Guyer, of *Essays in Kant's Aesthetics*, and the author of papers in the philosophy of art and of the forthcoming *Art and Other Intimacies: American Perspectives*.

Colleen Crangle is a Research Associate at Stanford University and the co-author of papers in semantics.

Jonathan Dancy is Senior Lecturer in Philosophy at the University of Keele and the author of *An Introduction to Contemporary Epistemology*, *Berkeley*, and papers in ethics and epistemology.

David Heyd is Senior Lecturer in Philosophy at the Hebrew University of Jerusalem. He is the author of *Supererogation* and papers in ethical theory.

Jennifer Hornsby is a Fellow of Corpus Christi College, Oxford. She is the author of *Actions* and papers in philosophy of language and philosophy of mind.

Anthony Kenny is Master of Balliol College, Oxford. His publications include *Action, Emotion and Will*; *Will, Freedom and Power*; *Freewill and Responsibility*; *The Aristotelian Ethics*; *Aristotle's Theory of the Will*; *Descartes*; *The Anatomy of the Soul*; *The Ivory Tower*; *Reason and Religion*; *The Heritage of Wisdom*; and numerous papers in philosophy of mind and history of philosophy.

Peter Kivy is Professor of Philosophy at Rutgers University and the author of *The Seventh Sense, The Corded Shell, Sound and Semblance*, and papers in aesthetics.

J. M. E. Moravcsik is Professor of Philosophy at Stanford University. He is the author of *Being and Meaning in the Sophist* and papers on Greek philosophy and philosophical logic, the editor of *Aristotle* and *Patterns in Plato's Thought*, and co-editor of *Plato on Beauty, Wisdom, and the Arts*.

Dan Sperber is Maître de Recherches at the Centre National de la Recherche Scientifique, Paris. He is the author of *Rethinking Symbolism, On Anthropological Knowledge*, and papers in anthropology. He is also co-author, with Deirdre Wilson, of *Relevance* and papers in pragmatic theory.

Patrick Suppes is Lucie Stern Professor of Philosophy at Stanford University. He is the author of *Probabilistic Metaphysics, Logique du probable, A Probabilistic Theory of Causality, Studies in the Methodology and Foundations of Science*, and numerous papers in philosophy of science, mathematical psychology, and educational applications of computers.

C. C. W. Taylor is a Fellow of Corpus Christi College, Oxford. He is the author of *Plato, Protagoras* (translation and commentary), and papers in ethics, philosophy of mind, and history of philosophy. He is also co-author, with J. C. B. Gosling, of *The Greeks on Pleasure*.

J. O. Urmson is Emeritus Professor of Philosophy at Stanford University and an Emeritus Fellow of Corpus Christi College, Oxford. He is the author of *Philosophical Analysis, The Emotive Theory of Ethics, Berkeley, Aristotle's Ethics*, and numerous papers in many areas of philosophy (see "Philosophical Writings of J. O. Urmson" in this volume).

Bruce Vermazen is Professor of Philosophy at the University of California, Berkeley, and the author of papers on aesthetics, philosophy of mind, and philosophy of language. He is co-editor, with the late Merrill B. Hintikka, of *Essays on Davidson: Actions and Events*.

Kendall L. Walton is Professor of Philosophy at the University of Michigan. He is the author of papers in aesthetics and of *Mimesis as Make-Believe: On the Foundations of the Representational Arts* (forthcoming).

Bernard Williams is Professor of Philosophy at the University of California, Berkeley. He was formerly Provost of King's College, Cambridge, and Knightbridge Professor of Philosophy at Cambridge University. Before that he taught at London and Oxford universities. He is the author of *Problems of the Self, Descartes, Morality, Moral Luck*, and *Ethics and the Limits of Philosophy*, and papers in philosophy of mind, ethics, and history of philosophy. He is also co-author, with J. J. C. Smart, of *Utilitarianism, For and Against*.

Deirdre Wilson is Reader in Linguistics at University College, London. She is the author of *Presuppositions and Non-Truth-Conditional Semantics* and papers in linguistic theory; co-author, with Neil Smith, of *Modern Linguistics: The Results of Chomsky's Revolution*; and co-author, with Dan Sperber, of *Relevance* and papers in pragmatic theory.

HUMAN AGENCY
Language, Duty, and Value

J. M. E. MORAVCSIK

Introduction

The papers collected in this volume deal with four topics: epistemology, philosophy of language, ethics, and aesthetics. Thus they represent the fields to which J. O. Urmson, to whom the volume is dedicated, has contributed so much over the years. The influence of his work in philosophy is reflected as well in several other unifying features of the volume. The first of these concerns philosophical method.

Classical modern philosophy is associated with thinkers such as Leibniz, Spinoza, and Descartes. These philosophers erected systems of thought within which interrelated answers were given to questions about the nature of reality, the self, human knowledge, and the foundation of morality. The nineteenth-century theorist Hegel was even more ambitious, since he made sweeping predictions about human history and destiny as well. Today most philosophers are wary of grand schemes and large philosophic systems. Their reluctance has at least two sources. One of these is skeptical epistemology, which questions claims of knowledge that go much beyond empirical evidence on the one hand and the tautologies of logic on the other. The other source is the success of the natural sciences, the rise of the social sciences, and the era of specialization that emerged as a result of these phenomena.

The pressure toward specialization in philosophy is especially notable in the so-called analytic tradition that dominates the Anglo-American philosophic world today. Philosophers in this tradition tend to focus on specific conceptual problems within subfields of philosophy dealing with reference, belief, action, and similar topics. Between the grand schemes of the system builders of the past and the highly specialized work of the new philosophic experts, however, there is room for philosophizing that looks at a variety of problems related to the human condition and offers solutions that recognize the connections between these problems without resulting in grand schemes that one has to accept or reject in toto. The ability to resist overspecialization, to preserve the insight that the subfields of philosophy are interrelated, and to address problems of reasonable scope has been exemplified in an outstanding way by Urmson. At faculty teas at Stanford it was fashionable to ask people about their subjects and fields of specialization. Urmson's answer to both questions was inevitably, "I am a philosopher."

The philosophic retreat to relatively narrow, allegedly purely conceptual problems is caused in part by worry about how to carve out for philosophy a domain that would distinguish it from other disciplines. One can, however, refuse to worry about how to draw sharp departmental frontiers, or a sharp line between the conceptual and the empirical. This opens up the possibility of talking about such problems as those of the successful moral agent, the knowledgeable individual, or the successful rational explanation in a way that helps people in all walks of life to cope with some of their problems. Aristotle is a prominent example of a philosopher who theorizes in this manner. It is small wonder, then, that many current practitioners of this method, including Urmson and most of the contributors to this volume, have either worked on interpreting some parts of Aristotle's philosophy, or at least derived many of their problems from Aristotle's way of parceling things out. This method is, then, one of the bonds that unites the essays collected here.

Another, key bond is that they all regard the various distinctly human potentialities from an agent's point of view. In this volume, the main concern is with humans as doers, rather than as just another species with a fixed essence waiting to be defined, or as mere observers. This viewpoint will become clearer as we take a brief look at the four topics of this book.

One can look at knowledge as something possessed by a human in an ideal state. The task of the philosopher, according to this conception, is to characterize this state in terms of the logic of evidence. Alternatively, one can construe the task of philosophy as clarifying what it is to speak and act knowledgeably and competently with regard to a certain subject matter. This involves spelling out the justifiable ways of ascribing ability and competence to human agents in various contexts.

Language can, on one hand, be viewed as an abstract system of sound, form, and meaning that is somehow mastered and utilized by humans. The philosophic task here is to reflect on the theoretically interesting properties of these abstract systems. On the other hand, we can look at language as an aspect of what is involved in linguistic processes; that is, as an aspect of what is involved when humans perform various actions by the use of language. We use language to perform such actions as asking, asserting, commanding, and promising. The philosophic task here is to understand what we do when we use language in these ways, and how we do it.

Similarly, ethics can be viewed as a set of rules and principles that humans at their best follow. The philosophic task on this view is to try to uncover the right rules and principles. Alternatively, we can view the philosophical study of ethics as having the primary goal of characterizing what it is to be a good human agent. It will include such topics as friendship, heroism, and care, as well as the obeying of certain rules in some contexts. The sharing of emotions and communal living are not exhausted by the following of moral rules. The good human agent can transcend in various ways the limits of the merely useful.

The freedom to transcend utility is also shared by the artist and the appreciator of beauty. One could, on one hand, think of philosophical aesthetics as having the main task of defining "beauty." On the other hand, we can conceive of the task as clarifying various aspects of the activities of the artist and his audience. The essays on aesthetics in this book take the second path. These brief remarks should help to show what it is to view knowledge, the use of language, morality, and art as salient aspects of human activity and human agency, and how such an approach differs from others taken occasionally by philosophers.

Finally, the essays assembled here, taken together, show how these four aspects of human agency are interrelated. To ascribe knowledge and competence to someone is to make normative claims that are very similar to the ones we encounter in ethics.

The nature of these evaluative activities has to be understood in comparison with other linguistic activities by a comprehensive philosophy of language. Language, in turn, is one of the media of art, to be understood in comparison with other modes of symbol producing.

In his three critiques Kant, too, dealt with knowledge, with the practical and obligatory, and finally with the aesthetic. This volume, however, although the problems it considers are at the core of philosophizing and of general human concerns, does not assume an overall, Kantian scheme within which each of these aspects of human thought fits. A survey of some of the salient aspects of what it is to be human can stand on its own without any superstructure.

The volume begins with some remarks about knowledge. Much of recent epistemology construes knowledge as belief strengthened to the point at which the evidence backing it is complete, in ways that philosophers can specify. Both J. L. Austin and Urmson rejected this view, and the inspiration for their stance came to a large extent from the teaching of H. A. Prichard. According to the proposed alternative, which Urmson develops in his essay, to say that one knows something is to give certain warrants and assurances for the claims one makes. This interpretation construes knowledge less as a mental state than as a status in a community that seeks understanding. To say that someone knows is to ascribe to that person certain qualifications whose interpretation is a communal task. This way of viewing knowledge claims enables one to apply this notion both to the theoretical and to the practical. In his philosophic works Urmson applied the same point of view to the analysis of language. Thus, for example, reference is not just a matter of how a part of language fits reality, but of the aptness of phrase in the context of communicating with different types of persons.

Making knowledge claims and ascribing qualifications to oneself and to others involves various uses of language. The study of the whole variety of language uses and acts that we perform by the use of language is the topic of the next set of essays. These papers consider not only truth and the assertoric use of language but also uses such as questioning, promising, and commanding. They pave the way toward a general theory of language use. At the same time, several of the essays show that specific meaning can be assigned to human utterances only in context, and that even this task, if carried out thoroughly, is of formidable complexity.

Language use involves both process and product. Deirdre Wilson and Dan Sperber's essay deals with the product, while Jennifer Hornsby's essay and that of Patrick Suppes and Colleen Crangle deal primarily with aspects of the processes constituting language use.

Theories of language and theories of action must be—as Hornsby shows—related to each other. This can be seen especially in the case of so-called performatives; that is, utterances such as "I promise," in which we do not so much describe a part of reality as perform a certain social activity, in this case, that of making a promise. In spelling these matters out Hornsby's essay shows also how a general philosophic theory about language use can lead to specific predictions and explanations.

The paper by Suppes and Crangle attacks the task of assigning meanings to verbs that play prominent roles in what they call the "language of action." This language includes not only positive notions but also verbs like "avoid," and it contains commands as much as assertions. Carrying out a task successfully is a matter of executing procedures. Thus it is reasonable to represent meaning in the analysis of the language of action as a set of procedures. The assignment of procedures to action verbs is carried out within specific contexts, and different pragmatic contexts require different procedures. Suppes and Crangle conclude that one cannot assign meaning to these verbs in general, that is, apart from context.

This conclusion resembles that reached by Urmson about aptness of reference. Urmson's approach, however, is that of a naturalist—a matter of studying several cases. Suppes and Crangle are more like biologists, since they aim at a general, rigorous theory. The comparison shows that in the study of language use we can hope that the naturalist and the biologist will converge on the same evidence. Urmson and Austin have always urged us to study first the simpler cases and only then move on to the more complex. This attitude also informs the work of Suppes and Crangle, since they start with theories for instructable robots on the ground that in these simplified contexts we can get a hold on the fundamentals in a more perspicuous way.

The third paper on language, by Wilson and Sperber, contributes both to the semantics of moods such as the interrogative and the imperative, and to the study of illocutionary force, that is, the interpretation of what a human does and accomplishes in producing a given utterance in a given pragmatic context. The paper shows that we cannot read off the linguistic force of an utterance from its linguistic form. At the same time it reveals that a semantics of mood can provide the foundations for an interpretation of force. The semantics of mood that Wilson and Sperber provide relies on notions such as the desirability, potentiality, and relevance of utterances. Thus they demonstrate that though the analysis of mood underdetermines linguistic force, the analysis can be given a general form, and it can contribute to the understanding of force.

The treatments of the first two topics emphasize the social aspects of language use and the making of knowledge claims. The papers in the remainder of the volume look at other kinds of human interactions. Although many human relations might be interpreted as being based on self-interest or desire for gratification, these essays single out human bonds and relationships that can transcend such limitations.

To choose human relations that transcend mere utility and satisfaction of desires is to assume that humans are not mere "pleasure machines" dominated by the desire to maximize pleasure and minimize pain, but have a more complex attitude toward pleasure, satisfaction, and enjoyment. Aristotle, for one, proposed such a more complex attitude. Thus reconstructing and interpreting his view is an important task for those philosophers whose conception of human agency requires this rich account of agent and motivation. Urmson has done much to clarify critically the Aristotelian account, and C. C. W. Taylor's contribution to this volume carries the enterprise further.

One such complex relationship is genuine friendship, which inspires loyalty even in the absence of mutual utility and gratification. The possibility of this kind of friendship was stressed by Aristotle; hence, recent efforts to revive the central role of this phenomenon in thinking about human values rely on the Aristotelian analysis. Still, a number of conceptual puzzles are left to us by Aristotle's account. In my own essay I attempt to deal with some of these. We typically assume that genuine friends will be loyal to each other "no matter what." My essay attempts to clarify this rider, and to make the notion of personal loyalty intelligible. In the course of this we also encounter the problem of vulnerability that friendship of this sort places on us. Deep involvement with others means feeling great pain when the loved ones suffer or when the bond between us breaks. Constructive ways of dealing with this problem suggest that different views of friendship and its fragility involve us in different conceptions of the self. Laying out these conceptual problems about friendship helps us to confront crucial questions in our lives. When others hurt us, do we react with grudge and resentment, or seek to repair our bonds with others in constructive ways? This question is beyond both matters of obligation and calculations of utility. Hence it forces us to think about fundamental choices among human ideals, ideals that Greek drama and philosophy were preoccupied with but which do not play central roles in most of contemporary ethical philosophizing.

In addition to views of friendship and the varieties of enjoyment, the notion of duty or obligation affects in an important way our conceptions of how humans should interact. One can think of duty and a system of rules that prescribes and organizes our whole range of duties as constituting all the notions needed for a moral life. But many thinkers have gone beyond that, and have seen that rule following cannot exhaust the content of morality. For there are saints and heroes who act morally even though they do not simply obey the rules but go beyond them. Their acts are acts of supererogation. This human possibility and reality is vital to those who see morality as not just a matter of applying a rule system, or following—to use Stuart Hampshire's felicitous phrase—the "geometrical model," but rather as a way of viewing others and ourselves in our actions and attitudes that affect other human beings.

Urmson, more than anyone else, brought the phenomena of hero and saint to philosophic attention. In the present volume the essays of David Heyd and Jonathan Dancy are devoted to this topic. Heyd argues that though morality involves following rules, in the last analysis it is the supererogatory that is the concrete and genuinely human aspect of the very subject matter of morality. Dancy considers supererogation in the context of examining moral realism, that is, the view that acts have moral qualities in the same objective sense in which they have temporal or sensibly perceptible qualities. If acts need to be ordered according to both deontic and evaluative properties, which sort the more specific qualities of acts into different structures of varying saliency, will this not cause problems for moral realism, which seems to assume a unitary view of all of the moral qualities of acts? Supererogation is the key evidence for the need to posit both the deontic and the evaluative, while acknowledging their distinctness. Dancy shows how a correct account of supererogation systematically relates the evaluative and the deontic and shows that the difference between them need not be an obstacle for the moral realist.

There is a temptation to think of moral agents as starting life with the same opportunities for excellence, and of moral rules as a unitary, homogeneous system. This temptation is resisted in the essays of Anthony Kenny and Bernard Williams, which bracket the other papers on ethics.

Kenny's paper deals with "moral luck," the notion that not all humans are in equally favorable positions to achieve moral excellence. For example, we do not all start out with the same character and personality. Kenny compares the treatment of moral luck in Kant with that in Aristotle's writings. While Kant could not tolerate this notion, Aristotle discussed various cases of it, and left room for them in his framework for delineating human flourishing.

Kenny suggests that while one might be tempted to regard the Christian framework as more egalitarian than the Aristotelian one, it has to be admitted that we can find the analogue of moral luck also in Christian thought. For not all humans have an equal chance to develop into the kind of person who will accept God's grace. The chances are better for the person who is born into a Christian family than for the person who is part of a pagan family. At the end, Kenny expresses his preference for the Aristotelian as opposed to the Kantian framework, and shows that as long as we assign praise and responsibility accordingly, moral luck need not be viewed as unfair.

Williams's essay distinguishes intuitionism in the sense of having a plurality of first principles from intuitionism in the sense of an epistemological doctrine. He points out that the epistemological model need not take mathematical knowledge as its paradigm; it could construe moral judgment as analogous to perceptual judgment. After a careful review of alleged shortcomings, Williams ends by presenting a new and original defense of the thesis that we have a plurality of first principles.

As we noted above, still another distinctive aspect of humans as agents is their production and appreciation of works of art. Art is one of the few cultural universals; that is to say, no known culture is without it. It is reasonable to suppose, then, that this practice reveals something important about human nature. Like language, art involves both product and process. There is, on the one hand, the work of art, and on the other, the processes of creation and enjoyment.

Bruce Vermazen's essay deals with the concept of aesthetic satisfaction. Such satisfaction, he argues, is not a feeling but a logical state holding between psychological states. One of these is a cognitive state, which links to aesthetic satisfaction the notion of aesthetic criteria. Vermazen discusses the notions of relevant aesthetic criteria and of what fine art is. Illuminating these notions turns out to be a partly historical enterprise, for they change from epoch to epoch. This raises the question of how much of this process of development is governed by general rational principles. Vermazen's suggestion that answering this question will require a lot of detailed fieldwork rather than sweeping a priori pronouncements is very much in line with Urmson's approach to such questions.

For some art forms, production can be divided into the process of creating the work as a pattern of elements and the process of performance, in which these patterns are realized for specific audiences on specific occasions. The two essays in this volume that deal with music, those by Peter Kivy and Kendall Walton, discuss how both of these processes relate to the product.

Kivy's essay relates the work of art to the creative process of the composer. He argues that the composer's intentions that go into the creation of a musical work of art are also relevant to the appreciation of the work. Though this thesis may not sound revolutionary to those not familiar with recent aesthetic theory, it is in fact a much-needed corrective to recent efforts to construe a work of art as self-sufficient, requiring for its interpretation no account of the artist's intentions.

In Walton's essay the key question is the relation between the musical work of art and its performances. A preoccupation with the concrete and empirically given might tempt one to think that it is primarily the performances that attract musical attention. Walton argues for the alternative thesis that the work of art as a pattern is also the proper object of musical attention. His account helps us to see the differences between the relation of the musical work and its performances on the one hand, and the literary work and its copies on the other.

The concluding essay spans aesthetics and ethics. In this paper Ted Cohen, considering certain aspects of sports, discovers in our appreciation of the athlete elements that are analogous to our appreciation of art and the artist. The comparison centers on the kinds of difficulty that are appreciated in the achievements of both artist and athlete. He then considers the "true fan," the person who enjoys team sports and is loyal to a team regardless of its rate of success or other extrinsic considerations. He finds in the loyalty of the true fan an analogue of the kind of altruism that is the foundation of many of our moral attitudes and activities.

In summary, the essays in this volume explore what it is for humans to act knowledgeably, to use language, to be friends, to act heroically, to be morally fortunate, and to produce as well as to appreciate art. This kaleidoscopic picture helps us not only to catch a glimpse of current work in the central areas of philosophy, but also to understand some of the salient aspects of human action and human agency. The volume is, therefore, also a particularly appropriate tribute to J. O. Urmson, a philosopher who has contributed significantly to many of these areas, and who so signally displays that complex of admirable and amiable qualities for which "humanity" is the most appropriate designation.

J. O. URMSON

Prichard and Knowledge

When I first started to study philosophy, at Oxford in 1935, things were in many ways different from how they are fifty years later. Philosophy, and particularly Oxford philosophy, was a much smaller world. There were vastly fewer professional philosophers than now; those there were often had far less inclination or incentive to publish than their successors. Moreover, Oxford was philosophically very much a closed community that saw little need to publish and relied mainly on viva voce discussion. One was aware of Russell and Moore at Cambridge and of William James in America, but to look further was to cultivate a specialized interest, somewhat like breeding cacti. Consequently it really was much easier to keep abreast of developments and controversies, and still easier to believe that one was doing so, than in these days of philosophical mass production.

My introduction to philosophy was via what was called "Mods. logic" (i.e., logic for Oxford classics students in their second year). I went to the lectures of H. H. Price, then still a tutor of Trinity College; what he taught was the traditional syllogistic logic as contained, for example, in H. W. B. Joseph's *Introduction to Logic*, and inductive logic as contained in Mill's *System of Logic*. That nobody was taught modern formal logic in those days at Oxford (and W. C. Kneale was probably the only man there capable of teaching it) is certainly regrettable, but to learn the technical vocabulary and logical presuppositions of all western philosophers from Aristotle until the twentieth century was an advantage the lack of which can lead to curious misunderstandings of the European tradition.

At Oxford the school of John Cook Wilson, called realist since it was in reaction to the near-Hegelian idealism of F. H. Bradley and H. H. Joachim, was then still dominant. Cook Wilson was dead and Joseph had recently retired, but H. A. Prichard and various lieutenants still were in command. Any venturing into divergent paths was frowned on as being inevitably a lapse into error. It must have been about 1935 that the John Locke Scholarship, the most coveted distinction for young graduates, was not awarded, on the ground that no candidate of sufficient merit had presented himself. A. J. Ayer and J. L. Austin were two of the candidates who did not impress the examiners. It was, with some exaggeration, held to be impossible to gain an Oxford doctorate in philosophy in those days, since the statutes of the university required for the degree an original contribution to knowledge. But what was presented by a candidate was either already known to Prichard and therefore not original, or else mere opinion and therefore not knowledge. There can be little doubt that the scruples of Prichard and other like-minded Oxford philosophers were a principal cause of the changes subsequently made in the D.Phil. statutes.

Prichard was no doubt a menace in many ways—dogmatic, repressive of all divergent thinking, and, on the whole, sterile. But he was a very able man and not an unmitigated disaster. If he was dogmatically dismissive of heresy in debate, *in foro interno* he was endlessly questioning himself, and what at one time was publicly proclaimed to be obvious to anyone willing and able to think might later come to be equally firmly rejected. Thus he earlier espoused direct realism in perception, but later held that we see colored patches, which we mistake for physical objects. Since much that Prichard stood for is now very unfashionable—some of it rightly so—and also frequently misunderstood, a few words about him might be worthwhile. I attended his lectures and classes and occasionally had the opportunity to talk to him in private (when he was much less repressive and dogmatic).

An ultimately Aristotelian view about knowledge was basic to Cook Wilson and Prichard's position. Nowadays it is fashionable to attempt to define knowledge in terms of belief; to them it seemed obvious that belief must be defined in terms of knowledge. Some states that are called belief seemed to them to be of little philosophical interest; thus the more or less behavioral acceptance that they called thinking without question or taking for granted, such as our "belief" when we run a bath that water rather than sulphuric acid will emerge from the tap, seemed to them a fact about human nature outside the scope of rational thought. But if we have in mind rational belief, which they usually referred to as opinion, then we must, they held, agree that there is no such thing as immediate, intuitive rational opinion. Rational opinion must be based on evidence. The evidence for a rational belief may itself be not knowledge but rational belief, in which case it must also be based on evidence. As Wittgenstein was later to say, justification must come to an end; but there are legitimate and illegitimate places to come to an end. Rational belief by its very definition cannot be the end point, and surmise or supposition is no justification. The only legitimate starting place is knowledge.

One alternative view was, indeed, known to the Cook Wilsonians, the view of the idealist enemy. According to this view rational opinion was an element in a coherent set of mutually supporting beliefs, none of which were absolutely basic and none absolutely derivative. The set of rational beliefs was the most comprehensive of such sets. But this view was believed to be demonstrably false, since for any set of beliefs $p_1, p_2, \ldots, p_n$ there will also be an equally large set comprising not p_1, not $p_2, \ldots,$ not p_n. There can be no reason to accept one set rather than the other if we may have recourse to nothing but coherence. This is but one of the battery of arguments fired remorselessly against the coherence theory in the early years of this century.

Hence, as Aristotle had taught long ago in the *Posterior Analytics*, the Cook Wilsonians claimed that there must be some nonderivative knowledge, which they called apprehension, to serve as a foundation to all other knowledge and to all opinion. Knowledge acquired by apprehension was not based on evidence or argument, and so did not need to be defended by evidence or argument. Indeed, to ask for an objective test of apprehension implies a contradiction, since to pass such a test would be precisely to be based on external grounds—we should know that p was the case because q, the objective test, was the case. One could, no doubt, point out absurdities arising from the denial of an apprehended truth, as Aristotle did with regard to the law of contradiction; but basically the only thing to do was to hope that others would have the same rational insight as oneself and be led to the light by the mere opening of the intellectual eye.

So Prichard's dogmatism was not a mere personality trait. In his view, to invite an opponent to think again, to clear his mind of cant and prejudice, was the only rational possibility when discussing issues of immediate apprehension. That was the only way to gain basic truth. But Prichard knew that he, like other men, was fallible; it was incumbent on him as on others to exercise vigilance and to make sure that his mind also was free from distorting prejudice. Hence his continual self-examination and occasional spectacular recantations.

This view about knowledge was the basis of his view of moral philosophy. Moral philosophy, regarded as the attempt to provide a basis and justification for common morality, was a mistaken enterprise because the essentials of common morality were immediately apprehended and required no justification. One can apprehend that to lie or to break a promise is as such wrong, so that any attempt to show that it is wrong because it offends against the general welfare, or self-realization, or anything else one may care to mention must be wrongheaded. Philosophers can doubt anything when in their studies. But as Hume denied that they could sincerely doubt the existence of physical objects outside their studies, so Prichard thought that in concrete moral situations one could not doubt the wrongness of injustice and deceit in their own nature.

The claim for direct or immediate apprehension outlined above has its well-known difficulties. It is disturbing that Prichard had, or claimed to have, an immediate intuition of the truth of the Euclidean axiom of parallels and of the falsity of all non-Euclidean geometries. To some of us this would suggest the extreme fallibility of claims to such apprehension. It also disturbs me that Prichard denied that I could know that I am now using a typewriter and similar facts since they were not matters of which immediate apprehension was possible. But it is very hard to discard the Prichardian view completely. Does the fact that I sometimes accept a fallacious argument as valid (claim the immediate apprehension of an argument as valid when it is in fact fallacious) show that I can never recognize an argument to be valid? And if a claim to see a fallacy is never admissible, since there is no immediate apprehension, and accusations of fallacy must always be proved, will one not have to apprehend the validity of this proof? Or are we to demand an infinity of metaproofs?

I do not intend to plunge now into these treacherous philosophical waters any further than to suggest that Prichard's views require emendation rather than wholesale rejection. But I do have much sympathy with the view of Cook Wilson and Prichard that, while the nature of belief has to be elucidated in terms of its relation to knowledge, knowledge has to be contrasted with belief or opinion rather than being treated as a special case of belief. I now, therefore, turn to that issue, since Prichard's view is opposed to the orthodoxy of recent years. By the view that knowledge is a special case of belief I have in mind accounts of knowledge that hold that a person knows *p* if he both believes *p* and also satisfies certain other conditions. This view has been objected to by Edmund Gettier and others on the ground that nobody has been able to state satisfactorily what these other conditions are. Whether these Gettier-type objections are good or not I do not now ask. I wish to raise difficulties of quite a different sort, and to draw attention to some features of our use of the terms "know" and "believe," which will both tend in that direction and, I hope, be of interest in themselves.

One of the prime uses, perhaps the central use, of the expression "I believe" (first-person present indicative) is as a cautionary signal when one is giving information. One may offer, or supply if requested, the information that it is too late by saying "I believe it is too late," or "It is too late, I believe." By adding "I believe" to the information, one indicates that one does not regard it as wholly reliable. I do not now elaborate this point; I mention it in order to note that ordinarily there is no corresponding use of "I know." Expressions of the type "I know that such and such is the case" are quite rare; they normally are used in rather special circumstances, and they are used when the purpose of speech is to impart information only in quite exceptional circumstances.

I cannot, obviously, give a proof of this universal negative; but reflection on a variety of circumstances in which one might wish to impart information suggests to me that in general it would be odd to do so with the prefix "I know that." Thus, let us suppose that you know that there is to be a concert tomorrow in a certain auditorium, that you believe that I would like to know about it and decide to give me the information. In such circumstances you might well say to me "There is a concert tomorrow," or "The concert will be tomorrow in the main auditorium," or many similar things. What you certainly will not say, in a context that is purely one of supplying information, is "I know that there is a concert tomorrow," or "I know that the concert will be tomorrow in the main auditorium," or anything else containing the expression "I know that."

When, then, might one say "I know that such and such is the case"? Here are a few examples that I find convincing:

1. You think I know all about a certain concert about which you have some, but insufficient, information. You come to me and say "I know the concert is tomorrow, but can you tell me where it is to be?" The function of "I know" here is not to impart information, but to indicate that you do not need to be told the particular thing that follows. You do, of course, inform me that you do not need to be told, but that is not what you say that you know.

2. You tell me that there is a concert tomorrow; I reply "Yes, I know that there is." I let you know that your information is superfluous, but clearly do not inform you about the concert.

3. I back into your car in a parking lot; I do not confess. You say to me "I know it was you who backed into my car." You do not inform me of my action.

4. Your nephew has been very cheeky to his mother; you have a present for him and say to her "I know he doesn't deserve it, but I'll let him have it." Here you ward off a possible objection and indicate that you have not overlooked his behavior. You are not telling the mother that he does not deserve the present.

5. You say to me "I know that you think I am mistaken," thereby informing me that I have not concealed my attitude, not that I think that you are mistaken.

6. You search vainly in a drawer for some article; you say, with great emphasis, either to yourself or to a bystander, "I *know* I put it here." This is said to forestall or repress doubt, not to give information.

These cases differ from each other considerably. Certainly there is nothing that is *the* point of saying that one knows. What they have in common is the negative feature of not communicat-

at least 60 percent. I think that this is perfectly analogous to many situations in which "Do you believe that p" is asked. When this question is raised, what is often at issue is not whether one's mental state can most accurately be described as belief rather than knowledge or some other state but whether one either believes (or is in some yet stronger position) or disbelieves. It is this fact that can justify the answer "Yes" when one in fact knows. The answer "Yes" no more shows that knowledge is a case of belief than the former example shows that 80 percent is a special case of 60 percent. I say that I believe or that the probability is 60 percent because it would be misleading to do anything else in the context, though I would regard the one as an inaccurate account of my state of mind and the other as an inaccurate statement of the probability.

Two additional remarks about *knowledge that* before we turn to other related matters. First, let us note that there are further types of circumstance in which one can legitimately say that somebody knows something but not that he believes it. Thus the examiner in an oral examination may say to the candidate such things as "Come on, now, you know the answer very well!" and will say "There you are, you knew all the time but just lacked confidence." Here we could certainly not say that he believed all the time that he had the answer. We could compare the example given me by Nancy Cartwright—"I know I'm growing old, but I can't believe it"—although the two cases are not identical.

The second supplementary remark is about Wittgenstein. I remember hearing him say and repeat with great emphasis that it was a philosophical absurdity to say "I know I am in pain." Let me now tell a story. I build a long, straight road along a flat, open desert—no side-turns, just a long, straight road. Every few hundred yards I set up a traffic light permanently set at green. If asked what they are for I answer that they are to indicate that it is safe to proceed; if they are justified anywhere, they are justified here, I claim. Well, it is absurd to set up the traffic lights and it is absurd to say (in most contexts) that one knows that one is in pain. But not for the sort of reason that Wittgenstein had in mind. The traffic light analogy could be pursued further: the reader might care to consider what would be lost if we abolished the words "know" and "believe" from our language and merely carried with us a little green light to shine when we would now say that we knew and a little yellow light to shine when we would now say that we believed.

But there are other relevant idioms beyond "I know that." I have not in mind the use of "know" with a direct object such as a person or place; the connection between this and "knowledge that" seems to me tenuous and must seem even more so to those whose language contains *savoir* and *connaître*, or *kennen* and *wissen* (or to our forefathers, who possessed the verbs "to ken" and "to wist"). But there are uses of the verb "to know" other than "I know that," which uses involve some claim to a grasp or apprehension of the way the world is.

Gilbert Ryle directed our attention to the locution "know how," which may clearly be used in claiming some grasp of the world. But Ryle should not have selected "know how" as a solitary contrast to "know that," for there are other, equally important expressions to consider, such as:

> I know when to do it. I know when one should do it.
> I know where to do it. I know where one should do it.

Exceptionally, we also have "I know why one should do it" but not "I know why to do it," an anomaly of which I do not know the explanation.

It has often been suggested that to say "I know how to do so and so" is more or less the same thing as to say "I am able to do so and so," or it is said to be a claim to a skill. While this may be true of the colloquial noun "know-how," it will not do as an account of the verbal phrase. The gross falsity of this thesis in the case of certain types of illustration is not immediately apparent. If we consider such examples as "I know how to ride a bicycle" or "I know how to swim," we are indeed considering skills, and most people are better able to show that they possess these skills by an exhibition of the skills than in any other way. The falsity of the thesis is, however, apparent if one considers such examples as "I know how to address the Pope"; to know how to do this requires the possession of the relevant information, not of any knack or skill. I do know how to address the Pope; one should say "Your Holiness." By saying this I have exhibited that I know how; but I am not able to address the Pope because I have not the opportunity, and I might be too bashful if I did have the opportunity.

To be able to do something does no doubt require that one knows how to do it, but not conversely. Ability requires opportunity, capacity, will, and no doubt other factors. A retired horn player may know very well how to play high C but have lost his lip; I may know how to ride a bike but lack the time, or the bike, or the legs. I may know how to lose weight but not be able to do so because my will is too feeble.

Ryle, it seems, tended to move from the extreme error of supposing that knowledge how was always and only a matter of giving a verbal explanation to the opposite error of supposing that it always and only required the ability to execute. Both extremes are false, since there are many different ways, none essential, in which one may exhibit such knowledge. On one hand it is absurd to suppose that I do not know how to tie a bow tie because I most certainly cannot say how one should do it. On the other hand it would be lunacy to suppose that the only way one could show that one knew how to reclaim excessive tax payments would be to make such payments in order to go through the process of reclaiming them; in this case one's ability to say how to do it would be the best and normal proof that one knew how to do it. I think, incidentally, that in the case of skills that require a great deal of practice and bodily adaptation for their successful practice but have few principles to apply, such as the skill of the contortionist, it is more natural to use the verb "can" than to say that one knows how to do it.

It seems plain that the cases of knowing when to do something or where to do it are in all essentials parallel to the case of knowing how. Once again, the knowledge may be exhibited in action, as by the skilled tennis player who shows that he knows when to advance to the net by doing so on appropriate occasions, though he may well lack the coach's skill of enunciating the principles. But equally the lawyer may show that he knows where to sign the documents, not by signing them himself, which may be quite inappropriate, but by saying that they should be signed in such and such a place, or marking the place with a sign.

Ryle contrasted knowing how with knowing that, which may have been legitimate for his purposes. But, in a classification, "how" is not parallel to "that" but to "why," "when," "where," "who," "what," and "which." Moreover, Ryle had not all cases of knowing how in mind but only that of knowing how to do something. But I think that a useful distinction can be made between the following two classes:

1. *Knowing how, why, when, where, who, what, which* as followed by a clause in the indicative. Examples are "I know how he did it," "I know when he will do it," and "I know where he is doing it."

2. *Knowing how, why, when, where, who, what, which* as followed by a verb in the infinitive or a clause with the verb in the subjunctive. Examples are "I know how to do it," "He knows whom we should ask," and "You know what you should do."

We have already given some consideration to the second of these two classes. We have seen that knowledge in this kind of case can be exhibited in several ways, none more essential than the others, but one being more apt than another according to context. Most notably, I may either give a demonstration or else enunciate a principle in one of the many ways in which principles may be enunciated. How then do I exhibit knowledge of the first type distinguished above, as when I say that I know where something is or when something happened? Once again, there are at least two basic ways, though they may not be equally appropriate on all occasions. I may show that I know where the key of the door is by fetching it, and I may show that I know how to speak French by speaking it. These are both cases of exhibiting knowledge by performance, though not in an identical way, since one case is of demonstration, the other not. I may also show that I know how he did the conjuring trick by reproducing it. All these cases are different but may be loosely classed as exhibition by performance. But equally I may show the how, when, or where of an occurrence by saying that it happened in this manner, at that time, in this place. It would be hard to show that I knew when it happened by a demonstration, and hard to show that I know how a singer phrased a melody except by demonstration.

So it seems that the situation is not at all as Ryle represented it. On the one hand we have knowledge how, when, or where to do something. This can sometimes be most appropriately demonstrated by doing whatever it may be, sometimes by saying that one should act in a certain manner, or at a certain time, or at a certain place—also, no doubt, by apt criticism and many other ways. On the other hand we have the knowledge of the how, when, or where of a certain occurrence or state of affairs. This, too, may sometimes be more appropriately exhibited by action and sometimes by saying that something is the case or that one knows it to be the case.

So Ryle was correct in thinking that the conceptual function of *knowledge that* was very different from that of *knowledge how*, but he misdescribed both functions. If we take knowledge how to do something, this may sometimes be best demonstrated by action (tying a bow tie), sometimes by description (saying that one addresses the Pope as "Your Holiness"). Thus a statement of *knowledge that* (one should call him Your Holiness) is not parallel to a statement of *knowledge how* but is rather parallel to a demonstration or other performance as a verification of *knowledge how*. Similarly, knowledge how, when, or where something happened can be demonstrated either by appropriate behavior or by saying that it happened in this manner, at that time, in this place—that is, by exhibiting a piece of knowledge that. So both types of knowledge how, when, where, etc., can be exhibited either by some performance or by a statement how, when, or where, a statement of *knowledge that*. As we earlier noted, statements of *knowledge that* normally take the form of plain indicative statements, without the annexation of "I know."

One final point on this topic, of a linguistic character. In the case of statements beginning "I know how (when, where, why, what, etc.)," the verb "to know" is an ineliminable part of the basic structure of the sentence. For example, in the case of either "I know how to do it" or "I know how he did it" the expression "I know" cannot be removed from the sentence without making it syntactically incomplete. But in the case of *knowledge that* the verb "I know" is parenthetical and thus syntactically eliminable. Thus if one eliminates "I know" from "I know the cat is on the mat" one still has the complete sentence "The cat is on the mat." This linguistic fact reflects the conceptual facts that underlie and illuminate it. In the case of the basic knowledge claims, the verb "to know" is naturally ineliminable; if it be cut out from "I know how to write" we are left with a syntactically incomplete expression. But in the case in which we are merely exhibiting such basic knowledge by verbal statement the verb "to know" is not essential and, if added, is loosely attached and eliminable. Such utterances as are exemplified by "I know that he is at home" are neither so important nor required on half so many occasions as philosophers typically suggest, as I said earlier. When they are appropriate the speaker may be construed as saying such things as "He is at home—treat this as an exhibition of my knowledge where he is." "I know" is loosely attached like a label on a piece of luggage.

If we were omniscient, or if we either knew how, why, when and where or else were blankly nescient, we should have no use for the verb "to believe." This verb has an indispensable place in our vocabulary precisely because we sometimes neither know nor are wholly nescient. Knowing how, why, when, where, and the like are not special cases of believing how, why, when, and where since there is no such thing and the expressions are *voces nihili*. Philosophers, it seems, have been led to treat knowledge as a case of belief as a result of concentrating on the relatively unimportant locution "I know that," which has, no doubt, superficially similar uses to "I believe that." Prichard was right, I think, in holding that belief could be understood in the light of its relation to knowledge and not vice versa and in holding that, so understood, they could be seen to be clean different things. But I cannot claim that the arguments I have used are those that he himself would have used. No doubt some of them would have reduced him to the outraged speechlessness that I remember so well.

PART I
Theories of Language Use

JENNIFER HORNSBY

Things Done with Words

In his paper "Performative Utterances," J. O. Urmson presents a useful summary of J. L. Austin's principal doctrines about performatives and a careful account of their development. He goes on to put forward his own answer to the question how performatives should be characterized, and concludes that "performatives should not be classed as speech-acts."[1] This is a surprising conclusion on the face of it. For Austin initially introduced performatives as those bits of speech that constitute acts. And if he came to doubt whether performatives could be sharply singled out, this was not because he doubted that uttering a performative sentence is going in for speech and for action: what worried him was that one goes in for action whenever one goes in for speech.[2] Of course Urmson's conclusion is more surprising when stated this baldly than it is in the context of his paper, as he meant it. I shall make a suggestion about how the conclusion is to be interpreted within a framework for accounts of language use arising out of *How to Do Things with Words*.

The framework is a useful one for setting out a range of issues in the philosophy of language. I shall say something about explicit performatives, about the relations between theories of meaning and theories of force, about *stating*, and about non-indicatives. But I should note at the start that there is nothing new about the framework;[3] in discussing it here, I try to make explicit some connections between Austin's work and subsequent theorizing about language and about action. I begin by paying critical attention to the use of the notion of a speech act.

Austin's "Preliminary Isolation of the Performative"[4] rested on a distinction between constating and performing: performatives are sentences in using which we perform rather than constate; when one employs a performative, one is doing something rather than stating something. But, as Austin saw, this contrast cannot be maintained. We cannot say that someone who states something does *nothing*: one thing done by someone who states that *p* is *state that p*. Any use of speech for whatever purpose is a person's doing something. Indeed in any use of speech "lots of things will have been done."[5]

Here is a list of a few of the things that might have been done on an occasion when someone used a sentence: *vibrate the vocal cords, move the mouth in a particular way, emit such and such sounds, say "the bus ought to have arrived by now," state that the bus ought to have arrived, complain about the bus company,* and *cause Harry to look at his watch*. Allowing that someone on occasion might do all these things, we must make a distinction between people's doings of such things as these, and such things as these, which people do. This is the same distinction, here restricted to speech in its application, as Urmson once made, in a quite different connection, between act tokens and act types. Urmson asked how we should interpret Mill's claim that actions are right in proportion as they tend to promote happiness.[6] If Mill's actions are Urmson's tokens, then the claim is that individual doings alone are assessed for rightness, as the act utilitarian says; but if Mill's actions are Urmson's types, then the claim is that the things that rules of conduct prescribe or proscribe may themselves be right, as the rule utilitarian says. What Mill meant—on which side of the distinction his "actions" fall—remains controversial. But on which side *speech acts* fall need not be controversial. The list of things that someone might have done is surely a list that includes speech acts. Yet things on that list were to be distinguished from people's doings of them (or actions, or tokens). So the class of speech acts consists of some of those things that Urmson called act types.[7]

Speech acts, therefore, correspond to groupings of uses of speech—that is, to groupings of speech actions, or utterances. If one were able to say something systematic about sorts of speech acts and relations between them, one would be organizing the ways there are of classifying utterances, and thereby supplying a general framework for accounts of the things that language users do.

To point out that speech acts are things people do is to say what sort of thing they are. In order to assess Urmson's claim that performatives are not speech acts, we shall need to know *which* things of the relevant sort they are. (As for "performative," I shall use this word only of sentences, although this cannot be how Urmson used it: when he denied that performatives are speech acts, he did not mean merely to deny that sentences are acts. What he denied, I take it, is that acts specifically associated with uses of performative sentences are speech acts.)

"Things done *with words*" might seem to be the obvious answer to the question "What are speech acts?" But this answer in itself may not determine any category of things people do. We saw that one thing someone can do using words is *cause Harry to look at his watch*; yet we know that this is something that can be done otherwise than by using words. And it seems that some of the things customarily thought of as speech acts, such as *warning*, are things of which we cannot say once and for all that they are "done with words."[8]

Perhaps we should not expect to be able to say straight off whether *causing Harry to look at his watch* or *warning* is a speech act. We might think that this is something that we have to assess with respect to an occasion: whether *warning*-on-occasion is a speech act depends on whether speech was involved on that occasion, and, perhaps, whether the person who spoke had warning someone of something as part of her purpose.[9] If this is right, then the notion of a speech act must be taken to be really a relational one. If someone warned someone of something, but either did this otherwise than by using language or did not do this intentionally, the relevant pair of the thing she did and her action of doing it would not be a speech act. In a case in which language was used and in which *warning* was something the speaker meant to do, the relevant pair—this thing she did, in relation to her doing of it, as it were—does qualify as a speech act. Admittedly one never finds this sort of relativity explicitly registered by those who have used the term "speech act." But it does seem to be suggested by many of the things they say.[10]

Still, no relativity seems to be suggested by Urmson when he says that performatives are not speech acts; and we need a nonrelational notion to interpret his claim. We could think of speech acts as those things that are typically done intentionally, and of which *every* doing is a doing of that thing with words. Speech acts are then those things that are always done (perhaps *have* to be done) by using words. Of course doubts can be raised whether this gives a necessary condition of a *speech act*, because it obviously excludes such things as *warning*. But it certainly seems to be sufficient. What more could we require of a speech act than this?

The feeling that we do have a sufficient condition here will explain our initial puzzlement over the claim that performatives should not be classed as speech acts. When Urmson makes the claim, it concerns only the use of sentences from which Austin began his discussion (which Warnock has called Mark I performatives[11]): "I take thee . . ." as used in marriages, "I name . . ." as used in official naming ceremonies, etc. Urmson's failed candidates for speech act status, then, are *getting married (as it is done in England), naming a ship,* and *offering a wager.*[12] Are we not surprised to be told that these things are not speech acts, because we know that people typically do them intentionally and regularly use words to do them? Urmson contrasts these things with others, which Austin came on to later and which are also done using what he called explicit performatives—sentences starting, for instance, with "I warn" or "I promise." These other things—*explicitly warning, explicitly promising,* etc.—Urmson thinks *are* speech acts. For instance, he says of *warning people by conveying information labeled as a warning,* which I have just called "explicitly warning," that it is a speech act.[13] But this may puzzle us further. We may wonder what is supposed to make all the difference to the question whether we have a speech act.

Still, to say all this is not yet to attend to what gives Urmson's prima facie surprising claim a foundation. Urmson's point was that the conventions in virtue of which uttering certain words counts as marrying, or as naming, are not linguistic conventions. In order to get married in a foreign country, one needs to know the conventions that obtain there, and it is not enough to know the language spoken there. It seems that Urmson wishes to count as speech acts only things that are embraced by a study of language use as such. His claims can be seen as making his point if speech acts are defined as those things people do that need to be mentioned in setting out a distinctively linguistic classification of speech actions.

This definition can also provide a rationale for Urmson's contrast between Austin's two categories of performatives. Some people have said that the meaning of an explicit performative sentence determines the force with which it is used, so that conventions governing meaning, which obviously do have a place in a distinctively linguistic classification of speech actions, are the determinants of certain utterances' being explicit warnings, or explicit promisings. But if explicit performatives are to be thought of as requiring knowledge only of *linguistic* conventions for knowledge of what is done by using them, there is a point in thinking, as Urmson does, that the idea of an explicit performative carries with it a distinction between what is a speech act and what isn't.

I suggest, then, that Urmson's claim that (certain) performatives are not speech acts is best viewed in the light of the framework we touched on, which provides for the organization of speech acts. When such a framework is theoretically conceived as providing a schema for the linguistic component of accounts of the practices of human communities, some rough and ready line has to be drawn between what a study of language properly concerns and what it doesn't. In an account of the English language, we have to accommodate utterances of "I take thee . . ." along with utterances of all the other sentences of English; in an account of the practices of English people, we have to recognize certain utterances as being conventionally acts of marriage; but we do not have to talk about *marrying* in the linguistic component of any description of what anyone gets up to.

Greater definiteness may be introduced into the framework now by registering distinctions we have had to recognize to accommodate Urmson's claims about performatives. We may suppose that within a complete account of the linguistic practices of any community, a portion will be special to their particular language and concern itself with the conventional significance of its sounds, and a portion will deal with language use, whatever the language. Thinking of these two portions as constituting a whole account of the use of a language, we see that there is no room within it for things people do which, for all that they depend upon the use of language, and for all that they are conventional, are in the category to which Urmson refuses the title speech acts. The division between the two portions seems natural when we reflect that an account that treats of the sounds coming from the mouths of English speakers manifestly has no application to the sounds of, say, French speakers, yet there are many things that may be done equally well with English words and with French ones, in virtue only of the fact that English and French are, equally, human languages.

Austin's own classification of speech acts provides for this sort of divided account within the domain of the linguistic. At the level of determinable speech acts, Austin spoke of six: phonetic, phatic, rhetic, locutionary, illocutionary, and perlocutionary. We need be concerned only with three of these. The phatic act can be left out of account, because it will be no great cause for concern if we blur the distinction between phonetically adequate and syntactically adequate descriptions of utterances, which Austin marked with the phonetic/phatic distinction. The locutionary act can be left out of account, because Austin said at one stage that he meant by it simply the sum of the phonetic, phatic, and rhetic. Finally, the perlocutionary act can be left out of account, because determinate perlocutionary acts for the most part will be things that by Urmson's lights do not count as speech acts at all. The division between the two portions of an account of language use, conceived now as dealing with phonetic, rhetic, and illocutionary acts, then comes simply at the midpoint, with the rhetic act. Austin used Frege's terms to mark the division: he spoke on the one hand of the sense and reference of vocables—to be given in the specification of the rhetic act—and on the other hand of the force accruing to the use of vocables—to be given in specifying an illocutionary act.[14]

A complete account of the use of a language might be thought of as a sort of theoretical counterpart of the ability to know, on hearing a speaker do a particular phonetic thing, which particular determinate illocutionary things that speaker has also done. But when someone is accustomed to using some language, she can be assumed to have the wherewithal to get from rhetic to illocutionary acts, and what she lacks that she would need in order to make sense of what goes on in the use of a language foreign to her is only knowledge how to get from phonetic acts employing the foreign language to rhetic acts. Thus we can think of an extricable component of an account of the use of a language that says, for any particular phonetic act, which rhetic act is being done by doing it. It will take us, as Austin himself once explained, from *oratio recta* reports of speech to plain *oratio obliqua* reports.[15] It has become usual to speak of this component of an account of the use of a language as a theory of meaning for the language. I shall be concerned with the question how theories of meaning fit into the Austinian framework when I have dealt with challenges to the picture as so far presented.

John Searle once denied that "Austin was completely successful in characterizing a locutionary-illocutionary distinction."[16] More particularly, he questioned whether anything definite was marked by the locutionary act—or, as I shall go on saying, the rhetic act.[17] If we agreed with Searle about this, we should have to doubt whether there could be such things as theories of meaning in the sense just alluded to.

Searle found a difficulty with Austin's speaking[18] of the rhetic act as an abstraction from the total speech act. But granted what has been said about the notion of a speech act, the total speech act can only mean everything done on an occasion of language use, and the idea of an abstraction from it may then be only the idea of one thing done. There seems to be no problem about this. And we might find it fitting to use the word "abstraction" for the rhetic act because we know that only someone with the abstracted purposes of a theorist will wish regularly to speak of rhetic acts. The theoretical abstraction envisaged connects the *saying* that figures in particular rhetic acts with the idea of the literal meaning of words. It is true that in the ordinary course of reporting speech, there are more interesting things to be told about what a speaker achieved or intended to achieve than what her words literally meant, or what she said in the plain, thin, abstracted sense of "say" that goes with the rhetic act. But this point ought to cast no doubt on the possibility of making rhetic act reports.

Still, Searle's main doubt was whether rhetic acts can be kept suitably separate from illocutionary acts. He wrote: "The concepts [*rhetic*] act and *illocutionary* act are indeed different, just as the concepts *terrier* and *dog* are different. But the conceptual difference is not sufficient to establish a distinction between separate classes of acts, because just as every terrier is a dog, so every [rhetic] act is an illocutionary act."[19] In saying here that every rhetic act is an illocutionary act, Searle may only have meant what Austin put more accurately when he said that "to perform a [rhetic] act is . . . also and *eo ipso* to perform an *illocutionary* act."[20] This is to say that doing one thing (of a rhetic sort) is doing another thing (of an illocutionary sort): each speech action is of (at least) two kinds—rhetic and illocutionary.[21] But that has no tendency to show that a rhetic act can be an illocutionary act, as Searle asserts. And it suggests that Searle's analogy with dogs is not very apt; the statement that all terriers are dogs is hard to construe in parallel with the claim that all rhetic acts are illocutionary acts, because animals are particulars and speech acts aren't.

Presumably the thought that suggested the analogy to Searle was that the determinables "rhetic" and "illocutionary" subsume the same classes, or subsume overlapping classes, of determinate acts. Searle makes it clear that he was led to this thought by considering the case of explicit performatives, where, in his view, locutionary meaning determines illocutionary force.[22] What this means is that one cannot do the locutionary thing without its being determined that one has therein done a certain illocutionary thing; one cannot, for example, say that one promises to return the book without thereby promising to return the book. But even if this is right, it does not yield any general conclusion, like Searle's, about "*every* rhetic act." And in particular cases, it shows only that given that some particular rhetic act was done, one can know that some particular determinate illocutionary act was done, which is not to say of any rhetic act that it *is* an illocutionary one. Just as we can distinguish the kind *terrier* from the kind *dog*, even though every animal that is a terrier is a dog, so we can distinguish two speech acts, even in cases in which every utterance that is of one act is of the other: we can distinguish, for instance, *saying that one promises to return the book* from *promising to return the book*.

It seems then that Searle's analogy leads in an unintended direction when we compare like with like: his distinction between a difference of concepts and a difference of acts cuts no ice when it is recognized what sort of thing speech acts are. Picturing two theoretical taxonomies, one for animals and one for utterances, we imagine *dog* taking its place above *terrier* in a hierarchy of levels, but we may imagine *saying that one promises to return the book* and *promising to return the book* as on some same level in the other taxonomic hierarchy. These two speech acts are subsumed by the rhetic and the illocutionary act respectively, and the rhetic and the illocutionary act are both at some same (high) level. (It is the contrast between two taxonomic pictures that shows up here which has led me to use the talk of determinables and determinates in the case of speech acts.)[23]

It appears now that the claim that, in certain cases, meaning determines force is no obstacle to persevering, even in those cases, with a rhetic/illocutionary distinction. But if one returns to Austin, one finds another possible source of the kind of doubt Searle had in the case of explicit performatives. Austin held two theses about utterances of explicit performative sentences: they are not statements; they do not have truth values. Either of these theses might be thought to make a difficulty for the idea that there is a rhetic act when an explicit performative is uttered. For it may be asked, If no statement is made with an utterance, is anything really said? And it may be asked, If nothing true can be said with an utterance, and nothing untrue can be said with it, can anything be said?

Underlying the first of these questions is the view that only statements are sayings. But in the plain, thin sense of "say" that occurs in rhetic act reports, this is wrong: it is easier to say three impossible things before breakfast than to make three impossible statements before breakfast; I could be fully serious if I said, asking you to reflect on the idea, that a transcendental self owns each of us, but this is not something that I could in all seriousness state. Perhaps it is forgotten that reports of sayings need make no commitments about statements. Or perhaps too much weight is placed upon reflections about how we should ordinarily report utterances of "I promise that I'll return the book." (Ordinarily of course we should report "She promised," and not "She said that she promised.")

But even if the argument from the non-statement-making function of explicit performatives is flawed, it appears to start well enough. The sort of use explicit performatives are cut out for may actually be incompatible with a statement-making use. If someone states that p, then (usually) it is possible to take her to be coming out with her words because she believes that p; but if someone says that she promises to return the book, then (usually) her intention is to make it the case that she has in speaking promised this. If this is right, our view of someone who explicitly promises stands in the way of supposing that she makes a statement. Someone starts on the sentence "I promise . . ." which means that p. Can we *both* think that she intends thereby to bring it about that p, which apparently requires that we think that she think that it is not yet the case that p, *and* think that she will thereby state that p, which apparently requires that we could think of her as thinking already that it is the case that p?[24]

If the non-statement-making function of some performatives is allowed, the other argument against the possibility of giving rhetic act descriptions of their utterances must be assessed on its merits. In fact, however, the two sorts of arguments have probably been conflated: the non-constative nature of uses of performatives and their failure to have truth values certainly seem to have been linked in Austin's mind.[25] The dissociation of *saying* from *stating* may work to sever any supposed link between being statable and being such as to be true or false. And the dissociation having been effected, we can ask what reason there might be for thinking that one does not speak truly if one says that one promises. If no reason is offered, then all the positive reasons for supposing that utterances of explicit performatives do have truth values can come into their own.[26] What is more, the account of why performatives are *not* used for stating[27] appears to require that they *are* assessed for truth. An explicit performative is used with the intention of bringing it about that p; when successful, the speaker has brought it about that p. But success then consists in the truth of the utterance, which is after all a saying that p.

This last point depends on the truism that if someone says that p, then all that is required for the truth of her utterance is that p. A related truism tells us that if an utterance characterizable as of the phonetic act *saying s* is characterizable also as of the rhetic act *saying that p*, then all that is required for the truth of her utterance is that p. These truisms are relied on by those who, seeing the special properties of Tarskian theories of truth, have come to claim that such theories can subserve theories of meaning.[28]

The distinction between the locutionary and the illocutionary portions of accounts of language use has been taken here as a distinction between language-specific things and something not language-specific: a theory of locution is a theory for English or for French or for whichever language, but an account of illocution will serve any language. It should be acknowledged, though, that we can imagine regularities in language use that are not ubiquitous, yet that are assignable neither to locutionary matters (having to do with the conventional significance of sounds) nor to matters that we can readily regard as extralinguistic. This means that there could be things to include in the illocutionary portion of an account of the use of some language that do not have universal application. Still, if there are such regularities, then they can be associated with communities of speakers, rather than with languages per se; and the correct locutionary theory for a language will remain as something that can be set out independently of the particular illocutionary practices of particular speech communities. The line between locution and illocution, which comes at the point of the rhetic act, seems then to be a firm line; it is firmer than the line that I suggested Urmson drew, between what is genuinely illocutionary and what requires language only incidentally or accidentally.

If we thought of an account of language use as equipped to record what speech acts there were on occasion, then the illocutionary portion of that account would be bound to lack the systematic character of the locutionary portion. For whereas the question which rhetic thing would be done by someone who did some particular phonetic thing is a question that can be answered more or less automatically (without recourse to contextual factors save those that, intuitively, bear on the interpretation of words), the question which illocutionary things would be done by someone who did some particular rhetic thing is affected by countless factors that are contextual in the broadest sense and on which the extralinguistic purposes of speakers bear. (This is part of the reason why the line between what a study of language properly concerns and what it doesn't cannot be very firm.) It is not that there are no good questions of a theoretical sort about illocution. We can ask, What sort of thing may be conveyed when certain sorts of things are said?[29] and, What is the nature of determinate illocutionary acts, such as *stating* or *promising*? What we cannot hope for is a theory that regularly says exceptionless things of the form: if there were an utterance of such and such rhetic kind, then it would also and *eo ipso* be of such and such illocutionary kinds. (It may be doubted whether something of that form is right even for explicit performatives; if it is right, then they provide a special case.)

When it comes to locution, we do hope for systematic theory. A theory of locution should provide one with all that is necessary to move systematically from reports of the phonetic acts that utterances are of, to reports of the rhetic acts they are of; from an instance of (P) to the correct instance of (R).

(P) An L speaker made these sounds: ----
(R) The L speaker said that * * * *

If theories of truth can be introduced into theories of locution, then that is because they can be devised to do the work of moving from (P)'s fillings to (R)'s. The target theorems of a suitably constrained theory of truth[30] are on the pattern of:

(T) ---- is true in L iff * * * *

I have envisaged a theory of truth as doing its work at the level of locution. One could, if one wanted, introduce the illocutionary act of *stating* or *asserting* into the scene. So it might be said: Where the target theorems of a suitably constrained theory of truth for L tells us such things as that s is true in L if and only if p, there we know such things as that s can be used by L speakers to *state* that p. Going straight to this formulation, one bypasses rhetic act reports; and it might seem an advantage to tie the notion of truth directly to illocutionary acts. For successfully using indicative sentences communicatively is ordinarily a matter of conveying truths. If truth is to be the central concept of semantic theory, is this not because truth enters essentially, in this way, into a properly purposive description of what people do when there is linguistic communication?

Well, the account of explicit performatives has reminded us that we must have room to predicate truth of indicative utterances that are not fit to make statements. And this point should not go unheeded. The notions of "stating" and "being true" seemed to have been closely linked in Austin's mind. It seems that they are closely linked in the mind of anyone who espouses a correspondence theory of truth, as such theories are traditionally conceived. If we proclaim that a statement is true if things are as the speaker, in making it, states that they are, and we reflect on this as telling us what we need to know about truth, then that may induce in us a picture of a range of things that must be matched with statements, so that the truth of the statements depends upon the existence of those things. What fact is it, we might then ask, whose existence must be investigated, if we attempt to evaluate for truth an utterance of "I promise to return the book"? The answer will seem to be, There is no fact whose existence it would be appropriate to try to ascertain, because the person who says "I promise to return the book" does not come out with something that purports to be matched to how things are independently of her. Here we see a conception of what it is to make a statement conspiring with a certain conception of truth to present the illusion that explicit performatives do not have truth values.

Of course it is not enough to free ourselves from a correspondence view of truth to point out that not all sayings are statings. For it is open to remark that a saying is true if things are as the speaker, in saying it, says that they are, and this (in which we write "say" where we had "state") might equally lead someone to suppose that things suitably independent of sayings, and corresponding to them, make sayings true. To be free from the correspondence conception we need to recognize that things' being as they are stated, or said, to be requires a relation of identity between how things are and how they are stated, or said, to be. (In the truism that if someone says that p, then all that is required for the truth of her utterance is that p, the words "that p" play the same role twice over.) Still, the line of thought that persuades people that utterances of explicit performatives cannot be true may rely upon a conception of truth exhausted by a conception of what we aim at when we aim at truth, and a particular vision of the aim of the statement maker may be what sustains the correspondence view of truth. In any event, we shall certainly need to have resisted the temptations of the correspondence view if we are to suppose that indicative sentences can, in general, receive semantic treatment in a truth-conditional theory.[31]

In placing emphasis on what Austin called the rhetic act, I do not mean to detract from the importance of the particular illocutionary act of *stating* (or *asserting*). Certainly *stating* cannot remain offstage for very long.

Granting that utterances are manifestations of minds, we may conceive of saying something, even in the thin sense of the rhetic act, as putting a thought into the open. If what is put forward is something that may be true or false, then one especially straightforward way to explain its being put forward is to suggest that this is done because as far as the speaker knows the thought is *true*. But when something is put forward because (inter alia) as far as the speaker knows it is true, then a statement is made. The simplicity of the connection between *saying* and *stating*, forged here with the notion of truth, may explain why *stating* has seemed to be the central illocutionary thing done with indicative sentences. When someone can be interpreted as stating that p, or as knowing that *state that p* is something another speaker has done, her knowledge of meaning is evinced as plainly as can be.[32]

Two further symptoms of *stating*'s central part are these. First, a great many illocutionary acts that might be done by saying that p—for example, *inexplicitly warning that p*, *conversationally implicating that q*, and *hinting that r*—if indeed they are to be done by saying that p, must be done (also) by stating that p. Second, some illocutionary acts, such as *hinting that p*, cannot be done by saying that p; and the reason seems to be that you can't both state that p *and* hint that p, and you can't get away with saying that p without stating that p—at least not if you can be taken to be in a position to get it across that p.[33]

Even if stating must be regarded as the central illocutionary act, there is a further reason why it can be salutary nonetheless to focus on Austin's rhetic act. With the rhetic act in mind, I think we may have a key to the proper treatment of *mood*—so that we shall be able to deal with utterances of imperative, interrogative, and optative sentences.

Theories of locution have been characterized here as theories that could enable one to know which rhetic things are done on the basis of knowing which phonetic things are done. But if the only sort of rhetic act were that which can be reported by using the "say" of (R), then this characterization would contain an oversight. There is no correct description on the (R) pattern of someone who uses a non-indicative sentence; and this ensures that a theory of locution that countenanced no other rhetic act

Things Done with Words 41

than that of *saying* would leave the use of non-indicative sentences out of account.[34] Yet non-indicatives surely must be treated in a theory of locution, because the phenomenon of mood is constituted by devices having a certain recurrent, conventional effect. And it seems wrong to suppose that non-indicatives can be assimilated to indicatives.[35] In order to provide an account of their use, then, I suggest we shall have to recognize new determinate rhetic acts, corresponding one to one with the moods found in a language.

In any non-indicative sentence, one may discern an indicative core and a device that indicates mood. An imperative-indicating device, for instance, can stand to record whatever transformation takes one from (e.g.) "You will shut the door" to "Shut the door" (or whatever other transformation or pattern of intonation does the same work). We may indicate the presence of the device in the latter sentence by rewriting it thus: !"You will shut the door"! What we can add now to an account of locution, subserved as before by a suitably constrained theory of truth, is that *L* speakers' utterances described as !s! are *imperative sayings* that *p*. More generally we can see to it that we have as many things on this pattern as there are moods introduced by transformations in the language:

(P*) An *L* speaker utters |s|

For any particular case of something on (P*)'s pattern (for any mood indicated at the place where "|" is written), we should arrange that we can get from it to something on the pattern of:

(R*) The *L* speaker says . . . -ly that *p*.

In the instance of (R*) that is correct for the mood indicated in some instance of (P*), we write at the place of " . . . " a word that expresses the property possessed by any utterance of any sentence in that mood.[36]

It will be asked with what justification we introduce these rhetic acts: do we have any right to the notion of an *imperative* or *interrogative saying*, or of someone's *saying imperatively* or *interrogatively*? Well, it has to be realized that *imperative sayings* are no more sayings than false pearls are pearls. If someone simply does not like the idea of such a modifier, he should invent a new term:

he can call *imperative sayings* "impings" if he wants, and where I should talk of speakers as *saying imperatively*, he will talk of them as *imping*.

My introduction of such terms as *say imperatively* and *say interrogatively* reflects two beliefs. First, our language contains a perfectly good word to serve in a theory of locution that treats all indicative sentences—namely, the "say" of (R).[37] Second, it may be that our language contains no words that can similarly serve in a theory of locution that treats non-indicative sentences. Even someone who disagreed with the first belief might accept the gist of what I have said about the treatment of indicatives; and if he did, he would need to introduce some term of art to replace the word "say" in (R). My second belief, on the other hand, represents acknowledgment that there may be no alternative but to introduce terms of art into the instances of (R*). Someone who disagreed with this would think that "saying imperatively" (or whatever) could be replaced with an honest English word. What is at issue, then, when it is asked whether we are entitled to such a notion as "say imperatively," is only whether the meaning theorist is at liberty to help himself, if need be, to words for what language users do whose correct application goes hand in hand with the use of the various moods that feature in the language.

If you understand speakers who use *indicative* sentences in some language, then you have the ability to tell what speakers are up to when they use them. And your ability is accounted for when (1) the contents of utterances of sentences you can recognize are specified, (2) it is specified that speakers, in uttering the sentences, *say* those contents (in the plain, thin sense of "say" that [R] uses), and (3) a general account is given that relates what substantive things a speaker may intentionally do on occasion by saying something with a particular content. If you understand any brand of non-indicative sentence, then you can recognize such sentences as transformationally related to their indicative cores, and you can come to know what substantive things speakers may do on occasion with utterances of sentences of that brand having cores with a particular content. Your ability is accounted for when (1') the contents of utterances of indicative cores you can recognize are specified, (2') it is specified that, in case a certain mood is recognizably present along with the core, speakers are related to those contents in a certain mode, and (3′) an account is given of what substantive things speakers may on occasion intentionally do by being related to particular contents in that mode. Now I think that in the case of any particular mood, you can call "the certain mode" that goes with that mood by any name you please, and that you can introduce any verb you like to relate speakers to contents when their utterances are related to contents in that mode. For I think that by reminding you of what is involved in your ability to understand sentences in that mood, and then claiming that your ability can be accounted for with (1′), (2′), and (3′), I have, by way of comparison with the indicative case, fixed what you will mean, whatever your choice of word. But if the sense of "say imperatively" (or whatever) is seen to be fixed even as it is seen how "say imperatively" can be used to achieve what an account of language use should achieve, there need be no complaint about its introduction.

To see this it may help to consider the position of someone who does not use or understand imperatives, or does not use or understand sentences in some other mood we may imagine we could discern in some language. She is a bit like someone who lacks a concept expressed by a word of speakers whom she wants to understand, and who must acquire the concept before she can understand them. (She would have acquired the concept if she had come to understand them.) But if she has an understanding of those terms from a theory of force that would be used at (3′) in connection with imperatives, then it ought to be easy to convey to her what she needs to know: one can describe to her the transformations by which sentences in the imperative mood are got from indicatives, one can tell her that utterances of the transformed sentences are *imperative sayings* of their contents, and one can give an account of the sorts of interesting things that speakers may intentionally do by *saying imperatively* that p. Provided she understands the last stage here, which of course will require an ability to engage in psychological explanation generally, she can come to know what it is to *say imperatively*.

Perhaps I can now remain agnostic whether English words can serve in the place of "say imperatively" and "say interrogatively." Some people may think that "tell that" and "ask whether" can serve in a theory of locution for imperatives and interrogatives.

The only question would be whether these words (or some others) do actually behave as the words whose behavior I have claimed to fix behave.

It might be held that no actual English verbs could be suitable for use in a theory of locution for (say) interrogatives, on the grounds that "ask whether," "inquire whether," and all such English verbs imply that utterances carry a certain force, and that nothing could guarantee any constancies between the use of a mood in sentences and the force accruing to their utterances. But of course if someone did maintain that "ask whether" could play the role of "say interrogatively," then it would be her view that "ask whether" is as plain and thin as the "say" that figures in rhetic act reports of indicatives, so that she would deny that describing an utterance as someone's asking whether *p* is already to describe it as having a certain force. She will say (rightly or wrongly) that the fact that a sentence in the interrogative mood need not be used by someone whose purpose is to question, but can be used by someone whose purpose is to command (for instance), does not show that there are uses of interrogatives that are not askings, but only shows that some askings are commandings.

Whatever the truth about words like "ask" and "tell," the point about the lack of constancy between mood and force is not to be forgotten. We have to allow not only that interrogatives can be used to tell people what to do, but also (for example) that a sentence in the indicative mood can be used with the force of a question, that a sentence in the imperative mood can be used with the force of a wish, and, perhaps, that on the stage a sentence of whatever mood may be used by an actress without her performing any *illocutionary* act in propria persona.[38]

Now in the paper considered above, Searle could find no room for any conception of a *rhetic* act except as something highly indeterminate and subsuming illocutionary acts. His eventual conclusion was that Austin's rhetic act should be replaced with a *propositional* act.[39] The lack of constant connections between mood and force shows that Searle's conclusion is correct up to a point: if one wants to isolate things done with words such that one can say that a speaker has done them without making any commitment to any illocutionary thing she has also done, then one must isolate the propositional contents of utterances. But it seems wrong to suppose that when a speaker has used a non-indicative, one should be confined to characterizing a propositional act in Searle's sense, which reveals only the content of an indicative core. The two sentences "The door is shut" and "Is the door shut?" are surely not distinguishable only at the level of illocution—as if someone might be in a position to tell what a speaker did with her words knowing only that the utterance was of the propositional act that the door is shut and without knowing which of these two sentences her utterance was of. My account agrees with Searle's insofar as the same propositional content is attributed to the utterances of both "The door is shut" and "Is the door shut?" But it distinguishes the two sentences insofar as their utterances are of different determinate rhetic acts. The lack of constancy between mood and force then seems to suggest that the rhetic act is an ineliminable part of a taxonomy of speech actions: it is impossible to isolate any class of determinate illocutionary acts that contains all and only those subsuming the utterances subsumed by some one determinate rhetic act.

The line insisted on here, between locution and illocution, is not a new one. What I hope is that the standpoint from which I have drawn it, exploiting an Austinian conception of a rhetic act, may encourage a particular view of the role of theories of truth and of the aspirations of accounts of language use.[40]

We imagined someone who does not use or understand imperatives, and that we might convey to her an understanding of the locutionary theory for a language containing imperatives by exploiting her understanding of terms from an account of force. But of course someone without an imperative device in her language might very well lack the concepts used in a theory of force in connection with imperatives; and then it seems that there is nothing we could tell her that would enable her to latch onto the notion of *saying imperatively*. A similar thought experiment can be tried for indicatives. Suppose that someone does not understand the "say" of the rhetic act, and lacks the concepts used in an account of force for indicatives. She cannot see any of the point of making utterances. Hers is the position of pre-linguistic children everywhere: unable to saying anything, they don't know what it is to say something. They are not in a position to acquire the knowledge that a theory of meaning for a language is fit to provide.[41]

If we had thought that a philosophically interesting account of language use should be capable of enabling someone to achieve what children achieve when they learn their first language, we should be disappointed now. And if we had thought that a theory of truth and a theory of force exhausted an account of language use, we should have had to remain disappointed. A theory of truth in itself says nothing whatever about what speakers do, and an account of force only says things of the form: a speaker can do this thing by doing this other. Put the two together, and one is told something about words themselves, and something else about what it is to do things; yet the something else takes for granted the idea of doing *something* with words. There is then a gap in the account. But when accounts of language use are separated into theories of locution and accounts of illocution (i.e., force), there should be no suggestion that we ought to try to fill the gap that would show itself here. This should be clear from the nature of the role of determinate rhetic acts. These are the basic significant linguistic acts.[42] With an ability to recognize rhetic acts, one knows the language-specific determinants of illocutionary, or force-endowed, acts. But it is only in the use of language that such an ability is gained or evinced. And if there is in fact no way to come to know what it is to do things with words except practically (by coming to do them), then one may suppose that the theorist who helps himself to rhetic acts only acknowledges that theory runs out here.

PATRICK SUPPES & COLLEEN CRANGLE

Context-fixing Semantics for the Language of Action

In this paper we develop the view that the specific interpretation of many ordinary English words can be fixed only within their context of use and not before. It describes an approach to the interpretation of natural-language commands in which the context of utterance is brought to bear on the interpretation of words used in the command. We also argue for a view of procedural semantics that is grounded in intentions. From this standpoint we outline the concept of a natural model for the interpretation of commands. Next we deal with those aspects of context we stress: the perceptual situation in which a command is given, the cognitive and perceptual functioning of the agent being addressed, and the immediate linguistic surround. The final section shows how our context-dependent view of the lexicon is integrated with the syntactic analysis of a sentence. Here we come into conflict with much conventional linguistic wisdom about the construction of grammars.

An important general point about much of the analysis in this paper is that it is done from the perspective of our work on instructable robots. The reasons for this emphasis are made explicit at the end of the next section.

Before turning to details we want to make some general remarks about context. The fundamental assumption of our work on the lexicon is that the precise interpretation of many words can be fixed only after the context in which the word is used has been taken into account. Contextual information, we claim, is an integral part of what a word means. Words do not in general have determinate meaning; their semantic significance is fixed by the actual occasions of their use.[1] Our purpose in this paper is to present evidence of the context dependency of ordinary words and to discuss the mechanisms by which the context fixes the precise interpretation of those words. We pay particular attention to the language of action—exemplified in imperatives—which places special demands on model-theoretic semantics. We argue that the language of action calls for a procedural semantics, and we discuss something of the potential of procedural semantics and the new problems it poses.

The fact that context must play a role in the interpretation of utterances has long been acknowledged. This is a familiar and obvious fact in the theory of demonstratives. A detailed logical treatment of their dependence on context is given by David Kaplan.[2] A more general analysis of context is given by Jon Barwise and John Perry,[3] who distinguish three aspects of context: the discourse situation (the time and place of utterance); speaker connections (a speaker's experiences, past and present, providing connections to objects, places, etc.); and resource situations (the use of one state of affairs to convey information about another). Our emphasis on the semantics of the lexicon leads in a direction that is orthogonal to the works of Kaplan and Barwise and Perry. A complete theory of context would need to include both kinds of analysis. Indeed, there is no general agreement on just what the complete role of context is. One prevailing view in both linguistics and philosophy is that an analysis of context is to be superimposed on the study of morphology, syntax, and semantics, all of which may be specified independently of the context of actual utterances. Our view is that context intrudes strongly at the lexical level and makes itself felt in ways that greatly affect traditional approaches to syntax. Suppes has examined some of these consequences for syntactic structure;[4] we examine them again in the final section of this paper, showing the expanded force of those arguments for the language of action.

Intentions

There is a fundamental point about the nature of intentions that is central to our analysis. When an intention is expressed, as in "Go to the other side of the room," the meaning of the expression does not include a detailed algorithm for executing the command. The particular path taken by the agent satisfying the command is not part of the meaning of the expressed intention. If it were, the meaning specificity of intentions and the commands expressing them would be computationally intolerable.

A vast array of scientific evidence is available to show that the central and peripheral nervous systems of humans (and other higher animals) are organized hierarchically, but also in a decentralized, pluralistic way.[5] Instructions for detailed movements that are part of some intended action are not transmitted from the central to the peripheral nervous system—again, the computational load of doing so would be intolerable. This decentralization of responsibility for the execution of details is well reflected in our intuitive ideas about the satisfaction of a command. In no sense do we compute a specific trajectory that must be followed in crossing a room or in carrying out any other sort of movement. Even in cases of instruction, we simply cannot verbally describe a specific trajectory. Most actions in fact execute a kinematic path in the four-dimensional space-time of classical physics, the details of which are quite beyond the descriptive powers of ordinary language.

Context enters these considerations in several different ways. Part of the decentralization of action execution is that the expressed intention satisfied by the execution ignores details of context that must be taken into account at a lower level of the agent's system in order for an action to be successfully carried out; for example, an action that required a path through several traffic lights would not ordinarily have been guided by any mention of the traffic signals in the verbal expression of the intention. But the traffic lights would automatically—in ordinary cases—be taken care of at a lower level. Notice that this sketchy character of the expressed intention with respect to any actual path taken is characteristic both of intentions expressed about one's own future behavior and of commands given to another agent.

However, if an agent—person or robot—is asked to fetch a book from a table on the other side of the room, and if the agent knocks over a chair in doing so, in ordinary circumstances we regard the movement of the agent as satisfying only partially or rather poorly the request made. Expressed intentions carry with them a bundle of ceteris paribus conditions that impose a variety of constraints on the specific procedures actually executed. These ceteris paribus conditions are not given concretely or in advance but depend on the particular context in which an action is carried out. From a psychological standpoint, these conditions become embodied in habits. Learning in all its forms is needed for the unspoken consonance between intentions and habits to develop. If someone is driving a car while thinking intently about some problem, the person will, as we say, *automatically* stop for red lights. Other cases of habit are even more ordinarily a matter of automatic, that is, unreflective, response. If I am walking somewhere on an errand, the motor control and perceptual feedback required for normal walking operate quite outside of consciousness. These habits are efficient but unconscious ones. Moreover, even if we try to reflect consciously on how we are walking, our cognitive insight into the details is poor unless we are specialists in the psychology and neurophysiology of such matters. And even specialists can be directly aware of only very limited aspects of their own procedures of movement.

The kinds of considerations just set forth support the view that habits take care of many contextual details of action execution—the *expected* details, we might want to add. Before we circle back to semantics, we will introduce a useful distinction about actions. The distinction we have in mind is familiar in the theory of events as ordinarily developed in probability theory. Suppose we roll two dice and bet on the *event* of a sum of eight coming up. Several different *outcomes* will realize this event, namely the pairs (6, 2), (5, 3), (4, 4), (3, 5), and (2, 6). In the elementary probability cases, the description of the outcomes is nearly as simple as the description of the event, but in more complicated, less regimented cases this is not so. If, for example, a meteorologist forecasts moderate rain tomorrow afternoon, he does not begin to describe the many different configurations of the atmosphere, that is, outcomes, that could produce this event. Notice that the elementary probability cases strip away by obvious convention most of the details of the outcomes. Essentially, the process of getting to an outcome is not recorded at all. Only the end result matters, provided—and this is an important proviso—the process satisfies a set of mostly unstated ceteris paribus conditions. The analysis of these conditions is no part of elementary probability theory, but is a necessary part of professional practice for those who love to shoot craps. The most obvious standard condition is that the dice must be thrown against the vertical side of the crap table opposite the shooter before coming to rest on the horizontal surface of the table. It has been known since the time of Poincaré that the detailed analysis of the motion of dice from the instant of their being thrown until they come to rest, that is, the analysis of the process of reaching the outcome, is a matter of great mathematical difficulty. The listing of the possible outcome *results* for the pair of dice is trivial, but the full listing or description of the possible outcome *processes* is in fact impossible.

In the case of actions, the initial distinction we have in mind is between an *event* and an action outcome or *specific action*. It will also be useful occasionally to distinguish between *process* and *result*. We therefore introduce the following technical terms: "event result," "event process," "specific-action result," and "specific-action process."

We can now turn back to semantics. The semantics of commands have, from a process standpoint, an appalling lack of concreteness. When Susan says to an agent "Bring me the book on the table," we naturally tend to think that the command's satisfaction is evaluated just in terms of the result—what we have termed the event result. Here we are close to the situation in elementary probability theory. In the pretty little model of elementary probability theory, the command to the crapshooter "Roll an eight!" has a simple result-semantics. The command is satisfied by any of the pairs listed above, and not satisfied by any of the other possible pairs. No context to worry about. No ambiguity. The same is true of the command "Bring me the book" if only the result-semantics consisting of the pair (brought the book, did not bring the book) is considered. But lurking in the background are those nebulous and troublesome ceteris paribus conditions. An ideal process-semantics of the book command should, at the specific-action process level, consist of all possible acceptable paths of movement to the table and back, together with a probabilistic measure of their likelihood of occurrence. But this is hard enough to do for the simple, idealized models of classical statistical mechanics. It is out of the question in a situation like the present one, in which the component forces determining the motion are so diverse and subtle. Something less detailed is essential; this is reflected in the inevitable vagueness of ordinary descriptions of such processes. Ordinary language, like ordinary conscious thinking, is oriented toward results, not processes.

Even this last claim is too general. There are many devices in ordinary language for distinguishing between process and result. The many distinctions of aspect and tense that are available in English and other languages reflect important semantic features that are essential for accurate and subtle communication. It is just that we do not usually think in terms of any very elaborate schemes for expressing at the appropriate level of detail the semantics of process referred to in ordinary talk.

Although the usual discussions of aspect in English center on the indicative mood, it is easy to generate imperative examples. Contrast the perfective (1) to the imperfective (2):

(1) Stop at the table.
(2) Keep going until you reach the table.

With respect to the process-result distinctions introduced above, we immediately think of (1) in terms of results. The case of (2) is less clear. The imperfective aspect suggests process, but all the same the primary semantic evaluation would probably be result oriented, unless the agent stopped on the way to the table. We are not really certain about this, but when possible a result is probably looked for.

In many cases, however, the only semantic possibility is to make some crude appraisal of process satisfaction. Consider these imperfective imperatives expressing a demand for habitual action:

(3) Take walks every day.
(4) Keep working regularly.

We would ordinarily accept very sketchy behavior reports to judge (3) or (4) satisfied—nothing like process specificity would be asked for. To use our earlier distinctions, we would accept event-process reports at quite a high level of generality.

Given the difficulties of these semantic problems, we have adopted a standard strategy. We have retreated to a simpler framework than that of human response to a verbal command or request for action. The simpler framework is that of instructable robots, which are vastly more simple and simpleminded than people—at least at present. Such robots accept commands in a natural language such as English and use those commands to extend their basic repertoire of actions. The kind of detailed semantic analysis required for instructable robots forces us to confront problems that may remain hidden in more abstract philosophical inquiries. Even here the semantic difficulties are daunting. Although our work in this area has been going on for some time, we are far from having anything definitive to show. Nevertheless, because we can lay out the underlying procedures in an explicit and systematic manner, our robot world, in spite of its severe limitations, provides an opportunity for a kind of detailed analysis that is not possible for human execution of commands. Many of our examples will reinforce this point, particularly those in the penultimate section, which discusses intentions and procedures for the robot that has been the focus of our recent work.

Natural Models for the Interpretation of Commands

In a recent phase of our work on instructable robots, we have used a robotic aid that was designed to assist the physically disabled. Earlier work made use of a robot that was taught elementary mathematics.[6] All instruction to these robots is interpreted relative to a set of models that define the agent to whom instruction is being given and the perceptual situation in which the instruction takes place. The command "Find the empty space" to the arithmetic robot of R. E. Maas and Suppes, for instance, is interpreted relative to the rows and columns of an arithmetic problem. That same command given to the mobile base of the robotic aid is interpreted relative to the configuration of objects and their parts in the room in which the instruction is taking place.

One natural semantical outcome of the viewpoint of experimental robotics is that one is not interested in the set of logically possible models satisfying a given utterance or piece of discourse. In all cases of the kind of work we are considering—and we would claim for almost all natural discourse—it is appropriate to take a subset of the set of possible models by holding rigid, at the very least, ordinary mathematics and physics, but in fact a larger body of knowledge about the real world. What this larger body of knowledge is and how it restricts the set of models may be expressed as a question about how one deals with the concept of something's being possible. We are not at all talking about the kind of possibility usually thought of in terms of logical possibility but about the ordinary notion of the possible that lies behind ordinary discourse. This notion of possibility assumes as given the kinds of fixed structures familiar in ordinary talk. Moreover, we really want to say something more radical. For the completely detailed and implemented semantic analysis needed in robotics work, we restrict even more severely the fixed set of models to ones that just encompass a particular environment, for example, the room and its physical contents in the case of the robotic aid for the physically disabled. In this set of models the frozen metaphors of abstract language so common in much ordinary talk would be ruled out. Only quite literal physical language would be understood, which means that the set of models is severely restricted to models of physical phenomena.

It is necessary, however, to include in the set of models a framework for the cognitive, perceptual, and motor functioning of the agent—person or robot—to whom the commands are addressed. This means that if we are talking about the robotic aid we are not simply restricting ourselves to the physical objects in the room but must have a way of integrating the models with the cognitive and perceptual states of the robot. The language of communication will, as we envisage it, be almost entirely physical in character. In a command like "Go to the table and pour me a glass of water," all of the terms have a direct physical interpretation. But satisfaction of the command in a set of models requires some apparatus to express as part of the model the cognitive state and perceptual and motor activity of the robot. This point has special plausibility when one considers the verbs "remember" and "look at" in commands such as "Remember where you placed the cup" or "Look at the chair to your left."

Reducing the possible set of models to a relatively small set helps to fix the context of an utterance. The semantic content of the lexical items is given in terms of these models, and the rules of semantic composition are expressed in terms of these models. But—and this is crucial—for many words, residual contextual factors remain and the precise interpretation of a word gets fixed only on the actual occasion of its use, and gets fixed normally, to use our earlier distinction, in terms of results, not processes. It is the residual contextual factors that are of special interest in this paper and are the subject of the next section.

Our use of a set of models to define the context of an utterance has something in common with the "commonsense metaphysics" approach to the lexicon[7] in which core theories are constructed about physical objects—and about time, space, material, and so on—and in which the lexical items are characterized in terms of those theories. Our work is different, however, in that we focus rather more closely on specific contexts of use, and we make provision in the lexical items for those contexts, at the time of utterance, to make their contribution.

In our work on the lexicon for the language of action, our search has been for semantic content that is specific and psychologically plausible in the context in which the language is being used. Consider the word "avoid," for instance, which in many of its ordinary uses carries the sense of evading or shunning or keeping out of the way of something. It is possible to give a general characterization of what this word means, a characterization that charts the interesting relationship between avoiding, evading, shunning, and keeping out of the way. However, such a characterization of the word is neither necessary nor sufficient in the language of action. It is not enough to enable an agent to understand in a detailed way a command such as "Avoid the chair." And the agent can understand and obey that command without ever understanding the words "shun," "evade," and "keep away from." Procedural or operational denotations are most appropriate for the language of action. Verbs such as "avoid," "look at," "put," and "remember" function semantically as operations on the natural physical models and are expressed in terms of the models that define the agent's cognitive, perceptual, and motor functioning.

The idea that a natural-language utterance may be represented semantically as a procedure performed by the language user is an old one, championed at one time by T. Winograd and supported in various ways in the work of S. D. Isard, G. A. Miller and P. N. Johnson-Laird, Suppes, and J. van Benthem.[8] But as yet little has been done to offer a theoretically grounded view of procedural semantics for natural languages comparable to the effort for programming languages that began many years ago with J. McCarthy and R. Floyd.[9] In principle, we would like to be able to answer the following question of adequacy: Why these procedures and not others?

We propose the following approach to procedural semantics as a way of answering that question. In broad outline, this is what we do. We describe, intuitively and informally, a class of intentions. These are intentions we want to communicate to the agent—human or robot—through the natural-language commands whose semantics we are concerned with. We then propose a set of procedures whose satisfactory execution should demonstrate that the intentions were successfully communicated. Next, we state satisfaction conditions for these procedures, that is, conditions under which the procedures can be said to have been executed satisfactorily. Finally, we construct proofs that these satisfaction conditions can be met, proofs expressed in terms of the set of models that define the robot's cognitive, perceptual, and motor functioning in the given instructional context.

In terms of the distinction stated above in the section on intentions, we intuitively tend to define satisfaction in terms of event results, the most general of the four categories we introduced. But as we said earlier, satisfaction of a command at this level assumes a variety of unspoken ceteris paribus conditions. When we are interested in a fine-tuning of behavior, as in many instructional contexts, we want to move all the way down to analyzing satisfaction in terms of specific-action processes. Take, for instance, the two commands "Go to the table" and "Go left to the table." The first command simply expresses the result we would like to see. The second command interposes a process condition—that the table be reached by moving to the left. Yet other commands are less clear about the result to be achieved. "Go left toward the table," for instance, may be satisfied even if the table is not reached. And other commands are specific about process: "Keep moving slowly to your left until you are at the table."

It is evident that the construction of proofs of adequacy will vary considerably according to the level at which satisfaction is characterized. Here is a pair of contrasting examples to make the point. Perhaps the most familiar construction of "turtle geometry" as represented in the programming language LOGO is the drawing of a circle, for which an instruction could be "Draw a circle by repeatedly going forward one unit then left one unit." In this case it is easy to prove, for a given unit of measurement relative to the display used, how nicely the generated polygon approximates a circle. However, for the command to the robotic aid "Go to the chair," which expresses the result we would like to see, what is of interest is not the particular path taken but whether the robot reaches the chair or not. We ordinarily judge the satisfaction of the command "Go to the chair," addressed to a person or a robot, in terms of results, not in terms of process—unless something alerts us to do otherwise. If, for instance, a bystander picks up the chair and carries it over to the person, we would be obliged to consider the process whereby the person came to be by the chair.

To what extent can these questions of adequacy be posed at the lexical level? Individual lexical items are themselves often thought to denote procedures, with rules of composition stipulating how these lexical procedures are combined to form a more complex procedure for the whole command. Can we ask of each lexical procedure, Why this procedure and not some other? Consider, for example, the following procedural denotation of the verb "avoid" taken in the context of our work on instructable robots. This procedure uses information about the robot's position and the position of the object to be avoided to generate a velocity vector away from the object. The magnitude of this vector is greatest when the robot is close to the object; it declines in proportion to the robot's distance from the object. At a distance greater than D standard units of measure from the object, the velocity vector is zero. When this procedure is being executed, the robot is never allowed to get within d units of the object. But equally plausible, in the absence of further argument, is another procedure that generates a velocity vector away from the object only when the robot comes within d units of the object, thereby bouncing the robot around the perimeter of the region that surrounds the object.

If, as we propose, intentions are semantically primitive, the procedures that are of primary interest are those "at the level of" the intentions. What is required of the lexical procedures is whatever allows these higher-level procedures to be executed satisfactorily and is in accordance with the class of natural models. But is that the only semantic condition that lexical entries are subject to? Certainly not, and our concern in this paper is to present an important source of semantic constraints on the lexicon, namely, the context at the time of utterance. We emphasize that context plays a central role even at the most general level of satisfaction, that of event results.

To return to the original question of adequacy, it should be clear that the approach outlined allows the following restricted question to be answered: Why these procedures? It also implicitly shows why many other procedures would not be adequate: it would not be possible to give satisfaction conditions for them, conditions, that is, that could be proved to be met in terms of the class of models. The approach we advocate therefore allows a criterion of sufficiency, but not of necessity, to be met. This is as it should be. At the level of computational detail at which we are working—which is not the level of particular hardware and software or a particular neurophysiology but is the level of particular algorithms—we should expect to find more than one procedural account that is adequate.

What remains, of course, for procedural semantics as we conceive it is to show how the procedures associated with the intentions tie up with the English commands that express those intentions. This is where semantic grammars play their role. In a semantic grammar, rules of semantic composition are attached to the phrase-structure rules of the grammar to stipulate how the denotations of individual words are combined to produce a denotation for the whole expression. We return to this step in the final section of this paper.

Examples of Context Fixing

Context-dependent words are not hard to find. The examples of indexical and anaphoric pronouns and adverbs of place and time are familiar. Our claim is that these are the obvious examples of a pervasive semantic phenomenon, especially in the language of action. A first, straightforward example illustrates the role of the perceptual situation in fixing the interpretation of words. This example will come as no surprise; the words of interest in it— "left" and "right"—are generally understood to have context-dependent meaning.[10] The example is given here, however, in preparation for the examples that follow, in which the perceptual situation is required for the interpretation of words that are not as widely recognized to be context dependent.

Consider then the commands "Turn left" and "Move to the right of the chair." There are clearly several ways to interpret a command to turn left: is it to your left (the speaker's) or to my left (the one being instructed), or am I to turn left relative to some path I have been following, as one turns left along a footpath or road? Clearly, information about the orientation of the speaker, or the listener, or any path being followed, will be required for the precise interpretation of "left" in this command. For the command "Move to the right of the chair," since many chairs are thought to have their own left and right (identified by the position of the backrest), "right" could be interpreted relative to the chair and its orientation. But if the chair has no perceptually obvious front and back, "right" must be interpreted relative to the position and orientation of the speaker or relative to the position and orientation of the agent being instructed.

Contextual information is also required to fix the interpretation of intensive adjectives such as "big" and comparatives and superlatives.[11] Our treatment of an adjective such as "large" in the instructable robot project closely follows the analysis of Suppes and E. Macken in recognizing the existence of an underlying ordering relation on the objects referred to by the noun the adjective qualifies. The denotation of the intensive adjective "large" is thought of as a procedure that uses the underlying ordering relation of size to determine if an object, the one said to be large, stands in the appropriate size relation to some criterion object. While this ordering relation is often given by the perceptual situation, particularly for adjectives such as "red" and "large" that refer to physical attributes, there are contexts of use, even for a word such as "large," in which the ordering relation is not immediately accessible by perception—take the phrase "largest donation," for instance, as in "Our company gave the largest donation to the United Way." Our emphasis, however, has been on those uses of language for which the ordering relation is given by the perceptual context.

The criterion object for an intensive adjective is also given by the context. A simple example is provided by the adjective "large" in "large book." The criterion object will typically be different when the context is a shelf of dictionaries and when it is a shelf of poetry volumes. Perhaps the most striking example of the role of the criterion object is given by the phrases "large elephant" and "large ant." While the ordering relations for "large elephant" and "large ant" will both use some measure such as mass or girth, the criterion objects will be quite different. Here we see that the criterion object will sometimes be set not only by extralinguistic factors such as the perceptual situation but also by the immediate linguistic surround of the word: the words "elephant" and "ant" serve to limit the range of entities that may be used as the criterion object.

Many of the words we have encountered in the instructable robot project rely on the perceptual situation for their precise interpretation. We will discuss in some detail as our next example the word "next." This word is similar to the intensive adjectives in that it relies on an underlying ordering relation. There are several other words like this: the ordinals ("first," "second," "last," and so on), the adjectives "top" and "bottom," and the adjective "previous." The intuitive idea behind the semantics of "next" can best be understood if we talk about "the next x," where x may, for example, be "chair," "table," or "wooden chair." When we say "the next x," we are referring to the first x, by some ordering relation, relative to some present reference entity. Three things have to be fixed by the context for the interpretation of "next": the ordering relation, the class of x-type entities from which one will be selected, and some encompassing class of entities that are ordered by the relation. This encompassing class must be specified because it makes perfect sense to talk about the next x even when the present reference entity is not itself an x. A clear example is given by the arithmetic robot of Maas and Suppes. For most uses of "next" in the arithmetic instruction context, the ordering relation required by "next" is given by the relation *vertically below*, a strict partial ordering on the perceptual objects such that each perceptual object that has a successor has a unique immediate successor by this relation, and similarly for a predecessor. That is, in the usual contexts of use for "next," the robot has been, and is expected to continue, scanning down a column. Suppose the robot is focused on the blank space at the top of the tens column of an arithmetic exercise. That blank space plays the role of the reference entity for the interpretation of "next" in "the next number." Thus, for the blank space the robot is focused on to function as the reference entity for "next number," the blank spaces and the digits (numbers) in an arithmetic exercise must all stand in the relation *vertically below*.

Context-fixing Semantics 61

A command may explicitly fix the ordering relation required for the interpretation of "next." Consider, for instance, the command "Choose the next person in order of height," in which the ordering relation is given by the phrase "in order of height." In the absence of such explicit directions, the perceptual situation imposes its own choice of ordering relation in many cases. For instance, suppose the agent being instructed is in a room containing ten chairs arranged in a row. That very arrangement of objects will tend to establish an ordering relation for sentences in which the adjective "next" qualifies the noun "chair." If the agent were positioned alongside the second chair, facing down the row toward the third chair, and if there had been no prior discourse, the command "Go to the next chair" would probably be interpreted as a command to move to the third chair. It is clear that the appropriate ordering relation must not only be available perceptually (or by some other means such as memory), it must also be established as a focus of attention. (The robotic aid at present has no ability to adduce an ordering relation from the perceptual situation. The first time the adjective "next" is used to refer to objects of a certain type, the person instructing the robot is queried for help in fixing an ordering known to the robot. That ordering is subsequently used as the default unless explicit instruction changes it.)

Sometimes two of the three contextual factors required by "next" are set explicitly by the command. Consider again the room containing only the row of chairs, with the agent at the second chair in the row. Suppose the agent were being instructed to clean the wooden chairs by applying a furniture polish, and the row included two cane chairs, one of which was in the third position and the other in the eighth. The command "Clean the next wooden chair" would then direct the agent to the fourth chair in the row, the first wooden chair relative to the present chair. In this case, the adjective "wooden" specifies the class of wooden objects, of which one must be selected, and the noun "chair" specifies the encompassing class of chairs, both wooden and cane. Because there are no objects other than chairs in the room, the class of wooden objects is a subclass of the class of chairs. The restricting class given by the adjective will not in general be a proper subset of the encompassing class, given usually by the noun. In general, the intersection of the two classes must be found before the next x can be selected.

There are many different ways a command may specify the contextual factors required by "next." Consider the command "Go to the next chair to the left." Here "to the left" specifies the ordering relation, a relation, call it L, which could be defined informally as follows: for all a and b, aLb if and only if a is positioned to the left of b and within the compass of an arc of 30 degrees radiating horizontally from b. Consider, however, the command "Go left to the next chair." Here "left" does not make a contribution to the interpretation of "next"; it serves rather as an adverb directly qualifying the verb, acting as an extra constraint on where to go. There are many other examples like this. On one hand, in the command "Search for the next file in alphabetic order," the ordering relation behind the use of "next" is given explicitly by the phrase "in alphabetic order." In the command "Search from A to Z for the next file," on the other hand, that same ordering relation defines a direction in which to search, but leaves open the question of what ordering lies behind the use of "next."

There are also occasions on which the perceptual situation does not play a role in fixing the interpretation of the word "next," as in the phrase "Susan's next book." Here the underlying ordering relation is on publication date, something that is seldom available in the immediate perceptual situation.

Our last extended example in this section draws directly on the functioning of the robotic aid that is the focus of our current work in instructable robots. Here we will examine how the agent's cognitive functioning comes into play in the interpretation of the word "avoid," as used in commands such as "Go to the door, avoiding the cat on the rug" or "While avoiding the table, move three feet left."

As part of the robotic aid's basic repertoire of perceptual and motor functions, there is a procedure that provides the core interpretation for "avoid." This procedure was described earlier. It generates a velocity vector away from the object when the robot is close to the object and prevents the robot from ever getting within d units of the object. At a distance greater than D units from the object, the velocity vector is zero. As described earlier, the procedure has three parameters: the first specifies the object to be avoided and the second and third the distances d and D. The value of the first parameter is given by the interpretation of the object noun phrase in the "avoid" command. The values of d and D may also be fixed explicitly by the command. "Avoid the heating element by at least one foot" sets d to be one foot, for instance. In the absence of such explicit instruction, however, the context of utterance must provide values for these parameters of avoidance. While perceptual feedback may tell the robot when it is within d or D units of the object, it is the robot's cognitive functioning—specifically, the robot's knowledge of the object that is to be avoided—that will set these values appropriately. In general, different objects demand different parameters of avoidance: a fire and a delicate table lamp, for instance, require distinct d and D values. There are further complexities arising from objects that are part of other objects. If the object is physically part of a larger object (it is the back or the leg of a chair, for instance) and if the robot does not have the motor functioning to allow it to avoid the subpart independently of the larger object (the robot cannot, for instance, maneuver around the base or around and between the legs of the chair), the whole object must be used for the setting of the d and D parameters.

The significant point of this extended discussion of several examples is that for many ordinary words, there must be mechanisms for fixing the precise interpretation outside the language itself. In the final section we discuss how these mechanisms are brought into play in coordination with the grammatical analysis of a sentence. The next section examines in some detail, as required for the discussion in the final section, the procedural semantics developed for the robotic aid.

Intentions and Procedures

We turn now to the specifics of the mobile robotic aid operating in a room containing ordinary items of household furniture. The robotic aid consists of a six-jointed arm mounted on the front of an omnidirectional mobile base. The base is fitted with sensor-equipped bumpers. The intentions we want to communicate to this robot concerning its movement across the floor are:

    that the robot go to a given region of the room
    that the robot move in a given direction
    that the robot avoid a given region
    that the robot stay within a given region

that the robot stop doing whatever it is doing at that time
that the robot perform any specific motion at a faster than normal speed
that the robot perform any specific motion at a slower than normal speed
that the robot speed up
that the robot slow down
that the robot pursue two goals simultaneously (the goals are not necessarily achieved simultaneously)
that the robot pursue one goal after another has been achieved
that the robot pursue a goal until a given condition is met (the pursuit of the goal will be interrupted)
that the robot repeatedly pursue a goal until a given condition is met
that the robot pursue a goal if a certain condition is met
that the robot pursue a goal when a certain condition is met
that the robot pursue a goal whenever a certain condition is met.

The conditions we want the robot to detect are:

that a given distance has been traversed
that a given time has elapsed
that the robot's bumpers are hit
that the robot is in a certain region.

In this discussion we are interested only in the movement of the robot across the floor. We therefore restrict our attention to the omnidirectional base of the robot. This mobile base can best be described as a collection of simultaneously executing motor, perceptual, and cognitive processes that communicate with each other under the control of a scheduler. This scheduler has seven modes of operation, corresponding to the following seven procedures (presented here in the notation that places the procedure name followed by its arguments in parentheses):

($Sequence\ A_1\ A_2\ \ldots\ A_n$)   Execute A_1, then A_2, and so on in sequence to A_n
($Parallel\ A_1\ A_2\ \ldots\ A_n$)   Start $A_1, A_2, \ldots, A_n$ executing simultaneously
($If\ X\ A$)   Execute X, and if X returns True, execute A
($When\ X\ A$)   Repeatedly execute X until X returns True, then execute A
($Whenever\ X\ A$)   Repeatedly execute X until X returns True, then start A's execution and begin repeatedly executing X as before
($Do\ A\ X$)   Start the execution of A and repeatedly execute X until it returns True, then interrupt A's operation

Context-fixing Semantics 65

(*Repeat A X*)   Repeatedly execute *A* and then *X*, until *X* returns True

Each of these seven procedures (also known as *control structures*) specifies a temporal order for the execution of its argument procedures, along with any logical connections that hold between the procedures. Each *A* can itself specify a control structure, or one of the robot's primitive procedures (described below). Each *X* specifies a test procedure that returns the value True or False. One test procedure available to the robotic aid is *DistanceCovered*, a procedure that takes two arguments. The first argument specifies a distance in inches; the second gives the direction along which distance is measured. The procedure returns True if the distance covered since the procedure began to be executed is greater than or equal to the distance specified, False otherwise. Another test procedure is *RobotInRegion*, a procedure of one argument that returns True if the robot is in the region specified by the argument, False otherwise.

The overall motion of the robot base results from the simple linear sum of motions contributed by the individual procedures operating at any time. A simple motion is expressed as a two-dimensional linear velocity plus a third component for rotation. Motions are relative to one of two coordinate systems: the first is embedded within the robot and the second is given by the room in which the robot is being instructed. The linear motion may be left or right, forward or backward in the robot coordinate system, and north or south, east or west in the room coordinate system. The rotation about the vertical axis may be clockwise or counterclockwise.

Three of the primitive procedures that contribute to the movement of the robot base are of interest to our discussion. The first, a procedure of three arguments, produces movement away from an object as described in our earlier remarks on the verb "avoid." We will return to this procedure in the next section. The two other primitive motion-procedures are *Piloting* and *Region-Seeking*. The *Piloting* procedure takes three arguments: the first specifies whether the movement is linear or rotational; the second specifies the direction of movement (north, for instance); and the third specifies whether the default speed of the mobile base is to be increased, decreased, or not changed at all. The call (*Piloting Shift Left* +), for instance, starts a process that shifts the robot to the left at a speed one unit greater than the default speed. Calls to the *Piloting* procedure such as this one are usually embedded in a *Do* structure, with the result that the robot stops moving to the left only when the condition specified by the *Do* structure becomes true. The *RegionSeeking* procedure takes three arguments: the first specifies a region whose nearest point the robot moves toward or away from; the second argument indicates whether that movement is toward or away; and the third argument specifies speed as for the *Piloting* procedure. The procedure stops executing as soon as the robot reaches the region.

While we will not offer satisfaction conditions for these procedures or proofs that the conditions can be met, we want to communicate a sense of such proofs by showing the extent to which the commands, the intentions, and the procedures fit together. Consider the following three commands.

Move toward the table.
Move three feet forward.
Continue going toward the door until you have moved forward six feet.

Each of these commands expresses a distinct intention, and consequently in our analysis, despite the fact that the verb "move" occurs in each command, distinct procedural interpretations are produced. The first command uses the *RegionSeeking* procedure for "move," the second the *Piloting* procedure, and the third the procedure *DistanceCovered*. The partially specified interpretations of these commands are as follows. (We use square braces for the denotations; the denotation of "forward," for instance, is shown as [forward]. The speed arguments of *Piloting* and *RegionSeeking* are omitted for simplicity.)

Move toward the table.
(*Sequence* (*RegionSeeking* [the table] *Toward*))

Move three feet forward.
(*Do* (*Piloting Shift* [forward]) (*DistanceCovered* [three feet] [forward]))

Continue going toward the door until you have moved forward six feet.
(*Do* [going toward the door] (*DistanceCovered* [six feet] [forward]))

Consider also the command "Move three feet north west." (It is convenient semantically to treat "northwest" as two separate words.) The robot's *Piloting* procedure knows only about the four compass directions of north, south, east, and west given by the room coordinate system. The only way to accomplish movement in the northwest direction in response to this command is to simultaneously execute (*Piloting Shift* [north]) and (*Piloting Shift* [west]). A *Parallel* structure is thus embedded within a *Do* structure with the test procedure (*DistanceCovered* [three feet] *Trajectory*). The second argument value, *Trajectory*, specifies that distance is to be measured along a straight line (computed off a map) from the robot's position at the time the command was given to its present position.

> Move three feet north west.
> (*Do* (*Parallel* (*Piloting Shift* [north]) (*Piloting Shift* [west])) (*DistanceCovered* [three feet] *Trajectory*))

As a final example, consider the command "Go left toward the table." In response to this command, the robot will simultaneously execute (*Piloting Shift* [left]) and (*RegionSeeking* [the table] *Toward*) embedded within a *Do* structure with the test (*RobotInRegion* [the table]). Note that a simple *Parallel* structure of *Piloting* and *RegionSeeking* is not adequate. With that interpretation, *RegionSeeking* would end when the robot reached the table, but *Piloting* would not, and the robot would continue moving left. Note too that it makes sense to issue this command only if in moving leftward the robot would indeed reach the table.

> Go left toward the table.
> (*Do* (*Parallel* (*Piloting Shift* [left]) (*RegionSeeking* [the table] *Toward*)) (*RobotInRegion* [the table]))

One could argue that the command "Go left toward the table" does not necessarily express the intention that the robot move all the way to the table and then stop but merely that it begin to move leftward in the direction of the table. It could be seen as semantically incomplete from the point of view of the intentions listed at the beginning of this section, since it specifies neither how far to move exactly nor for how long. However, if the robot did not stop moving when it reached the table but sailed on past it or, even worse, bumped into it, we would in ordinary circumstances consider the command to have been poorly understood or inadequately obeyed.

This observation takes us back to our earlier remarks, in the sections on intentions and the interpretations of commands, about the distinction between process and result and about the unstated ceteris paribus conditions that often accompany verbal commands. We have already noted the extent to which process conditions are present in some commands and absent in others. Satisfaction of a command that primarily expresses a desired result is not without process constraints, however, as our examples have shown. The question how these constraints are gleaned from the context is a major challenge in our work and one we have made a small start on by recognizing the role that interaction plays. So the command "Go left toward the table," for instance, will in fact not immediately be interpreted as above, but will initiate a dialogue between the robot and the speaker to determine the speaker's intent.

We end this section with some further remarks on lexical procedures and the context. As suggested by our extended discussion of "next" and other words, the context of use should fix certain details of a lexical procedure's operation. What is in fact required for the denotation of many words is a procedural *schema*. In the next section we show how procedural schemata for "next" and "avoid" are used to produce a procedural interpretation for the command "Avoid the next chair." We close this section with a brief discussion of the verb "pick up" as used in a command such as "Pick up the cup."

If one particular procedure functions as the interpretation of "pick up," a procedure that stipulates exactly how a cup is picked up, the details of that procedure will be inappropriate for many commands, for there are indefinitely many ways to qualify a command and so modify the action associated with it. Consider, for instance, the commands "Pick up the cup without using the handle," "Pick up the cup by its handle," and "Pick up the cup at its rim directly across from the handle." In general, it seems as if any procedure that serves as the interpretation of a verb of action must be open to an indefinite number of modifications in its actual execution. At the same time, however, the interpretation of a command such as "Pick up the cup" is in most circumstances subject to various ceteris paribus constraints—that the vertical orientation of the cup not be disturbed, for instance. The question we must face is whether or not the notion of a procedural schema allows the appropriate degree of procedural variation for verbs of action such as "pick up." One additional way of looking at this problem is to identify a default way of performing each action, recognizing that in certain contexts the default must be overridden. Under this view, the study of context would have to embrace an analysis of "normal" circumstances given by partially unstated ceteris paribus conditions in which the default holds, and other circumstances in which the default is to be overridden.

On the question how defaults are overridden, one approach is to embed procedures in a highly parallel processing environment. The special circumstance that signals the override of a default will then contribute its own procedure and the parallel execution of procedures will produce the appropriately modified action. There are cases in which this approach works and cases in which it does not. Again we draw on the robotic aid for an example. On the one hand, the procedure for "go to," as used in the commands "Go to the table" and "Go to the table without hitting the chair," produces straight-line motion of the robot toward its goal. The procedure invoked by "without hitting the chair," on the other hand, produces motion that avoids the chair. Together, these procedures have the effect of modifying the robot's direct movement toward the table, allowing it to skirt around the edge of the chair. However, not so successful a story can be told for the "pick up" command. If the default action for picking up a cup has the robot grasping the handle of the cup, and if "without using the handle" keeps the robot's gripper away from the handle, the overall effect is that the cup is not grasped at all. Much remains to be done to develop a sense of context that characterizes normal circumstances, default actions, and ways to override default actions.

Grammars and the Lexicon

The process governing the synthesis of lexical procedures to form a complex procedure for the whole sentence is as follows. A semantic tree is generated from rules of semantic composition, called semantic functions, that are attached to the phrase-structure rules of the grammar.[12] A simple example illustrates the main ideas. Although the example features a simple context-free grammar, the process is not restricted to such grammars. The grammar currently in use for the robotic aid in fact has its phrase-structure rules augmented with constraint equations, in the spirit of lexical-functional grammars and the unification-based formalisms of S. M. Shieber, F. C. N. Pereira, L. Karttunen, and M. Kay.[13]

Consider the following parse tree for the imperative "Avoid the next chair." The non-terminal labels shown are I (for imperative), VP (for verb phrase), NP (for noun phrase), V (for verb), N (for noun), DA (for definite article), and ADJ$_{ord}$ (for ordering adjective).

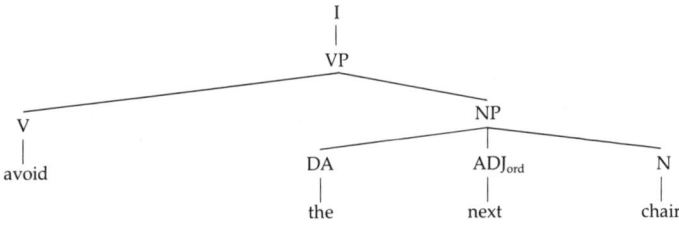

This parse is produced by a context-free grammar that we extend by assigning at most one semantic function to each production rule of the grammar. The resultant grammar is called a *potentially denoting* grammar, following Suppes.[14] In the grammar, we use square braces to show denotations. For instance, [NP] stands for the denotation of NP, [chair] for the denotation of "chair." The lexical denotations are, following our general strategy, relative to the set of models that define the agent being instructed and the perceptual situation in which instruction takes place. Without going into the details of the models, let us again use for our example the mobile base of the robotic aid. Suppose it is being instructed in a room containing several chairs arranged in a row. We will describe the denotations of "avoid," "next," and "chair." The definite article "the" is treated syncategorematically in this context.

Following our earlier discussion of "avoid," suppose the denotation of "avoid" is a procedural schema with three parameters that must be set to generate a specific procedure. Let us call it Proc1. The first parameter specifies the object to be avoided. The second and third are the perceptual parameters of avoidance discussed earlier: the first one establishes the minimal distance the robot must maintain from the object; the second fixes the region within which the robot's proximity to the object must be monitored. We use the familiar lambda notation for abstraction to represent procedural schemata. The schema for "avoid" is thus shown by the expression $(\lambda x\, y\, z)\text{Proc}1(x, y, z)$.

Suppose the denotation of "next" is a procedural schema, Proc2, with three parameters corresponding to the three contextual factors identified above in the section on context fixing. That is, the first specifies the objects—chairs or tables, for instance—of which one is to be selected as the next one relative to a present reference entity. The second specifies the ordering relation that holds for the encompassing class of objects. The third specifies that encompassing class of objects.

Finally, suppose the denotation of "chair" is a simple procedure, Proc3. We will not go into the details of how the robot picks out objects in its environment. We will suppose that Proc3 returns a list of all chairs in the given perceptual environment, each chair being designated by a triple $\langle x, y, \theta \rangle$ that specifies its position and orientation in a coordinate system that is fixed relative to the room.

The semantic functions below stipulate how the denotation at each node of the tree is obtained from the denotations of its daughter nodes. The extended context-free grammar for the sentence "Avoid the next chair" is as follows. Note that not all contextual parameters are set within the command itself. The notation y_c indicates the parameter value y given by the extralinguistic context of utterance.

Production Rule	Semantic Function
I → VP	[I] = [VP]
VP → V + NP	[VP] = [V]([NP], y_c, z_c)
NP → DA + ADJ$_{ord}$ + N	[NP] = [ADJ$_{ord}$]([N], v_c, w_c)
V → avoid	[V] = [avoid] = $(\lambda x\, y\, z)\text{Proc}1(x, y, z)$
N → chair	[N] = [chair] = Proc3
ADJ$_{ord}$ → next	[ADJ$_{ord}$] = [next] = $(\lambda u\, v\, w)\,\text{Proc}2(u, v, w)$

The extended grammar yields the following semantic tree for "Avoid the next chair." To the left of the colon at each node is the terminal or non-terminal label. To the right of the colon is the denotation of that label.

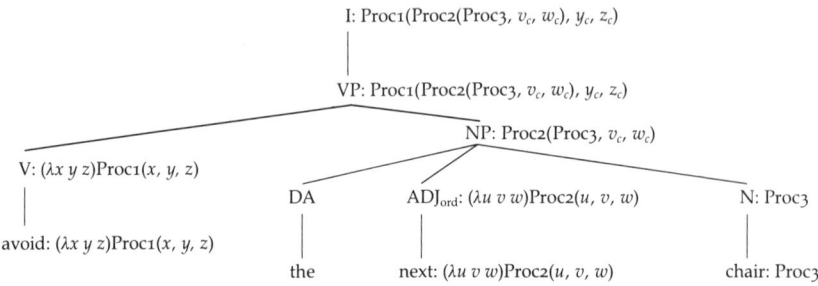

At the top of the tree we have a procedure specified for the command "Avoid the next chair," stated in the imperative mood. We call this the semantic interpretation of the sentence. If the sentence were a declarative, such as "The next chair is empty," the semantic tree for it would specify a procedure that determines the truth or falsity of the declarative. Although this example uses only one operation in its semantic functions—namely, function application—in general other operations are also used.

As the semantic functions show, not all parameter values are set within the semantic tree. In examining several examples in the section on context fixing, we saw how the precise interpretation of a word may be fixed by any of several means: the immediate linguistic surround, the perceptual situation, or the cognitive functioning of the agent. We see that same variability in this example. While the VP rule given above, for instance, is required for the sentence "Avoid the next chair," the sentence "Avoid the next chair by six inches" would require a rule such as the following one to produce the result shown on the right. Here the phrase "by six inches" sets the parameter that determines the minimal distance the robot must maintain from the object.

VP → V + NP + AdvPhDist   [Avoid the next chair by six inches]
[VP] = [V]([NP], [AdvPhDist], z_c)   = [avoid]([the next chair], [six inches], z_c)

Once the semantic tree has identified the parameter values still to be set, mechanisms must be invoked for obtaining those values from the perceptual situation, from the agent's cognitive functioning, and from interaction with the user. The theory of such mechanisms is as yet not very well developed, and many would regard their consideration as outside the proper domain of semantics. But given the drastic incompleteness of meaning if context-fixing mechanisms are not invoked in most ordinary conversation and communication, we take a contrary view. Moreover, a working understanding of these mechanisms is essential for developing adequate language capabilities in instructable robots. A central point of this paper is to show how essential they are. In other publications already mentioned we have begun a more detailed study of their nature.

Some final remarks have still to be made. The example in this section is but one of many in which the appropriate semantic interpretation of a command requires syntactic rules that are not in accord with many standard approaches to syntax. Several other examples from the instructable robot project can be found in Crangle and Suppes's report;[15] we mention one here briefly.

Consider the command "Go three feet left." Its interpretation by the robotic aid is given by the following procedure: *(Do (Piloting Shift* [left]) *(DistanceCovered* [three feet] [left])). Note that "left" makes a contribution to both the *Piloting* procedure and the *DistanceCovered* procedure. In *Piloting* it gives a direction of movement. In *DistanceCovered* it supplies a direction along which distance must be measured. (The path traced by the robot's movement may wind and turn—a point more easily seen with the command "Go three feet left while avoiding the cat"—but the intention is for the robot to move left three feet, and it is distance traversed in the leftward direction that must be measured, not distance along the path.) If "left" is to make its contribution in a straightforward way to both procedures, a relatively flat tree structure is called for in the parse of this sentence, a point we will return to in some detail in the next section. We of course want to claim that our syntactic rules are not merely the result of an inappropriate assignment of semantic content to words. To produce support for our use of what we call *semantically driven grammars*, we close this paper with a final section on grammars and the lexicon.

Perhaps the most unusual feature of the semantically driven grammars we have developed is the flatness of the derivation trees for sentences. We can illustrate our approach by considering a pair of simple sentences. What we prove for this pair is this. If the denotations of the lexical items are just the natural sets they should be—"tables" denotes a set of tables, and so forth—and no sets of the hierarchical kind characteristic of Montague grammars are permitted, then the trees must be flat.[16] Both philosophical and scientific intuition support this restricted view of sets. Philosophically there is a natural skepticism about sets of sets of sets, and other sets higher in the hierarchy. We never talk about them in any natural concrete way. Moreover, in the part of mathematics most powerfully adapted to quantitative science, namely, classical analysis, there is only a low-level hierarchy of numbers, vectors, and functions. It seems highly unlikely that the qualitative formulations so characteristic of natural language would have in back of them a more elaborate hierarchy than is required for classical physics. A modern structuralist point is that the mind must reflect the structure of the world—at least that part we most often encounter. Perceptual language and naive physical language seem most naturally analyzed semantically by a low-level hierarchy of sets.

The analysis we give of the following pair of sentences can be extended to more complex cases:

(1) If all tables are empty, stop!
(2) If some tables are empty, stop!

In fact, for complete simplicity, we restrict ourselves just to the antecedents of (1) and (2), that is,

(1′) All tables are empty.
(2′) Some tables are empty.

First, some concepts need to be explicitly defined, even if they are familiar. A *model structure* of a grammar G with terminal vocabulary V_T is a pair (D, v) in which D is a non-empty set and v is a partial function from V_T to a *hierarchy* $H(D)$ of sets built up from D by closure under the operations of union, intersection, and other set-theoretic operations. A model structure (D, v) of a grammar G is *Boolean* if and only if for any string s of V_T^+ for which v is defined, $v(s)$ is a subset of D. (V_T^+ is the set of all finite sequences of terminal symbols, minus the empty sequence.) A potentially denoting grammar G is Boolean if and only if for any Boolean model structure (D, v) of G, every semantic function of G has as its value a subset of D whenever its arguments are subsets of D.

We also need a Boolean formulation of the Frege function for the top of the tree. Using U for the universal quantifier function and E for the existential quantifier function, we have for any set A:

$$U(A) = \begin{cases} D \text{ if } A = D \\ \phi \text{ if } A \neq D \end{cases}$$

where ϕ is the empty set, and

$$E(A) = \begin{cases} D \text{ if } A \neq \phi \\ \phi \text{ if } A = \phi \end{cases}$$

To show how a flat Boolean grammar works, we have the following top-level rules and the associated semantic functions:

$S \to UQ + NP + VP \quad [S] = U(\neg[NP] \cup [VP])$
$S \to EQ + NP + VP \quad [S] = E([NP] \cap [VP])$

Note that the non-terminal symbols UQ and EQ for the universal and existential quantifiers have no denotation but operate as control-structure words at the top level. The non-terminal label S is for sentences.

Probably most linguists think of "all tables" and "some tables" as noun phrases, and consequently assign a complex denotation to such phrases, at least when pressed semantically. We do not deny there are good reasons for wanting "all tables" and "some tables" to be noun phrases, just as there are good reasons for wanting the semantics of simple sentences like (1') and (2') to be Boolean. There is a natural clash between grammar and semantics here. Our point is that the clash cannot be avoided.

We sketch the argument behind this claim.[17] Rather than the rules just given for a flat grammar, let the top-level rules be:

$S \to NP + VP$
$NP \to UQ + N$
$NP \to EQ + N$
$VP \to Copula + Adj \quad [VP] = [Adj]$

The semantic functions for the first three rules are our object of study. Suppose there were Boolean semantic functions for these three grammatical rules. Then, without any loss of generality we may assume that UQ and EQ themselves do not denote, so we must have semantic functions h, f, and g such that:

$[S] = h([VP], [NP])$ for $S \to NP + VP$
$[NP] = f([N])$ for $NP \to UQ + N$
$[NP] = g([N])$ for $NP \to EQ + N$

What we can then show is that there are Boolean models of (1′) and (2′) such that the Boolean functional equations in terms of h, f, and g cannot simultaneously have a solution.

The Boolean analysis just given generalizes to relation algebras. In particular, if lexical denotations are held down to sets of physical objects and relations among such objects, then the same argument given above forces the use of flat trees for prepositional phrases, as in "Go to all empty tables" and "Go to some empty tables." The technical details of this semantic analysis of prepositional phrases is rather lengthy, and so it is not given here. But the message for the lexicon is clear: there is an uneliminable tension between syntax and semantics.

DEIRDRE WILSON & DAN SPERBER

Mood and the Analysis of Non-declarative Sentences

How are non-declarative sentences understood? How do they differ semantically from their declarative counterparts? Answers to these questions once made direct appeal to the notion of illocutionary force. When they proved unsatisfactory, the fault was diagnosed as a failure to distinguish properly between mood and force. For some years now, efforts have been under way to develop a satisfactory account of the semantics of mood. In this paper, we consider the current achievements and future prospects of the mood-based semantic program.

Distinguishing Mood and Force

Early speech-act theorists regarded illocutionary force as a properly semantic category. Sentence meaning was identified with illocutionary-force potential: to give the meaning of a sentence was to specify the range of speech acts that an utterance of that sentence could be used to perform. Typically, declarative sentences were seen as performing assertive speech acts (committing the speaker to the truth of the proposition expressed), and imperative and interrogative sentences were seen as performing directive speech acts (requesting action and information, respectively). Within this framework, pragmatic theory, the theory of utterance interpretation, had at most a supplementary role: to explain how the hearer, in context, chose an actual illocutionary force from among the potential illocutionary forces semantically assigned to the sentence uttered.

The speech-act semantic program foundered on cases in which sentence meaning and illocutionary-force potential come apart. For instance, declarative sentences are not always used to perform assertive speech acts. They "occur unasserted"—and without change of meaning—in metaphor and irony, acting and impersonation, fiction and fantasy, jokes and example sentences, loose talk and rough approximations, and free indirect speech and thought; and as constituents of complex sentences, for example, in conditionals and disjunctions, or as subject or object complements. The fact that a sentence may retain its meaning though used without any of the potential forces semantically assigned to it is an argument against identifying meaning with force.

The correct conclusion seems to be that illocutionary force is a purely pragmatic category, a property not of sentences but only of utterances. What is it, then, that distinguishes declarative, imperative, and interrogative sentences on the purely semantic level? The answer one finds increasingly in the literature is that it is not force but *mood*.

For this answer to convince at all, "mood" must be taken not in its traditional syntactic sense, in which it refers to verbal inflection (e.g., indicative, imperative, optative), but in a semantic sense, in which it refers to the semantic or logical properties that distinguish, say, declarative sentences from imperative, interrogative, and exclamative sentences. In the narrow syntactic sense, English has no interrogative or exclamative mood; in the semantic sense, at least if the mood-based semantic program is to go through, it must. That is, each syntactic sentence type must be seen as determining a proprietary semantic mood common to literal and non-literal, serious and non-serious, embedded and non-embedded utterances of tokens of that type.[1] And, at least in non-literal, non-serious cases, determining the force of an utterance can no longer be a simple matter of choosing among a range of potential forces semantically assigned to the sentence uttered.

The new mood-based program has two interdependent tasks: to characterize the semantic moods, and to describe the relation between mood and force. A crucial constraint on the overall theory is that it must make it possible to see why utterances have the forces they do. As Donald Davidson says, "[A satisfactory theory of mood] must assign an element of meaning to utterances in a given mood that is not present in utterances in other moods. And this element should connect with the difference in force between assertions, questions, and commands in such a way as to explain our intuition of a conventional relation between mood and use."[2] Sentence meaning, and in particular the meaning of mood, must interact with contextual assumptions and pragmatic principles to yield a satisfactory account of how utterances are understood.

The new, mood-based program, then, is really a combined semantic and pragmatic program. Differences in the semantic characterization of mood often result from differences in assumptions about the nature and role of pragmatics. The more pragmatic rules or conventions there are, for example, the less intrinsic semantic content need be assigned to the moods; the fewer, and the more general, the pragmatic principles, the greater must be the intrinsic semantic content of the moods.

We will argue that most existing mood-based proposals are in fact empirically inadequate. We will briefly sketch an alternative account. This alternative account, however, casts doubt on a fundamental, though implicit, assumption of the mood-based program, and thus on this program's general feasibility.

Characterizing Imperative Mood

Given a powerful enough pragmatic theory, the moods themselves might be treated as semantically primitive, mere notational inputs to rules or conventions of pragmatic interpretation. This is how we propose to understand the claim that mood is a conventional indicator of force. On this account, though mood is distinct from force, there is nothing more to understanding a mood than simply knowing the range of speech acts it is conventionally, or standardly, used to perform. According to R. M. Hare, "When we say that 'The cat is on the mat' is a typical indicative (when we mention its mood, that is), we identify the type of speech act which it is standardly used to perform. Thus mood signs . . . classify sentences according to the speech acts to which they are assigned by the conventions which give meanings to those signs."[3] The whole burden of interpretation is left to pragmatic theory, which must describe not only the range of "standard" forces, and how the appropriate member of this range is chosen in context, but also how, in "nonstandard" cases, the conventional correlation between mood and force can break down, and what the effects of the breakdown will be.

The conventional correlation between mood and force is generally seen as breaking down in two main ways: in non-literal or non-serious utterances, and under embedding. For the moment, we will leave these cases aside, and consider various proposals about the standard or conventional force of imperative mood.[4]

Take the claim that imperative utterances are standardly used with directive force, where a directive act is defined as an attempt to get the hearer to perform the action described by the proposition expressed. The following look like clear counterexamples, in that a main-clause imperative is literally and seriously used without the predicted directive force.

Advice

(1)(a) PETER: Excuse me, I want to get to the station.
(b) MARY: Take a number 3 bus.

Here, Mary is advising Peter what to do. There is no reason to think she cares whether Peter follows her advice, and hence no reason to analyze her utterance as an attempt to get Peter to take a number 3 bus.

Permission

(2)(a) PETER: Can I open the window?
(b) MARY: Oh, *open* it, then.

Here, Mary is giving Peter permission to open the window. There is no reason to think she cares whether Peter performs the permitted action, and hence no reason to analyze her utterance as an attempt to get him to open the window.

Threats and dares

Mary, seeing Peter about to throw a snowball, says threateningly:

(3) Go on. Throw it. Just you dare.

Mary's utterance is not an attempt to get Peter to throw the snowball—on the contrary.

Good wishes

Mary, visiting Peter in the hospital, says:

(4) Get well soon.

Since the "action" described is not under Peter's control, there is no reason to analyze Mary's utterance as an attempt to get Peter to perform it.

Audienceless cases

Imperatives can be used in the absence of an agent or hearer, as when Mary looks at the sky and says:

(5) Please don't rain,

or gets into her car and mutters:

(6) Start, damn you.

The absence of both hearer and agent makes it hard to see these utterances as attempts to get someone to perform the action described.

Predetermined cases

Imagine a child, sent to apologize to someone, thinking to herself as she reluctantly approaches his door:

(7) Please be out.

Or a mother, whose notoriously ill-tempered child has been sent to apologize to someone, thinking to herself as the child arrives home:

(8) Please don't have made things worse.

Here, not only is there no hearer, but the events described have already happened (or failed to happen), and cannot be affected by what is said. Again, the predictions made by the directive analysis of imperatives are not borne out.

We know of no analysis of imperative mood as a conventional indicator of force that deals satisfactorily with the full range of examples listed above. For instance, Susan Schmerling, who discusses many of them, offers the following alternative: a serious, literal imperative counts as an attempt by the speaker to bring about the state of affairs described by the proposition expressed (but not necessarily an attempt by the speaker to get the hearer to bring about this state of affairs).[5] While this proposal would deal with good wishes, audienceless cases, and predetermined cases, it does not handle advice, permission, threats, or dares.

John Searle defines directive speech acts as attempts by the speaker to get the hearer to perform *some* action (not necessarily the action described by the proposition expressed).[6] While this proposal would deal with threats and dares, it sheds no light on our other categories of example. It also creates a new problem: how does the hearer decide which action the speaker wants him to perform?

One could, of course, abandon the search for a unitary analysis, and say simply, as Jennifer Hornsby seems to do in this volume, that the imperative mood in English can be used with the force of a request, command, advice, permission, threat, dare, good wish, and so on. This squares with the description of mood as a *conventional* indicator of force. However, it also means abandoning any attempt at an explanatory account of the relation between mood and force. Why, in language after language, do imperative sentences have just this cluster of uses? We should surely be looking for a characterization of mood that enables us not merely to describe, but to explain, these facts.

We conclude that mood cannot be satisfactorily analyzed as a conventional indicator of force. However, this is not the end of the mood-based program. It might be possible to assign the moods some intrinsic semantic content that would lay a satisfactory foundation for an explanatory account of force. Truth-conditional semanticists typically look for some analogue of truth conditions for non-declarative sentences. For example, Colin McGinn treats imperatives as having not truth conditions but fulfillment conditions, which are satisfied if and only if the state of affairs described by the imperative is "made the case."[7]

Could this semantic characterization interact with contextual assumptions and pragmatic principles to yield an explanatory account of force? It is hard to tell, since little is said about the pragmatic principles with which the semantic characterization is supposed to interact. Standardly, a connection is made, via a pragmatic maxim of truthfulness (e.g., "Do not say what you believe to be false"), between declarative utterances and expressions of belief. Let us suppose there is an analogous maxim connecting imperative utterances with expressions of desire, so that the speaker of an imperative utterance would be understood as communicating a desire that the state of affairs described should be "made the case." Then advice, permission, threats, and dares—which, as we have seen, need communicate no such desires—are counterexamples to this analysis. But then again, if there is *no* connection between imperative utterances and expressions of some attitude at least akin to desire, it is hard to see why the hearer of an imperative utterance should *ever* recognize that the speaker wants him to bring about the state of affairs described.

Even assuming that this problem could be solved, some of our examples (1)-(8) would still be troublesome for a framework such as McGinn's. With good wishes such as "Get well soon," audienceless cases such as "Please don't rain," and predetermined cases such as "Please don't have made things worse," the state of affairs described is under no one's control, and so nothing is made the case. Nor is there any obvious reason to regard these utterances as non-serious or non-literal. We conclude that McGinn's analysis, and any analysis in terms of fulfillment, obedience, or compliance conditions, is empirically inadequate.

Martin Huntley makes a more radical semantic proposal.[8] The distinction between declarative and imperative sentences, he argues, is a special case of a more general semantic distinction between indicative and non-indicative mood. Semantically, indicatives "involve indexical reference to the actual world," whereas non-indicatives (i.e., imperatives, infinitival clauses, and nonfinite "that" clauses) do not. As a result, non-indicatives, and imperatives in particular, can "represent a situation as being merely envisaged as a possibility with no commitment as to whether it obtains, in past, present or future, in *this* world."[9] This proposal is a radical departure from those considered so far, in that it makes no reference, however indirect, to notions from the theory of force. The question is, as Huntley acknowledges, whether it lays an adequate semantic foundation for the prediction of illocutionary force.

It seems to us that it does not. It is hard to see why a hearer should conclude, from the mere fact that the speaker is envisaging a certain situation as a possibility, that he is being requested, advised, permitted, etc., to bring it about. There is a crucial difference between imperatives and infinitival clauses in this respect. As Huntley predicts, the speaker of the infinitival utterances (9)(a) and (9)(b) can envisage a certain state of affairs without necessarily representing it as either achievable or desirable:

(9)(a) To spend all one's life in the same room. Imagine.
(b) To meet the president of the United States. Hmm!

Thus, as one might expect, (9)(a) and (9)(b), and infinitival clauses in general, can be seriously and literally uttered without imperatival force: that is, without being intended or understood as orders, requests, advice, permission, good wishes, or any of the other speech acts standardly performed by imperatives. By the same token, Huntley's analysis predicts that imperatives can be seriously and literally uttered without imperatival force. But of course, they can't. We conclude that imperatives and infinitival clauses cannot be treated as semantically equivalent.

We believe that the crucial semantic and pragmatic differences between imperatives and infinitival clauses are linked to the notions of achievability and desirability. The semantic analysis of imperatives must make reference to these notions; the semantic analysis of infinitival clauses does not. This is not to say that infinitival clauses can never be used with imperatival force. When can they be so used? When it is clear in the context that the state of affairs "envisaged as a possibility" is both achievable and desirable. Why do serious, literal imperatives have the imperatival forces they do? Because the notions of achievability and desirability are there from the start, as part of the meaning of imperative sentences themselves. We believe that this semantic characterization can interact with additional contextual assumptions and general pragmatic principles to yield an explanatory account of the full range of imperative utterances, including those in (1)–(8). Here is how an account along these lines might go.

Thoughts can be entertained, and the utterances that express them can be used, as descriptions (i.e., truth-conditional representations) of states of affairs in different types of worlds. In particular, they can be entertained or used as descriptions of states of affairs in the actual world or in alternative possible worlds; as descriptions of states of affairs in desirable worlds; and as descriptions of states of affairs in potential worlds, that is, worlds compatible with the individual's assumptions about the actual world, which may therefore be, or become, actual themselves. Different linguistic constructions may be semantically specialized for different types of description. We claim that imperative sentences are specialized for describing states of affairs in worlds regarded as both potential and desirable.

Let us make the simplifying assumption that imperatives are invariably used to describe a state of affairs regarded as potential and desirable by the speaker herself. (As we will show in later sections, this assumption only holds for serious, literal utterances.) Notice that the expression of desirability is a three-place relation—x regards y as desirable to z—and that what the speaker regards as desirable to one person she may regard as undesirable to another. Normally, in using an imperative, the speaker has some specific person (typically, either herself or her hearer) in mind, and expects the hearer to recognize who this is and interpret the utterance accordingly. The semantic characterization of imperatives is thus compatible with a number of different, more specific, pragmatic interpretations. We claim that serious, literal imperatives fall into two broad pragmatic categories, depending on how this semantic indeterminacy is pragmatically resolved.

With requests, commands, orders, good wishes, and audienceless and predetermined cases, the indeterminacy is resolved in favor of the speaker, who is understood as indicating that the state of affairs described is desirable from her own point of view. Within this broad category of cases, additional contextual assumptions are needed to distinguish the sub-categories familiar to speech-act theorists.

For example, if the hearer is manifestly in a position to bring about the state of affairs described, the utterance will have the force of something like a request, command, order, or plea. These sub-categories are distinguished from each other by manifest assumptions about the social and physical relations between speaker and hearer, and about the degree of desirability of the state of affairs described.

Good wishes fall into the same broad category as requests, but require two additional assumptions: first, the speaker manifestly believes that neither she nor her hearer is in a position to bring about the state of affairs described, and second, she manifestly regards this state of affairs as beneficial to the hearer. Audience-less and predetermined cases are also types of wish, though here the assumption is that the state of affairs described will be beneficial to the speaker, and there need be no hearer present at all.

Advice and permission belong to the other broad category of imperative utterances, in which the semantic indeterminacy is resolved in favor of the hearer: the speaker communicates that the state of affairs described is desirable not from her own point of view but from her hearer's. When Mary advises Peter to take a number 3 bus, she indicates that from his point of view it would be desirable to do so, given that he wants to get to the station. With permission, the indeterminacy is again resolved in favor of the hearer, but what is at issue is the potentiality of the state of affairs described rather than its desirability. When Peter asks Mary if he can open the window, he represents a certain state of affairs as desirable from his point of view, but expresses doubts about its potentiality (given that Mary can refuse to let him open it). By saying "Oh, *open* it, then," Mary incidentally concedes the desirability (to Peter) of this state of affairs, but more importantly, guarantees its potentiality, thus removing the only obstacle to Peter's opening the window.

We are suggesting, then, that the relation between linguistic form and force (or, more generally, pragmatic interpretation) is mediated by a direct semantic link between linguistic form and representations of propositional attitude. The intrinsic semantic properties of imperative form are characterizable in terms of a complex propositional attitude, itself analyzable into two more elementary attitudes: the belief that a certain state of affairs is potential, and the belief that it is desirable. These elementary attitudes recur in the analysis of other linguistic constructions. For example, the difference between hortatives and optatives seems to be that while both involve beliefs about desirability, only hortatives involve beliefs about potentiality: one can wish for, but not exhort someone to bring about, states of affairs that one knows to be unachievable. The proposed treatment of imperatives might thus form the basis for a much more general account.

Notice that our proposed semantic characterization makes no reference to terms from the theory of force. However, we have shown that unlike Huntley's characterization, it does lay an adequate foundation for an explanatory account of force. The force of an imperative utterance is determined, on the one hand, by the fact that the speaker has represented a certain state of affairs as both potential and desirable, and on the other, by manifest contextual assumptions. So far, we have said nothing about the general pragmatic principles by which contextual assumptions are selected and semantic indeterminacies resolved. Our answers to these questions will be sketched below.

Explaining Non-literal, Non-serious Cases

Most work on the semantics of non-declarative sentences treats the interpretation of non-literal, non-serious cases—for example, metaphor, irony, impersonations, jokes, and example sentences—as a purely pragmatic matter: it is assumed that, semantically, there is nothing to distinguish them from literal, serious cases. Since we think these non-literal cases hold the key to the analysis of interrogative sentences, we will discuss them briefly here.

In our recent book, *Relevance*, we argued that there are two fundamentally different types of representation, and therefore two fundamentally different uses to which thoughts or utterances can be put.[10] On the one hand, there is *descriptive*, or truth-conditional, representation, which is a relation between thoughts or utterances and states of affairs. On the other hand, there is *interpretive* representation, or representation by resemblance, which is a relation between thoughts or utterances and other thoughts or utterances that they resemble. The notion of descriptive representation is quite familiar; the notion of interpretive representation less so. We believe that interpretive representation plays a fundamental role in the analysis both of non-literal utterances and of interrogatives.

Any object in the world can, in the appropriate conditions, be used as a representation of some other object that it resembles—that is, with which it has properties in common. You ask me what shape Brazil is, and I point to an appropriately shaped cloud in the sky; I invite you to a drink by imitating the act of drinking; I make fun of someone by imitating his walk.

An utterance, like any other object, may be used to represent another object it resembles. For example, in direct quotation an utterance is used to represent another utterance with which it shares linguistic properties; in translation an utterance is used to represent another utterance with which it shares semantic properties; in paraphrase, an utterance is used to represent another utterance with which it shares logical properties—that is, with which it shares analytic or contextual implications.[11]

Any object with a propositional content—a thought or utterance, for example—may have analytic and contextual implications. The analytic implications of a proposition are its non-trivial logical implications; they are invariant from context to context. The contextual implications of a proposition are determined by the contextual assumptions used to process it. The contextual implications of a proposition p in a context C are those propositions logically implied by the union of p and C, but by neither p alone nor C alone. Any thought or utterance may thus be used to represent another thought or utterance that it resembles in propositional content—that is, with which it shares analytic or contextual implications. When a thought or utterance is used in this way, to represent not a state of affairs but another thought or utterance that it resembles, we will talk of *interpretive* resemblance and *interpretive* use.

Interpretive resemblance is a matter of degree. At one extreme, two objects may bear no interpretive resemblance to each other—that is, they may share no analytic or contextual implications. At the other extreme lies full identity of analytic and contextual implications. Let us say that when a thought or utterance p is interpretively used to represent another thought or utterance q, p is a *literal* interpretation of q if and only if p and q share all their implications. Literalness, so defined, is just a special case of interpretive resemblance.

Utterances are interpretively used to represent the thoughts of the speaker. Most philosophers of language assume that an utterance is fully acceptable only if it is a literal interpretation of the speaker's thoughts, in the sense just defined: this is what a maxim, or norm, or convention of truthfulness is supposed to guarantee. We reject the maxim of truthfulness, and with it, the assumption that non-literalness is a departure from some communicative norm. In *Relevance*, and in our paper "Loose Talk," we argued that the expectation crucial to communication is one not of truthfulness but of optimal relevance, where an optimally relevant utterance is one that communicates enough contextual implications to be worth the hearer's attention, and puts the hearer to no unjustifiable effort in obtaining them.[12]

Loose talk and metaphor may satisfy the expectation of optimal relevance in the following way. The speaker communicates only a subset of the total analytic and contextual implications of her utterance (that is, her utterance is a less-than-literal interpretation of her thoughts). This subset is rich enough to be worth the hearer's attention, and there is no other utterance that would have communicated this subset more economically.

To illustrate, consider the following metaphorical imperative:

(10) Build your own road through life.

In interpreting this utterance, the hearer's task is to satisfy himself that the speaker intended to communicate some subset of its analytic and contextual implications: a subset that she might rationally have thought worthy of his attention, and that could not have been more economically communicated by means of any other utterance.

By processing (10) in the context of his encyclopedic knowledge of road building, the hearer might obtain such implications as: "Do not follow the lead of others," "Make up your own mind what to do and where to go," "Plan your life," "Aim at consistency and continuity," "Be constructive," and so on. These are all implications that a speaker aiming at optimal relevance might have intended to communicate by means of this utterance. Other implications—for example, "Buy a steamroller," "Take a course in engineering," and "Submit your plans to the Department of Transport"—are inconsistent with information given elsewhere in the sentence (e.g., the instruction to build a road *through life*), or with manifest assumptions about what a rational speaker, in the circumstances, might have wanted to communicate.

In *Relevance*, we showed that every utterance has at most one interpretation consistent with the assumption that the speaker was aiming at optimal relevance: the first interpretation tested and found consistent with this assumption is the only such interpretation. In deciding which contextual implications the speaker intended to communicate, the hearer should thus select the *minimal* (because most easily recoverable) set of implications consistent with the assumption that the speaker was aiming at optimal relevance. In other words, he should take the utterance to be fully literal only if nothing less than full literalness will do. For example, if a rational speaker aiming at optimal relevance could have intended to communicate some, but not all, of the implications of (10), then that is how she should be understood.[13]

Every utterance, then, is interpretively used as a more or less literal representation of the thoughts of the speaker. But thoughts themselves may be descriptively or interpretively used: they may be entertained as descriptions of states of affairs in actual, possible, potential, or desirable worlds, or as interpretive representations of other thoughts (or utterances) that they resemble. For example, Mary may entertain the proposition that Peter is unhappy, not as a description of the actual world, but as a representation of what he said or implied. She may indicate this explicitly by saying "Peter says he is unhappy"; or (in the appropriate circumstances) she may use a form of free indirect speech and say, simply, "Peter is unhappy," implicitly representing her beliefs, not about Peter's actual mental state, but about what Peter said or implied. In free indirect speech (or thought), the speaker implicitly attributes a thought to some other person or type of person. Such implicit attributions we call *echoic*.

Echoic utterances are used not just to attribute thoughts but to express the speaker's attitude to them, and to the person, or type of person, who holds them. In echoing an opinion, the speaker may indicate by gesture, tone of voice, or facial expression, or merely leave the hearer to infer, that she approves or disapproves of it, accepts or rejects it, welcomes or resents it, is amazed or amused by it, and so on. In *Relevance*, we argued that verbal irony is a special case of echoic use.[14] The speaker echoes an opinion while implicitly dissociating herself from it, with anything from mild amusement to savage scorn.

To illustrate, consider the following exchange:

(11)(a) PETER: Can I open the window?
   (b) MARY: Go ahead and let in some nice Arctic air.

Here, Mary's utterance would probably be intended as ironical. She is not giving Peter permission to open the window. On the contrary, she is suggesting that it was ridiculous of him even to think of asking her permission. He could only have done so, she implies, if he thought she liked to be freezing cold. By caricaturing this attributed thought (that is, by offering a less-than-literal interpretation of it), Mary makes it clear that she dissociates herself from it and finds it ridiculous. Irony is thus a special case of echoic interpretation.

So far, we have considered two main types of interpretive use. An utterance may be a more or less literal interpretation of the speaker's thought, which may itself be an echoic interpretation of an attributed thought. Utterances of example sentences in linguistic or philosophical discussion illustrate a third type of interpretive use. The example token may be interpretively used to represent an utterance or thought type that it resembles—that is, with which it shares analytic or contextual implications. For instance, we used example (10) above to represent a certain type of imperative utterance or thought. This example, though interpretively used, was not used to attribute a thought or utterance to any actual person or type of person: it was used to represent a possible, or potential, but non-attributed utterance or thought. In the next section, we will argue that interrogative sentences belong to yet another category of interpretive use: they represent not descriptive thoughts, nor attributed thoughts, nor possible or potential thoughts, but *desirable* thoughts.

Characterizing Interrogative Mood

The literature on interrogatives parallels the literature on imperatives: some people treat interrogative mood as a conventional indicator of force; others try to assign it some intrinsic semantic content that would interact with contextual assumptions and pragmatic principles to yield an explanatory account of force. We will argue that most existing analyses are empirically inadequate.

Take the claim that interrogatives standardly or conventionally have the force of questions, where questions are defined as requests for information. In the words of Kent Bach and R. M. Harnish, "Questions are special cases of requests, special in that what is requested is that the speaker provide the hearer with certain information."[15] This is perhaps the standard speech-act account of interrogatives. Let us assume that a speaker cannot appropriately request information that she already has, or that she knows the hearer is unable to provide. Then even when non-serious, non-literal, and embedded cases are left aside, the following look like clear counterexamples, in that a main-clause interrogative is literally and seriously used without the predicted force:

Rhetorical questions

Peter has made a New Year's resolution to give up smoking. As he lights up on New Year's Day, Mary says to him:

(12) What was your New Year's resolution?

It is clear in the circumstances that Mary knows the answer, and that her utterance is not a request for information. Intuitively, such rhetorical questions function as reminders, and do not call for any overt response.

Exam questions

Examiners usually know more about the subject than examinees, and it would be odd to treat exam questions as requests for information.

Guess questions

Mary hides a sweet in her hand, puts both hands behind her back, and says to Peter:

(13) Which hand is it in?

Her utterance doubly fails to fit the standard speech-act account: the questioner already knows the answer, whereas the hearer doesn't and can at best make a guess. These cases bear obvious similarities to exam questions.

Surprise questions

Consider the following exchange:

(14)(a) PETER: The president has resigned.
  (b) MARY: Good heavens. Has he?

It seems inappropriate to describe Mary's utterance as a request for information, which she was given only a few seconds ago. Intuitively, (14)(b) expresses Mary's surprise or incredulity at the information she has been given. As such, it is a counterexample to the standard speech-act account.

Expository questions

Often, a writer or speaker asks a question to arouse the audience's interest in an answer that she plans to give herself. At the beginning of this paper we asked two such expository questions. They are better seen as offers of information than as requests for information.

Self-addressed questions

When Mary says to herself "Now why did I say that?" she is better seen as wondering why she said what she did than requesting herself to answer.

Speculative questions

When Mary thinks to herself, or asks Peter idly, "What is the best analysis of interrogative sentences?" there is even less reason to analyze her utterance as a request for information. Mary may know that she does not know the answer; she may know that Peter does not know the answer; she may know that no one knows the answer. On the speech-act account, there is no point in asking a question unless you think your hearer may be able to provide the answer. This rules out all speculative questions, that is, all questions that are of more than passing interest.

Martin Bell, who discusses many of these examples, proposes a weakened speech-act account on which "standard" questions are treated as requests to tell rather than to inform, the assumption being that one can appropriately request a hearer to tell one something one already knows.[16] While this would deal with exam questions and guess questions, it does not handle rhetorical questions, surprise questions, expository questions, self-addressed questions, or speculative questions.

John Lyons, in a more radical departure from the standard speech-act account, argues that interrogatives are conventionally used not to ask questions but to "pose" them: "When we pose a question, we merely give expression to, or externalize, our doubt; and we can pose questions which we do not merely expect to remain unanswered, but which we know, or believe, to be unanswerable."[17] The problem with this proposal is that not all interrogative utterances are expressions of doubt (at least doubt about the correct answer). In exam questions, guess questions, surprise questions, expository questions, and many types of rhetorical question (e.g., [12] above), the speaker is in no doubt about the correct answer, and a different type of analysis is required.

We conclude that interrogative mood cannot be satisfactorily analyzed as a conventional indicator of force: interrogative sentences must instead be assigned some intrinsic semantic content that will lay an adequate foundation for an explanatory account of force.

Within truth-conditional frameworks, some analogue of truth conditions has been sought for interrogatives, as for imperatives. C. Hamblin, for example, treats interrogatives as denoting their sets of possible answers, and Lauri Karttunen treats them as denoting their sets of true answers.[18] The main problem with this approach is that it provides no obvious explanation of the pragmatic differences among positive questions such as (15), negative questions such as (16), and alternative questions such as (17):

(15) Did you see Susan?
(16) Didn't you see Susan?
(17) Did you or did you not see Susan?

Each of these questions has the possible answers yes and no, and a true answer to any one is a true answer to all. For Hamblin and Karttunen, (15)–(17) should thus be synonymous. Why is it, then, that while utterances of (15) are generally neutral in tone, the speaker of (16) suggests that she had expected the hearer to see Susan, and (17) sounds impatient or hectoring?[19]

Dwight Bolinger develops this point at length, with a wealth of convincing examples.[20] He goes on to argue that indirect questions introduced by "if" are not synonymous with those introduced by "whether": the former are embedded versions of yes-no questions such as (15) and (16), the latter are embedded versions of alternative questions such as (17). This indirectly supports the claim that yes-no questions are not synonymous with their alternative counterparts.

Bolinger concludes that yes-no questions such as (15) and (16) are semantically very similar to conditionals: "Both conditionals and YNQs [yes-no questions] are hypotheses. A condition hypothesises that something is true and draws a conclusion from it. A YNQ hypothesises that something is true and confirmed, amended or disconfirmed by a hearer."[21]

While Bolinger's criticisms of existing approaches seem to us well founded, his own account is empirically inadequate. In the first place, if interrogatives and hypotheses are semantically equivalent, they should be identical in illocutionary force. Yet typically, to make a hypothesis is to invite one's hearers to accept it as true and see what follows from it, whereas to ask a yes-no question is to invite a consideration of whether the proposition it expresses is true or false. Bolinger's account offers no explanation of these differences in force. Moreover, there are yes-no versions of rhetorical questions, guess questions, surprise questions, exam questions, expository questions, and audienceless cases; contrary to what Bolinger predicts, none of these is a request for confirmation, disconfirmation, or amendment by a hearer. Nor is it obvious that Bolinger's account of yes-no questions can be generalized to handle "wh-" questions (questions containing words such as "who," "what," "where").

It seems, then, that there is no satisfactory existing analysis of interrogative mood. We believe there is a reason for this failure. Interrogatives do have some intrinsic semantic content in virtue of their interrogative form. However, this content is not analyzable in anything approaching truth-conditional terms. Interrogatives are semantically specialized not for descriptive but for interpretive use. In the simplest, most intuitive terms, interrogatives are interpretively used to represent what the speaker regards as relevant answers.

On this account, interrogative utterances, like echoic utterances, are doubly interpretive: they interpretively represent a thought of the speaker's, which itself interpretively represents another utterance or thought. However, while echoic utterances are used to represent attributed thoughts, interrogative utterances are used to represent desirable thoughts.[22]

What makes a thought desirable? In *Relevance*, we argued that a thought is desirable only if it is relevant—that is, only if it is rich enough in cognitive effects (e.g., contextual implications) to be worth the individual's attention. To regard a certain thought as desirable to someone is thus to regard it as relevant enough to be worthy of his attention. The claim that interrogatives represent desirable thoughts thus amounts to the claim that they represent not possible answers, nor true answers, but *relevant* answers.

How does the hearer decide what answer the speaker would regard as relevant? In the case of yes-no questions, the solution is straightforward. A positive question expresses a positive proposition, a negative question expresses a negative proposition, and an alternative question expresses both a positive and a negative proposition. The most natural assumption for the hearer to make, and thus the assumption favored by considerations of relevance, is that the speaker has chosen to express the very proposition she would regard as relevant if true. That is, a positive question such as (15) indicates that a positive answer would be, if anything, more relevant than a negative one, a negative question suggests that a negative answer would be, if anything, more relevant than a positive one, and an alternative question such as (17) indicates that a positive and a negative answer would be equally relevant. Although we have not the space to show it here, this analysis should interact with considerations of relevance, and in particular with considerations of effort, to account for the pragmatic differences among utterances of (15)–(17).

Although "wh-" questions do not express complete propositions but merely incomplete logical forms, we claim that they are interpretively used to represent complete propositions that they resemble. Which complete propositions? The natural assumption, and therefore the assumption favored by considerations of relevance, is that they represent completions of the incomplete logical forms they express. In other words, the speaker of a "wh-" question expresses an incomplete logical form and indicates that she would regard some completion of it, or an utterance expressing such a completion, as relevant if true.

On this account, interrogatives are the interpretive counterpart of imperatives, which are used to represent desirable states of affairs. Like imperatives, they are semantically indeterminate, and the indeterminacy must be pragmatically resolved by making some assumption about who it is that the speaker thinks would regard the thought in question as desirable. As always, the first assumption tested and found consistent with the expectation of optimal relevance is the only such assumption, and is the one the hearer should choose.

Like imperatives, interrogatives fall into two broad pragmatic types, depending on how the semantic indeterminacy is resolved. With requests for information, exam questions, guess questions, surprise questions, self-addressed questions, and speculative questions, the indeterminacy is resolved in favor of the speaker, who indicates that she would regard the answer as relevant to herself. Further contextual assumptions are needed to distinguish among the various sub-types of this broad type.

Consider the following exchange:

(18)(a) MARY: Where did I leave my keys?
(b) PETER: In the kitchen drawer.

Suppose that Mary manifestly regards an answer to her question as desirable to herself, manifestly expects Peter to know the answer, and manifestly expects him to supply it. Then (18)(a) would have the force of a request for information. Suppose that while Mary manifestly regards an answer as desirable to herself, she has not noticed that Peter is in the room, and is manifestly not addressing him. Then (18)(a) would have the force of a self-addressed question or speculation.

Still within the same broad pragmatic type of questions, suppose that Mary manifestly expects Peter to answer her question; but suppose, moreover, that she is manifestly in a better position than he is to know the answer—say, because she has just hidden the keys herself. Then (18)(a) would have the force of a request for an answer, but not a request for information. How can this be? Peter's answer (18)(b), like any utterance, expresses both a proposition and an attitude, and may be relevant in a variety of ways; for example, by providing evidence about the state of affairs it describes, or by providing evidence about Peter's beliefs about this state of affairs or others. If Mary's utterance had been a request for information, Peter's response would have been relevant in the first of these two ways; if, as we are imagining, Mary's utterance is a guess question, Peter's response might be relevant in the second way: by providing information about Peter's beliefs, his ability to predict Mary's actions, his willingness to cooperate with her, and so on. Exam questions might be dealt with along similar lines.[23]

With rhetorical and expository questions, the semantic indeterminacy is resolved in the hearer's favor: the speaker indicates that she regards the answer as relevant to him. Consider the following exchange:

(19)(a) PETER: Will they keep their promises?
(b) MARY: Have politicians ever kept their promises?

Here, Mary's utterance could be a genuine request for information. Suppose, though, that Mary manifestly regards the answer as relevant to Peter rather than to herself, manifestly knows the answer herself, and is manifestly prepared to give it. Then (19)(b) would have the force of an expository question or offer of information. Suppose, instead, that though she manifestly regards the answer as relevant to Peter, she also manifestly expects him to know it already, or to be in a position to work it out for himself without being told. Then (19)(b) would be a rhetorical question with the force of a reminder. Expository questions and rhetorical questions thus fit naturally into the framework.

In this section, we have tried to show that existing analyses of interrogative mood are empirically inadequate, and to present an alternative account that lays an adequate semantic foundation for the prediction of illocutionary force. Fundamental to our account have been the notions of interpretive representation and of a desirable (i.e., relevant) thought. Notice that our semantic analysis of interrogatives parallels our semantic analysis of imperatives in two important respects: first, it makes no direct reference to terms from the theory of force; and second, it relies heavily on semantic indeterminacy and the claim that such indeterminacy is resolved during the process of pragmatic interpretation.

On this account, the pragmatic force of an interrogative utterance is determined, on the one hand, by the fact that the speaker has represented a certain thought as desirable to someone, and on the other, by manifest contextual assumptions. How are contextual assumptions selected and semantic indeterminacies resolved? Here we have appealed to a single, general pragmatic principle, based on a notion of optimal relevance, and argued that in resolving semantic and contextual indeterminacies a rational hearer should select the first assumption (if any) tested and found consistent with the assumption that the speaker was aiming at optimal relevance. This completes our sketch of the semantics and pragmatics of imperatives and interrogatives.

Conclusion

The account just sketched is far from complete: we have ignored embedded cases, jokes, fantasies and fictions, threats and pseudo-imperatives, surprise questions and other types of echoic question, and "minor sentence types" (e.g., exclamative, optative, hortative). However, we hope to have shown that an approach along these lines is both feasible and generalizable. In this last section, we consider its implications for analyses based on mood.

We have argued for a direct semantic link between linguistic form and representations of propositional attitude. Imperative sentences (or rather, such characteristic features as imperative verb inflection, negative marking, and imperative particles such as "please") are linked to representations of potentiality and desirability. Interrogative sentences (or rather, such characteristic features as interrogative word order, intonation, and interrogative particles) are also linked to representations of desirability, in this case desirability of a thought rather than a state of affairs. Are we claiming, then, to have a satisfactory analysis of the semantic moods?

Not really—because we see no reason to assume that semantic moods exist. As we understand it, there is an implicit assumption behind mood-based approaches that we would want to question. The assumption is that the moods are unanalyzable and mutually exclusive semantic categories: that every sentence belongs to one and only one mood, which is not itself decomposable into more elementary moods.

It is easy to think of grounds for questioning this assumption. For instance, many languages have two types of interrogative sentence: those with an indicative verb, which expect an indicative answer, and those with a subjunctive verb, which expect a subjunctive answer. The Omotic languages of Southern Ethiopia have both indicative and imperative interrogatives—that is, interrogatives with an imperative verb, which expect an imperative answer. In each case, the meaning of the interrogative is a function of the meaning of the interrogative marker on the one hand, and of indicative, subjunctive, or imperative verb form on the other. On the assumption that every syntactic sentence type determines a distinct and unanalyzable mood, it would be surprising if a hearer encountering, say, an imperative interrogative for the first time was able to understand it. On our account, a hearer who already understood imperatives on the one hand, and indicative interrogatives on the other, should automatically understand imperative questions. This claim could be easily tested.

More seriously, what we see as the fundamental distinction between interpretive and descriptive use crosscuts any distinction among sentence types, and hence any distinction among semantic moods. As we have shown, every utterance—whatever its syntactic or semantic type—is in the first instance a more or less literal interpretation of the speaker's thought. This fact is not linguistically encoded in any way. Nor is the distinction between literal and less-than-literal interpretation. Although there are one or two linguistic indicators of non-literalness (e.g., hedges, or the use of "oh" in "There were, oh, a thousand people there"), it is in general left to the hearer, on the basis of considerations of relevance, to decide how faithful a representation has been attempted.

Similarly, any utterance, of any syntactic or semantic type, can be used as a second-order interpretation, and the fact is not normally linguistically encoded. Though there are linguistic indicators of echoic use (e.g., the "hearsay" particles used in many languages, or the French reportative conditional), it is in general left to the hearer, on the basis of considerations of relevance, to decide whether a second-order interpretation is involved, and if so, of what type.

Interrogatives, we have argued, do encode the fact that they are second-order interpretations of a certain type. But this does not prevent them from being used echoically too. Consider this:

(20) John sighed. Would she never speak?

The question in (20) is an example of free indirect speech. As such, it is triply interpretive: it is a more or less literal interpretation of the thought of the speaker or writer, which is itself an echoic interpretation of a thought attributed to John, which is in turn an interpretation of a desirable thought, namely, the answer to the question. Of these facts, only the last is linguistically encoded, and as this example makes clear, the encoding is indeterminate in two important respects: as to who regards the answer as desirable, and to whom.

The picture that emerges is thus both more complex and more highly structured than standard mood-based analyses would suggest. The echoic question in (20) is used to represent not a single propositional attitude but a stack of attitudes, each embedding or being embedded in another. An echoic imperative or declarative can involve a comparable array: it can, for example, be used in the appropriate circumstances to represent the speaker's view of what Bill suggested that Jenny regarded as an actual, potential, or desirable state of affairs. Moreover, the elementary attitudes that make up these complex arrays are not tied to any single sentence type: *any* sentence may be used as a faithful representation of the speaker's thought, or of an attributed thought, or of a possible but non-attributed thought. In *Relevance*,[24] we argued that even the sub-type of attitude encoded by interrogatives is shared in essential respects by exclamatives.

If we are right, then the linguistic form of a non-declarative utterance vastly underdetermines the way it is understood. In this, as in every other aspect of interpretation, considerations of optimal relevance play a vital constraining and enriching role. The greater the contribution of pragmatics, the less has to be attributed to linguistic semantics. Our claim is that the characteristic linguistic features of declarative, imperative, or interrogative form merely encode a rather abstract property of the intended interpretation: the direction in which the relevance of the utterance is to be sought.

PART II
Duty and the Moral Life

ANTHONY KENNY

Aristotle on Moral Luck

Each of us must have had, at some time or other, the thought "How lucky I am that I was not born in Nazi Germany." The thought is not simply that one is lucky not to have been subjected to the sufferings of those who lived under Hitler—that one was not a prisoner in a concentration camp, for instance. It is also the thought that one is lucky not to have been subject to the temptation to take part in all the wickedness that was practiced under the Nazis—that one was not, for instance, a guard in a concentration camp. "I am lucky not to have been born in Nazi Germany," we may think, "because if I had been I might very well have turned out horribly wicked."

The thought is a natural one, and yet it contains something of a paradox. How can a moral matter—such as whether someone turns out wicked or not—depend on luck? Philosophers often deny that it can: only what is within our control can be a proper subject for praise or blame; our moral responsibility cannot be affected one way or another by the good or bad luck involved in the consequences of our actions. Yet we are constantly meeting cases in practice in which our evaluation of our own and others' actions does depend on their luck. A drunken driver, if he is lucky, may get home without doing any damage to himself or anyone else; if he is unlucky enough to encounter an incautious pedestrian, he may kill him. It will be a matter of luck, then, whether he faces charges of drunken driving or of homicide, if his journey has attracted the attention of the police. The law is likely to punish him quite differently in the two cases, and yet the risks he took were the same in each case. Is this an imperfection in the law? Should our moral evaluation be exactly the same in the two cases? Or is it morally worse to kill someone while driving drunk than to drive drunkenly home with fortunate impunity?

The topic of moral luck was introduced into philosophy in recent times by Bernard Williams and Thomas Nagel.[1] Williams takes his start from the classical ideal of happiness as the product of self-sufficiency: what is not in the domain of the self is not in its control and so is subject to luck and the contingent enemies of tranquillity. In such a tradition the good man was immune to what might be called incident luck, but it was a matter of what might be called constitutive luck that one was a sage or capable of becoming one. In more recent philosophical traditions the goal of making the whole of life immune to luck has been abandoned, but there remains influential the idea that one supreme value in life, moral value, can be thus regarded as immune: the successful moral life is a career open not merely to the talents but to a talent that all rational beings necessarily possess in the same degree. On this Kantian view, any conception of "moral luck" is incoherent. Yet, Williams says, the aim of making morality immune to luck is bound to be disappointed. There is the constitutive luck that inescapably sets the conditions within which our moral dispositions, motives, and intentions must operate. But there is also—and this is the focus of Williams's attention—the incident luck that is involved in bringing any project of moral importance to a successful conclusion.

Williams considers in detail the case of a creative artist, such as Gauguin, who turns away from pressing human claims to live a life in which he can best pursue his art. In such a situation the only thing that will justify his choice will be success itself; if he fails, he did the wrong thing. There is no way of giving, prior to the outcome of the project, a justification in terms of moral rules or of utilitarianism. So Gauguin's justification is a matter of luck—though not equally a matter of all kinds of luck. If he failed through an accidental injury, that would not necessarily mean that he was wrong in his choice. What would prove him wrong in his project would not just be that it failed, but that he failed. Some luck is intrinsic to a project and some extrinsic; in Gauguin's case the intrinsic luck concerns whether he is a genuinely gifted painter who can succeed in doing genuinely valuable work. Intrinsic luck need not always lie within the agent, or the agent's control: the intrinsic luck involved in Anna Karenina's decision to leave her husband for Vronsky, for example, is something whose locus involves Vronsky as well as Anna.

Williams examines in detail cases such as these, in which an agent's eventual evaluation of her own decisions and actions will be decided partly by the good or bad luck she has had in the execution of *her* projects. He concludes that luck cannot be eradicated from the moral sphere, however much of a scandal this may be for the Kantian conscience. "Scepticism about the freedom of morality from luck cannot leave the concept of morality where it was."[2]

Nagel is more reluctant to consider jettisoning the Kantian concept of morality, though he fully recognizes both that luck is ineliminable from the moral sphere and that there is deeply rooted in our concept of morality the idea that one cannot be more culpable or estimable for anything than one is for that fraction of it which is under one's control. He sees the problem as parallel with skepticism about knowledge: if we take strictly the criteria that seem to distinguish cases in which claims to knowledge are justified, we seem to be left knowing nothing; if we take seriously the criteria for restricting the application of responsibility, responsibility seems to shrink to a point. The search for value that is non-accidentally good seems as doomed as the search for belief that is non-accidentally true. "The view that moral luck is paradoxical is . . . a perception of one of the ways in which the intuitively acceptable conditions of moral judgement threaten to undermine it all."[3]

The view that good or bad luck should not influence moral assessments was strikingly put in a famous passage of Kant's:

> If it should happen that by a particularly unfortunate fate or by the niggardly provision of a stepmotherly nature, the good will should be wholly lacking in power to accomplish its purpose, and if even the greatest effort should not avail it to achieve anything of its end, and if there remained only the good will . . . it would sparkle like a jewel in its own right.[4]

Nagel observes, in comment on this passage: "However jewel-like the good will may be in its own right, there is a morally significant difference between rescuing someone from a burning building and dropping him from a twelfth storey window while trying to rescue him."[5]

Nagel identifies four ways in which the natural objects of moral assessment are subject to luck:

> One is the phenomenon of constitutive luck—the kind of person you are, where this is not just a question of what you deliberately do, but of your inclinations, capacities and temperament. Another category is luck in one's circumstances—the kind of problems and situations one faces. The other two have to do with the causes and effects of action: luck in how one is determined by antecedent circumstances and luck in the way one's actions and projects turn out.[6]

I do not follow Nagel in thinking that free human actions can be determined by antecedent circumstances, so I shall not consider further his third kind of moral luck. The first, constitutive luck, is the matter of the kind of person one is at the beginning of one's moral life; this will depend partly on heredity and partly on environment, in proportions that nobody knows and everyone feels strongly about. Fortunately we need not settle the proportion, since both agencies have already done their worst before the individual is old enough to become a moral agent. The second we may call situational luck. The last kind listed by Nagel we may call executive luck. So we have three kinds of intrinsic moral luck: constitutive, situational, and executive (I think both situational and executive luck are varieties of incident luck).

Neither Williams nor Nagel claims to be able to reconcile the phenomenon of moral luck with the tradition in moral philosophy since Kant. Williams seems to view this cheerfully: he is happy to tap a further nail into the coffin of Kantian morality. Nagel sees the problem as merged into a greater overall one about human agency: how are we to relate the view of a moral agent to the view of a self as a thing in the world and acts as events?

I do not claim to be able to reconcile what Williams and Nagel have shown to be so far asunder. Instead, I want to look at the problem of moral luck from within a different moral tradition, that of Aristotle. For though in modern times the topic of luck in morality was hardly discussed before the 1976 symposium at which Williams and Nagel presented their papers, it was a topic that aroused interest in antiquity and, in a disguised form, in the Middle Ages. This essay, which is purely exploratory, is an attempt to relate what has been said in the modern debate to its ancient and medieval antecedents.

The form that the treatment of moral luck takes in the *Nicomachean Ethics* (hereafter *EN*) is a discussion of the relationship between luck and *eudaimonia*, which is, roughly, happiness. In chapter ten of the first book Aristotle asks whether a man can be called "happy" in his lifetime. Solon's dictum "wait to see the end" does not mean that it is the dead who are really happy: that is absurd, particularly if one defines happiness, with Aristotle, as the activity of the soul in accordance with virtue. Perhaps it means that it is not safe to call a man happy until he is dead and beyond the reach of misfortune: but this too seems open to objection. "Is it not paradoxical that at a time when a man actually is happy this attribute, though true, cannot be applied to him?" (*EN* 1100a34–35).

The reason that we are reluctant to call a man happy during his life is that misfortune may befall him. But it is quite wrong, Aristotle says, to make our judgment depend on fortune, "for fortune does not determine whether we fare well or ill, but is, as we said, merely an accessory to human life; activities in conformity with virtue constitute happiness" (1100b8–10). It is true that no state that is not durable deserves to be called happiness, but activities in accordance with virtue are the most durable and invulnerable of human activities. Although fortune can impede the activities of virtue and thus mar supreme happiness, a happy man can never be made wretched by fortune.

The man who is truly good and wise will bear with dignity whatever fortune may bring, and will always act as nobly as circumstances permit, just as a good general makes the most strategic use of the troops at his disposal, and a good shoemaker makes the best shoe he can from the leather available, and so with experts in all other fields. If this is so, a happy man will never become miserable; but even so, supreme happiness will not be his if a fate such as Priam's befalls him. (1100b35–1101a8)

If a man is equipped with all that is necessary for the exercise of perfect virtue at the present time, then he is happy. But he is supremely happy only if this state of affairs is going to continue until death, which we do not know. It will be true, then, that the word for supreme happiness, *makarios* or blessed, cannot be safely applied until a life is complete. And even those who finally deserve the accolade will not be blessed as the gods are: their happiness, even if in the end it survives intact, being a merely human thing will have been forever vulnerable throughout life (1101a15–21).

This familiar passage of the *EN* is relevant to moral luck because happiness is a moral concept for Aristotle; or rather, the concept of a worthwhile life that is expressed by the word *eudaimonia* includes as an element what we should call moral excellence. But Aristotle does not here discuss directly the relationship between luck and moral virtue: the good man on the rack may, because of his misfortune, cease to be happy (1096a1–2), but there is no question of his ceasing to be virtuous (1100b22–33).

It is not surprising, perhaps, that we find no treatment of executive luck in the *EN*. At least, it seems clear what Aristotle would say about executive bad luck, the case in which a moral agent, pursuing a worthwhile end, fails to achieve it because something goes wrong with the execution of his plan. If what goes wrong is something entirely external and incidental, then perhaps he is in the position of Priam, unable now to exercise the kingly virtues because of the collapse of Troy. But if what goes wrong is something intrinsic to his project—which was the case that Williams took as the paradigm of moral luck, and illustrated by the case of a Gauguin's failing in his Tahitian project because he could not bring off the kind of painting for which he sacrificed everything else—this is something that Aristotle will not count as ill-luck at all. According to him, the exercise of virtue involves not only moral excellence but also wisdom; so a person of good intentions who fails to translate them into virtuous deeds will lack wisdom and thus not be really virtuous. A Gauguin who threw up everything to develop his artistic talent in the South Seas, and then turned out to have only an extremely mediocre talent to develop, would be, for Aristotle, not somebody suffering from moral ill-luck but somebody lacking the self-knowledge that is an essential part of wisdom. Aristotle's attitude here seems to me correct. Even if we are prepared, as Aristotle no doubt would not have been, to regard the pursuit of artistic excellence as a proper overriding aim for a man's life, it is essential that the pursuit should be based on a sound estimate of the artist's talent if it is to be deserving of any moral respect.

There is perhaps, however, not a great difference between Williams's approach here and the one I have attributed to Aristotle.

For Williams agrees that if Gauguin had turned out to be unable to produce paintings of value then he would have been morally unjustified in what he did. Williams might claim to differ from Aristotle only in taking a more realistic view of the degree of uncertainty in which human decisions have to be taken, a degree of uncertainty that no wisdom can altogether eliminate.

So much, then, for incident moral luck in the *EN*. Constitutive luck receives one brief mention in the final book (1179b20–23). "Some people believe that it is nature that makes men good, others that it is habit, and others again that it is teaching. Now, whatever goodness comes from nature is obviously not in our power, but is present in truly fortunate men as the result of some divine cause." True good luck is to receive, from a divine source, the gift of whatever may be the natural element in virtue.

It is in his lesser known ethical treatises that Aristotle treats the topic of moral luck at the length it deserves. In the Middle Ages one of the most popular Latin versions of Aristotle was a small treatise called the *De Bona Fortuna*, popular enough to survive in 150 manuscripts (compared with 55 of the *Magna Moralia* [hereafter *MM*] in Latin, and not a single complete Latin manuscript of the *Eudemian Ethics* [hereafter *EE*]. It is composed of extracts from the *MM* (II.8) and from the *EE* (VIII.2). It has been published only partially;[7] the part of it that corresponds to the *EE* provides a better source for the reconstruction of the Greek original than do the surviving Greek manuscripts of the *EE*, which are in these passages corrupt.

According to the general Aristotelian theory, common to both the *EN* and the *EE*, happiness or welfare (*eudaimonia, eu prattein*) consists in the exercise of excellence, which involves the operation both of wisdom in the intellectual part of the soul and moral virtue in the appetitive part of the soul. The discussion in the *De Bona Fortuna* (*EE* VIII.2) starts from the consideration that not only wisdom produces happiness, but luck appears able to do so as well; and in general luck seems able to bring about the same results as knowledge. So we must inquire into the nature of good luck (*eutuchia*). Is it, for instance, by nature that one man is lucky and another unlucky (1246b37–1247a3)?

It seems beyond doubt that there are lucky people. There are those who do well in games of chance, and there are those who excel in matters like generalship and navigation, where skill is important, but where chance also has a major role. Now is being lucky an acquired disposition (*hexis*) like a virtue or a skill? Or is it something you are born with, like blue or brown eyes (1247a3–12)?

It is clear that luck is not a skill or species of wisdom; if it were, people would be able to give reasons for their lucky breaks. Is luck, then, a matter of divine favor: is being lucky a matter of having a guardian angel or *daimon* to pilot you through life? But why should God or an angel show special favor except to those who are best and wisest in their own right (1247a12–30)?

Well, if luck is not a matter of skill or of divine guidance, shall we say that it is something naturally inborn? But nature acts with regularity, while good luck is unexpected and irregular. Luck is contrasted with nature, so that if nature made people strike lucky—as having eyes of a certain color makes you see better or worse—then they should be called not *eutucheis* (blessed by luck) but *euphueis* (blessed by nature). A lucky man is one to whom chance brings good things; but if luck comes by nature is it not nature, rather than chance, that is the cause of these goods (1247a29–62)?

We meet a difficulty then in each of the hypotheses that we have explored: that luck is a skill, or a divine guidance, or a natural endowment. Shall we say then that there is no such thing as luck, and nothing is caused by luck? Is the notion of luck a cloak for our ignorance of causes? No: if there were an unknown cause in operation it would act with regularity; whereas luck is something that may strike once and not again. So, in spite of the difficulties we must maintain that there is such a thing as luck and that it is a cause (1247b3–18).

The key to the problem is this. There are in the soul impulses of two kinds: those that are the outcome of reasoning, and others that are more primitive and prior to reasoning, originating in unreasoning appetite. Just as there is a natural impulse expressed in the desire for pleasure, so there is a natural appetite for every kind of good. Just as there are some naturally musical people who sing well without being taught music, so there are some who, without reason, are impelled in nature's way and desire what they ought, when they ought, and as they ought. These people succeed, though they lack wisdom and reason, just as people can sing well without lessons. There will be one kind of lucky people, then, who are those who succeed in general, without reasoning; and these will indeed be people who are naturally lucky (1247b18–28).

But this is not the only kind of good luck. When things turn out lucky, what is done is sometimes in accordance with desire and choice; sometimes it is not, and may even be contrary to it. In the first case it is because the reasoning was incorrect that we say the people were lucky; in the second case the luck consists in obtaining a good that in one way or another you did not desire. In the first case we can indeed speak of natural luck: it was the goodness of the natural desire that kept the person out of trouble; similar reasoning joined to evil desire might have led to misfortune. This case, then, is natural good luck; but in the other case there is no desire, so we cannot say that good luck here is due to natural rightness of desire. So there must be at least two kinds of luck (1247b28–1248a15).

The crucial question is: what is the cause of a person's having the desire for the right thing at the right time? If luck is the cause of this, then it looks as if luck is the cause of everything, including thought and deliberation. We cannot say that deliberation is the cause of deliberation, under pain of setting off on an infinite regress. So what is the starting point of what goes on in the soul (1248a15–25)?

"The answer is clear: as in the universe, so there, God moves everything by mind: for the divine element in us is in a manner the cause of all our motions. The starting point of reason is not reason but something superior to reason. What could be superior even to knowledge and mind, except God?" (1248a25–29).

There are some who, without reasoning, succeed in their projects; it does not pay them to deliberate because they have within them a principle that is better than mind and deliberation: inspiration (*enthousiasmos*). In swiftness and sureness of judgment such people are not outdone by the wise and learned; they make use of the divine to give them foresight of the future (1248a29–b3).

"It is clear," Aristotle then concludes, "that there are two kinds of good fortune: one divine, in which it appears the lucky man succeeds through divine aid—this is the person who succeeds in accordance with his impulse, while the other is he who succeeds against his impulse. Neither owes his success to reason. The former kind is more continuous good fortune, the latter is not continuous" (1248b3–7).

This chapter in Aristotle presents many difficulties. In the first place, the text is often corrupt, and emendations can only be conjectural even with the aid of the better text of the *De Bona Fortuna*. In the second place, the argument is often cryptic, and in particular it is difficult to see which of the many distinctions Aristotle makes are meant to be equivalent to each other, and which are intended to further subdivide classes already divided.

There appear to be four possible classes of people who are candidates for being *eutucheis*. First, there are those to whom God gives a good nature, which leads, via reasoning, to virtuous action. These are the normally virtuous people: though the original gift of good nature is something outside their power, it is the whole foundation of moral virtue. This is the constitutive good luck of which the *EN* speaks; it is mentioned at *EE* 1248a17–29, but it is not really regarded as a case of luck there. Then there is the case in which God gives good nature, which leads via bad reasoning to a successful outcome: here it is the initial good natural desire that is the cause of the successful outcome (1247b37). Neither is this really luck.

The third and fourth cases are the two that Aristotle regards as genuine cases of luck, and lists as the two kinds at the end of the chapter. In the third, God gives us inspiration that leads from good desire to good outcome: there is no reasoning, but something more valuable. It may be that Aristotle here has in mind the unreasoned decisions that Socrates attributed to his *daimon* and that preserved him from wrongdoing. It is this luck that is described as divine in the *EE*, although constitutive luck is so described in the *EN*. This is continuous good luck (which means that it is only doubtfully worthy of the name, since irregularity is taken by Aristotle as one of the characteristics of luck). Finally we have the case in which somebody with bad desires performs good actions. This is a kind of luck; it is the non-divine, irregular kind mentioned last of all by Aristotle.

In the *EN* and the *EE*, then, Aristotle recognizes constitutive and executive luck as contributing to virtuous behavior. Situational luck is not mentioned in either as contributing to virtue; but it is mentioned in the *EN* as relevant to happiness—what Priam lacks is situational luck. But this kind of luck is in fact also relevant to virtue. It is a matter of luck whether we are placed in situations in which we have to choose between being a hero and being wicked (as in the case of someone forced by terrorists at gunpoint to plant a bomb, or a shipwrecked sailor who judges that he can survive only by killing and eating a cabin boy), instead of being able to steer a judicious course between the two as we usually do.

The constant reference to God in Aristotle's discussion of moral luck shows us where we should look for medieval treatments of the same topic. Aristotle's pagan luck is the equivalent of the Christian notion of divine grace. Divine luck, like divine grace, is a gift of God to humans, prior to all desert—the basis on which success or failure in the good life, salvation or damnation, is built. Grace is of several kinds, as Aristotle's luck is. There is the constitutive grace of being born and brought up in a Christian community, the sanctifying grace symbolized by baptism. The thoughts and primitive desires that precede all deliberation and choice and are the expression of the divine in us correspond to what theologians call actual graces. The inspirations that specially favored people like Socrates receive correspond to the *gratiae gratis datae* with which some of the saints, such as Joan of Arc, are favored.

Christianity is often contrasted with Aristotelian morality as being more egalitarian. The elitist picture of the *megalopsychos* in the *EN*, who needs wealth and power to display the greatness of his soul, is contrasted with the gospel religion of the poor and humble, equal citizens of the Kingdom of God.

The basic unfairness of the world is altered by Christianity, but it is not in fact eliminated. The widow's mite, we are told, is as valuable in the sight of God as the gift of the rich man: so the unequal opportunities for practicing munificence are evened out *sub specie aeternitatis*. But the unfairness of the distribution of terrestrial wealth has as its counterpart the inequality of access to heavenly riches. According to traditional Christian teaching, it makes a great difference to one's chances of salvation whether one is born before or after the arrival of the Messiah, into a God-fearing Christian family, or into a pagan milieu as part of a *massa damnata*.

The feature of moral luck that is most offensive to our modern notions is its opposition to the ideals of equality. Constitutive luck contrasts with the ideal of equality of talent, which very many people would like to be true, and which some people actually believe to be true. Situational luck contrasts with the ideal of equality of opportunity, which seeks to place people so far as possible in equal situations. (Equality of opportunity was originally pursued against a belief in inequality of talent; equality of opportunity was indeed designed to see that inequality of rewards matched inequality of skills, etc., and not inequalities of birth: the career was open to the unevenly distributed talents.) Executive luck points up the inequality of human achievement, both absolutely and in relation to desert.

The conflict between luck and ideals of equality seems more painful now than before given that the history of morality shows an ever greater weight being placed on those ideals. The topics covered in Aristotle's *Ethics* include much more than we would naturally think of as moral: there are the virtues of courage, wisdom, and temperance, as well as the virtue of justice. In the Middle Ages the virtues of faith, hope, and charity, none of which have anything to do with equality, occupied the center of the moral stage. We have gradually equated morality with the area covered by the cardinal virtue of justice; and even within the range of this virtue we have concentrated on distributive justice to the exclusion of retributive and other forms of justice, placing need rather than desert in the center of the picture.

When the notion of morality is thus circumscribed, and when morality is regarded as the supreme human value, the tension between luck and morality becomes excruciating. If, from an Aristotelian viewpoint, the Kantian type of moral value is seen only as one among others, then the tension is relaxed a little: the inequality of distribution of the wherewithal for moral goodness is perhaps no more and no less a scandal than the inequality of distribution of the wherewithal for intellectual achievement or artistic creation. But the inequality of the distribution of all these gifts is something that never ceases to disquiet us.

The Christian parable of the talents does not suggest that there is a basic equality of the most valuable human gifts; its moral is rather to reject discouragement at the development of a comparatively modest talent. The parable of the laborers in the vineyard suggests that however much effort one puts into the cultivation of these gifts, the distribution of achievement will in no way reflect the distribution of desert.

Neither ancient paganism, medieval Christianity, nor modern secularism has done anything to alter the conclusion that the world operates on principles quite other than those of fairness, and that no human institutions can radically alter the basic unfairness of the world.

Still, though we cannot eliminate it, we do try, at our best moments, to make our social arrangements compensate for the unfairness of the world in the distribution of non-moral goods. We try to bring up the most disadvantaged—not to equality—but to a minimum tolerable level of distribution of the goods accessible to society. We give special education to the intellectually subnormal, we give social assistance to the economically deprived, we make special provisions for access and mobility for the handicapped. Can we, and should we, make similar attempts to diminish the moral unfairness of the world?

Let it be observed first of all that there is nothing *unjust* in the operation of moral luck as I have described it. Moral luck, I have said, offends against our intuitions about responsibility and our sense of fairness. But the offense against responsibility would be genuine only if the recognition of moral luck involved holding people responsible for things when they had no choice about the outcome. It would be the moral equivalent of strict liability. One can recognize moral luck without doing that. In law there is not just the stark alternative between strict liability and restricting punishment to deliberate wrongdoing. The law punishes negligent and reckless wrongdoing as well as intentional crime: and what is thus punished is a mixture of choice and luck. Even when we punish the unfortunate Nazi guard or Irish Republican Army accessory who has chosen to kill rather than be killed, we are not punishing people who had no choice in the matter of their misdeeds. They had a difficult choice and the correct choice would have been a heroic choice; but nonetheless they had a choice, and they did what they did knowing that they were doing wrong and what the outcome could and would be.

The two principal ways in which moral luck seems unfair are these. First, we sometimes hold people equally responsible for equal deeds done under circumstances of unequal temptation, as we find guilty of murder the Irish Republican Army accessory as well as the cold-blooded murderer who had no similar temptation. This is a case of situational bad luck.

Second, we sometimes hold unequally responsible people who performed equally culpable acts (or were guilty of equally reprehensible negligences) when they have unequally bad outcomes (we don't find the lucky drunken driver guilty of manslaughter). This is a case of executive bad luck.

Is there injustice here? Let us consider first the question of deserts. There is injustice when someone gets less than his deserts, or is punished more than he deserves. That is not in question in either case: the driver is punished for the risk he took, and gets no more than he deserves; the lucky driver gets better than he deserves, but there is no injustice in this and it is supported by the principle of economy of punishment. So with the coerced accessory: he is guilty of murder, having preferred his own skin to someone else's, and there is good deterrent reason against letting him go.

But in addition to the justice that assigns just measure in accordance with deserts, is there not distributive justice, which aims at an equal or at least equitable distribution of goods? And should we not, in the interest of fairness, try to achieve a fair distribution of moral good as we do of the goods of health and strength and wealth?

Once one reflects on it, one sees that the goal of making everyone morally equal has not the prima facie attractiveness of making everyone equally rich, clever, and powerful. In fact, distributive justice has no application to the distribution of moral goodness. But with moral goodness as with other forms of goodness we do indeed wish to diminish the effect of luck. We should aim to take the maximum benefit to society from the good luck of those who are morally lucky, and minimize the damage to society of those who are morally unlucky. To make our moral judgments blind to the effects of luck would have exactly the opposite effect: if we marked down the lucky, we would diminish their incentive for using their heroism in our behalf; if we let off the unlucky altogether we would deprive them of their incentive to heroism.

A rational morality, then, is closer to the Aristotelian than to the Kantian one. Of morality as a whole we can say what Aristotle said of the good man: that he is like the cobbler who makes the best shoe with the bad leather he has. The best morality, then, is one that makes the best of the unfair world we live in. It is not one that denies the unfairness of the actual world, nor one that pursues fairness and equality in an imaginary metaphysical world of pure morality and pure goodwill.

C. C. W. TAYLOR

Urmson on Aristotle on Pleasure

While many of J. O. Urmson's writings have attained the status of classics in their various fields, his paper "Aristotle on Pleasure" has not attracted more than passing mention from other writers.[1] Yet that essay, brief though it is, raises an issue of major importance for our understanding not only of Aristotle's views on pleasure but of pleasure itself. That issue concerns the relation between the enjoyment of an activity and the having of pleasant sensations. Contrary to the empiricist tradition, which had tended to equate the two, Urmson both uses Aristotle to urge the distinction between enjoying φ-ing and enjoying sensations caused by φ-ing and finds fault with him for blurring that distinction. While taking issue with Urmson on both points, I count it a great merit of his paper that it focuses attention on a central and unexpectedly complex issue.

In that paper Urmson first summarizes Aristotle's discussion of pleasure in *Nicomachean Ethics* (hereafter *EN*) X, which he describes as "Aristotle's most mature and careful account," and then discusses some problems arising from it. His main conclusion, with which I broadly agree, is that in that discussion Aristotle offers an analysis of the enjoyment of an activity as something barely distinguishable from the activity, "more like the effortless zest with which the activity is performed than a result or concomitant of it."[2] This view of enjoyment, which is similar to Gilbert Ryle's, is opposed to any attempt to represent enjoyment as the obtaining of pleasant experiences accruing from an activity, of which the paradigm case is a pleasant bodily sensation caused by the activity. Urmson quotes a revealing example of the kind of misunderstanding to which the latter picture of enjoyment can lead: at the beginning of his discussion of temperance in *EN* III.10–12, Aristotle distinguishes the pleasures of the soul, for example, those springing from the love of honor or the love of learning, from bodily pleasures, pointing out that someone who experiences the former type "enjoys what he loves, his body being in no way affected, but rather his intellect" (1117b29–31). Enjoying intellectual activity, that is, or enjoying acting honorably, is not a matter of having any bodily sensations. Aristotle's commentator Aspasius, however, failed to see the point, protesting that pleasure and enjoyment are not in the intelligence but in the affective part of the soul.[3] It is natural to think in that way, Urmson suggests, if you take it for granted that pleasure and enjoyment are passive experiences connected only causally with any activity.

Aristotle, then, is in no danger of construing all pleasure as the occurrence of pleasant sensations. Rather, according to Urmson, he goes to the opposite extreme, attempting to make the experiencing of pleasant sensations itself a case of the enjoyment of an activity. This is seen from his discussion of bodily pleasures in *EN* III.10, where bodily pleasures are described as the enjoyment of different kinds of sense perception, enjoyment of pleasant colors, sounds, etc. The bodily pleasures that are the sphere of temperance (Aristotle's immediate concern in this passage) are those of touch and taste (1118a23–26) and primarily that of touch. The glutton and the drunkard are not interested in tasting what they are eating or drinking, as a wine taster or a cook might be, but in the sensation of the stuff actually sliding down the gullet (a26–31); hence Aristotle's anecdote of the glutton who wished that he had a throat longer than a crane's, so as to prolong the sensation of swallowing (literally, "since he enjoyed the touch" [a32–b1]). Similarly, and more plausibly, sexual enjoyment is all a matter of touch (a31–32). Urmson's account of this passage is as follows. What Aristotle is really doing is describing the intemperate man as one who goes in for excessive eating, drinking, and sex not because he enjoys those activities, but for the sake of the pleasant tactile sensations that they produce; but, lacking a clear grasp of that distinction, Aristotle misdescribes the intemperate man as enjoying the exercise of the sense of touch. This, according to

Urmson, is misleading, since enjoying the exercise of the sense of touch is quite different from having a pleasant tactile sensation. The latter is a passive experience, while the former is a kind of activity; an example of it would be the enjoyment of the tactile discrimination of different textures. A similar distinction holds in the case of each of the other senses; thus we can distinguish looking at x from seeing x, listening to x from hearing x, tasting (as in wine tasting) from having a taste in the mouth, and smelling (in the sense of sniffing at) from having an odor in the nostrils. In the case of each pair the enjoyment of the first member is a genuine enjoyment of an activity, but in the case of the second what is enjoyed is not an activity but a sensation. If in those cases an activity is involved, it is merely a means of obtaining the object of the enjoyment; it is not that object itself. An example of Urmson's makes the point clear: "We must surely recognize," he writes, "that one might smell roses not because one enjoyed smelling roses but because one enjoyed the smell—a passive experience to which the activity of smelling is but a means." Aristotle blurs this important distinction, and may therefore justly be censured for "the uncommon error of assimilating the enjoyment of feelings to the enjoyment of activity."[4]

I do not intend in this paper to discuss Aristotle's analysis of the enjoyment of an activity, or Urmson's account of it. Nor do I wish to take issue with Urmson's contention that in his discussion of bodily pleasures in *EN* III Aristotle assumes that the intemperate man overindulges in food, drink, and sex for the sake of pleasant bodily sensations caused by eating, drinking, and sexual activity. Rather I propose to concentrate on Urmson's doctrine (implied though nowhere explicitly stated) that when A φ's for the sake of sensation S, which A enjoys, A's enjoyment is always to be described as the enjoyment of S, *and never as the enjoyment of φ-ing*. The essence of Urmson's criticism of Aristotle, as I understand it, is that he tries to have it both ways: he describes the intemperate man as enjoying the activity of touching, while what he means, and therefore ought to say, is that the intemperate man enjoys tactile sensations, and therefore that his unseemly activities are not *what* he enjoys, but merely *means to* what he enjoys. I hope to show that that distinction does not hold, since the intemperate man's enjoyments are prominent among a range of cases in which it is true both (1) that A enjoys φ-ing and (2) that one of the features (perhaps the principal feature) in virtue of which A enjoys φ-ing is the occurrence of pleasant bodily sensations caused, in the appropriate way, by A's φ-ing.

I do not, of course, deny that *sometimes* when A's φ-ing causes a pleasant sensation S, A does not enjoy φ-ing. Such cases occur when the pleasant sensation is a relatively remote effect of φ-ing, for example, the glow of returning circulation produced by vigorous toweling after an agonizingly cold shower. Here the showering might cause the enjoyable glow, without being itself enjoyed; the glow is sufficiently remote from the shower, both temporally and causally, to be disqualified from being counted as a feature of showering in virtue of which showering is enjoyable. But now let us consider the glow in relation, not to the shower, but to the vigorous toweling, which *immediately* produces the glow. The toweling is no less *distinct* from the glow than the shower is; plainly, A's vigorously rubbing himself with a towel is not identical with the pleasant sensation that it causes. Yet when A rubs himself with vigor and enthusiasm, groaning with pleasure at the exquisite sensations of returning circulation, it seems quite artificial to insist that he is not enjoying *toweling himself*, but instead enjoying *the glow*. Here, while the toweling undeniably causes the glow, which is the focus of enjoyment, the temporal coincidence and the immediacy of the causal link seem to constitute the toweling as something that is itself enjoyed, *in virtue of its causing the glow*, rather than as a mere means to the real object of enjoyment, namely, the glow. That is, sometimes the occurrence of sensation S is, rather than a mere effect of φ-ing, a feature of φ-ing in virtue of which φ-ing is enjoyed; the pleasures of taste and touch, including sexual pleasure, provide the clearest examples of this type of situation.[5] This will become clear from more detailed consideration of an example drawn from this range of pleasures.

Suppose that I am a regular glutton for chocolates. I eat chocolates whenever I have the chance, smack my lips over them, can't keep my mind on anything else when there is a box in the vicinity, and so on. All this adds up to the characteristic Aristotelian-Rylean picture of someone who enjoys eating chocolates. Now you ask me why I enjoy eating chocolates, or, to put the same question another way, what it is about eating chocolates that I enjoy. I reply "I like the taste of chocolates." Having read your Urmson you then say "I see. You don't really enjoy *eating chocolates*. What you enjoy is the taste of chocolates, which is a sensation. The activity of eating chocolates is merely a means toward that sensation. So you have misdescribed what it is that you enjoy." Somewhat baffled, I ask you the following question: "You say that I don't really enjoy eating chocolates, since what I really enjoy is the taste of chocolates. What then would you count as a case of really enjoying eating chocolates, *as distinct from* enjoying the taste of chocolates?" Taking a hint from Urmson's wine taster, you reply "Well, for instance, the enjoyment experienced by a connoisseur of flavors, who enjoys identifying different chocolates by their taste, texture, etc., as opposed to someone like yourself who just wolfs down every chocolate in the box regardless of the differences between them." My rejoinder is this: "What you have done is to describe a chocolate fancier, that is, someone with a specialized interest in chocolates. I might agree at a pinch to describe him as enjoying eating chocolates, though it would be more precise to describe him as enjoying tasting or discriminating them. But there is absolutely no reason, and indeed it would be most misleading to *confine* the description "enjoys eating chocolates" to him and to refuse to apply it to me. We both enjoy eating chocolates, but for different reasons. I enjoy eating them for the taste, that is (suppose I am an extreme case), all chocolates taste the same to me, and it is a taste that I like. He enjoys eating them for the taste too, but in a different way, in that he enjoys the exercise of his powers of discrimination in respect of taste. It is as absurd to suggest that no one but a chocolate fancier really enjoys eating chocolates as it would be to suggest that no one but a beer connoisseur really enjoys drinking beer."

The defender of what I shall call the Urmsonian position[6] need not, however, regard this as a knockdown argument. While he might agree that, at the level of ordinary language, it seems very odd to refuse to describe me as enjoying eating chocolates, nevertheless, he might maintain, there is a logically compelling reason for this refusal. This is that there is merely a contingent connection between the activity of eating chocolates and the experiencing of the taste of chocolates. Thus, if we suppose that a drug could reproduce the taste of chocolates, though no chocolates were in fact eaten, one would get precisely the same enjoyment from taking the drug as one now gets from eating the chocolates. But, at least since Ryle, it has been commonplace to say that the enjoyment of an activity is unobtainable without the activity itself; one cannot get the enjoyment of gardening without actually gardening. So since, as our drug example shows, it is possible to enjoy the taste of chocolates without actually eating any, but logically impossible to have the enjoyment of eating without actually eating, enjoying eating chocolates must be a different enjoyment from enjoying the taste of chocolates, even in the case in which one enjoys eating them because of the taste.

In order to show why this argument will not work, we must distinguish two types of case in which one enjoys φ-ing by enjoying sensations caused by one's φ-ing: in the first type the occurrence of those sensations is non-contingently linked to the belief that one is φ-ing, whereas in the second those sensations can occur in the absence of the belief that one is φ-ing. Sexual enjoyment of mutual caressing is a particularly clear case of the first type. The pleasant sensations of caressing and being caressed are not "raw" sensations occurring in total independence of the context of beliefs in which they are felt. Being caressed feels pleasant in part because of the beliefs the person being caressed has about the person caressing, the nature of the situation, etc.; thus if the caressing were believed to be a prelude to torture it is unlikely that it would feel as pleasant as a "normal" caress, even supposing the physical stimuli to be identical. But this does not show that this kind of sexual enjoyment does not consist in part in the enjoyment of certain sensations; rather it shows that the holding of certain beliefs is a necessary condition for the occurrence of certain sensations. In order to have a soothing sensation, for example, it is necessary to be in a frame of mind conducive to being soothed, which requires that one should have certain beliefs and lack others. It follows that the only way in which sensations of that sort could be reproduced in the absence of the activity giving rise to them would be by the production of a total hallucination of the enjoyment of that activity, including the belief that that activity was being undertaken. But every instance of enjoyment, of whatever kind, could (theoretically) be thus reproduced. Hence if the bare logical possibility of the production of a total hallucination of the enjoyment of φ-ing were sufficient to show that what is actually enjoyed is not φ-ing, no one ever enjoys anything.

Since that is absurd, the defender of the Urmsonian position must concede that his thesis does not apply to cases of the first type.

He must, then, rely on cases of the second type, in which, as in the example of the drug-induced simulation of the taste of chocolates, the pleasant sensation could occur without even the belief that one was φ-ing. His argument is that, since *ex hypothesi* what one enjoys is precisely the same when one has taken the drug as when one is actually φ-ing, and since what one enjoys is not φ-ing when one has taken the drug, for then one is not φ-ing, what one is enjoying cannot be φ-ing in the case in which one actually is φ-ing. But this argument depends on a crucial ambiguity in the reference of "what one enjoys." It is the same *feature* that is enjoyed on either occasion, in that either situation is enjoyed because of the occurrence of F. But in the one case F is a feature of φ-ing, in which case one enjoys φ-ing because of F, while in the other F is a feature of a simulacrum of φ-ing, in which case one enjoys that simulacrum because of F.[7] So what one enjoys is not the same *activity* in either situation. Hence the argument is invalid, since the reference of "what one enjoys" is the feature F in the first premise, but the simulacrum of the activity in the second. The principle on which this defense relies, namely, that if one enjoys a situation because of the presence of F, one cannot really or strictly be said to enjoy anything other than F, is mistaken. One might as well argue that, if one admires a woman's looks because of her lovely hair, it is strictly speaking the hair that one admires, *and not her looks*. That is plainly false, even though the hair might be present, and admired, in the absence of the woman, when attached to a waxwork model of the woman, for example.

I am not, of course, maintaining that one can enjoy φ-ing without actually φ-ing, since I accept the Rylean position on that point. My claim is rather that if one enjoys φ-ing because of some feature of φ-ing, which we may label F, the fact that in certain circumstances one can get F without actually φ-ing does not show that, when one is actually φ-ing, one is not really enjoying φ-ing, but merely enjoying the occurrence of F. Someone who denies this claim is committed to the view that if I can get F either by φ-ing or by ψ-ing, I do not really enjoy either activity, but merely enjoy the occurrence of F. So if I enjoy both skiing and tobogganing because they are exhilarating, I do not really enjoy either, but just enjoy being exhilarated (whatever that means). Of course, it is true that I do not enjoy skiing just qua skiing, but qua exhilarating, and similarly for tobogganing. That is to say, there is some description of the feature(s) of the activity in virtue of which it is enjoyable more specific than "it is skiing" or "it is tobogganing." But it is clear that the application of the description "enjoys φ-ing" is not restricted to cases of enjoying φ-ing qua φ-ing, that is, to cases in which the question "What is enjoyable about φ-ing?" elicits no answer other than "It is φ-ing."

It is fairly clear what has gone wrong with the Urmsonian position. One begins by stressing, rightly, the importance of the distinction between the enjoyment of an activity and the experiencing of pleasant sensations consequent upon that activity. Urmson's example of doing geometry serves as an excellent illustration.[8] The enjoyment of geometry, as Aristotle pointed out (*EN* 1175a30–b6), is a matter of effortless concentration on geometry, which tends to make one a better geometer, whereas pleasurable sensations produced by geometry, for instance, a glow of excitement at the prospect of completing an important proof, may distract from one's geometrizing in the same way that an "extraneous" pleasure would, for example, hearing one's favorite tune from next door. One then proceeds to generalize this distinction, drawing the conclusion that if one undertakes an activity for the sake of some sensation(s), what one enjoys is not the activity, but the sensation(s). But this is to overlook the fact that the enjoyment of some activities is itself characterizable in part as the enjoyment of sensations. Thus (assuming that tastes are sensations) if one enjoys eating certain foods because one likes their taste, it is mistaken to suggest that what one enjoys is not eating, but some sensation consequent upon eating. That would correctly describe someone who was indifferent to what the food tasted like, but enjoyed certain digestive sensations occurring afterward, for example; it does not describe someone who relishes food for its taste. Again, if one enjoys sexual caressing because it feels pleasant, that is enjoying sexual activity, not enjoying sensations consequent upon it; the same is true, obviously, of enjoying intercourse because it feels pleasant. Urmson's "quasi-aesthetic enjoyment of textures"[9] is not the only kind of tactile enjoyment; there is also the active enjoyment of touching, stroking, etc., and the passive enjoyment of being touched, stroked, etc., whether in a sexual or a non-sexual context. In the former kind of enjoyment the occurrence of tactile sensations is an essential ingredient; necessarily, if one enjoys stroking the cat, it feels nice to stroke the cat. The latter, that is, passive tactile enjoyment, seems to be the enjoyment of (an activity of) having sensations aroused in one.[10] One can apply Urmson's own test to show that enjoyment of that activity is not to be separated from enjoyment of the sensation(s): it is surely absurd to suppose that enjoyment of the sensation of being stroked might distract one from being stroked, so that one should have to wait until that enjoyment passes off before getting back to concentrating on being stroked once again. Rather, to use Aristotle's terminology, the enjoyment perfects the activity (1174b23).[11]

I have here spoken of someone who enjoys sex because it feels pleasant to be caressed, etc., and have argued that given that description it is a mistake to separate enjoyment of sensation from enjoyment of activity. There is, however, another description of a sort of sexual activity, which allows that distinction to be made, namely, that according to which activities such as caressing arouse sensations located in the sex organs, which sensations are alone enjoyed. In that case one could properly be said to enjoy, not the activity, but just the sensation to which it gives rise. The difference between the two situations becomes clear when one reflects that in the second case it is not the stroking itself that feels nice, but the sensation that it arouses, which could be located in a quite different part of the body, whereas in the first case it is the stroking itself that feels nice. Clearly, either situation can occur; for what it is worth, I suspect that the former is the more common, but that is immaterial. What is important is that we should not assume that the second description is the only one available, and hence conclude that anyone who enjoys sex because it feels nice must be enjoying sensations and not activities.

To sum up, while it is always possible to distinguish enjoying φ-ing from enjoying sensations consequent on φ-ing, it is not always possible even in theory to distinguish enjoying φ-ing from enjoying the occurrence of some sensations, since φ-ing may be an activity the enjoyment of which consists, in part, in the enjoyment of certain sensations. The enjoyments of food, drink, and sex are characteristic examples of that kind of enjoyment, provided that we are prepared to reckon tastes as sensations. Nor, though a distinction exists, is it in every case clear just where the line is to be drawn between those sensations the enjoyment of which is constitutive of the enjoyment of the activity and those that are merely effects of the activity, of which the enjoyment is consequently separable from the enjoyment of the activity itself. Thus enjoying the taste of brandy is clearly not to be distinguished from enjoying drinking brandy. But what about the heart-warming glow that pervades the whole body after a glass or two? Is the enjoyment of that sensation part of the enjoyment of drinking brandy, or merely the enjoyment of a sensation produced by drinking? There neither is nor need be any clear answer to that question.

How, then, does this affect Urmson's criticism of Aristotle? The latter's doctrine is that the enjoyment of food, drink, and sex, or at least the kind of enjoyment of them that is characteristic of the intemperate man, arises wholly from the sense of touch. (This is a paraphrase of 1118a29–32.) Earlier I accepted Urmson's suggestion regarding what Aristotle means by this: what the intemperate man enjoys about eating, drinking, and sex is the occurrence of certain bodily sensations. I reject, however, the implication that Urmson draws from this, namely, that Aristotle therefore represents the intemperate man as not enjoying those activities themselves. As I have argued, it does not follow from the fact that you like sex for the sake of certain bodily sensations that you do not enjoy sex as such. But it may be true nonetheless that Aristotle in fact represents the intemperate man as not enjoying his intemperate activities themselves. We have to look at what he says. In the case of food and drink the intemperate man gets little or no enjoyment, in Aristotle's view, from the taste of what is eaten or drunk (nor does he say anything about enjoyment of the alcoholic effects of drink); the enjoyment lies wholly in the sensation of swallowing. Now, that sensation seems to me one of those that, like the warm afterglow of the brandy, are so intimately connected with the activity giving rise to them as not to be clearly separable from it. We can, if we choose, stipulate that someone who likes eating solely because he enjoys the sensation of swallowing is not to be said to enjoy eating, but that would be a stipulation, not an implication of the existing concept.

It is worth remarking on the odd reason that Aristotle gives for his assertion that the intemperate man gets little or no enjoyment from taste. The reason is that "to taste belongs the discernment of flavors, the kind of thing that wine tasters and cooks do. But they do not enjoy these things at all, or at least intemperate people do not; their enjoyment arises wholly from touch" (1118a27–31). What Aristotle has done here is to single out one specialized exercise of the sense of taste (one, moreover, that its practitioners do not, in his view, enjoy at all) and treat it as if it were the only exercise of that sense. He appears to think that if you do not enjoy tastes in that way, you cannot enjoy tastes at all. But that is simply false. Aristotle's view is even more extreme than the one I criticized earlier, according to which only a chocolate fancier really enjoys eating chocolates, which is a different enjoyment from enjoying the taste of chocolates. On Aristotle's view, only the chocolate fancier's enjoyment involves taste at all; the person who is greedy over chocolates, but is not a chocolate fancier, enjoys something altogether different, namely, the sensation of swallowing the chocolates. It may be sufficient to remark that on that view it seems impossible to account for the fact that people are very often greedy over particular kinds of food and drink while indifferent to others, since presumably it all feels much the same going down.[12] Aristotle's view perhaps depends on the assumption that the primary function of a sense is discrimination between objects of that sense, for example, that the function of sight is discrimination of color.[13] But that assumption does not lead to Aristotle's conclusion; for someone who is greedy over oysters, but indifferent to rice pudding, is at least discriminating oysters *from* rice pudding in enjoying the taste of oysters, though it may be no part of his enjoyment to make discriminations between the tastes of different kinds of oysters, as a connoisseur might.

We come now to Aristotle's account of the remaining "intemperate" pleasure, namely, intemperate sexual enjoyment. In saying that that is purely a matter of touch, Aristotle is clearly taking an unduly narrow view of sexual activity, ignoring such psychological factors as the pleasures of intimacy and tenderness, of dominating or being dominated, etc. But he cannot be interpreted on that ground alone as saying that the intemperate do not enjoy sexual activity, but only sexual sensations, since we have seen that in many sexual situations the enjoyment of the former consists, in part, in the enjoyment of the latter. There is, however, one further piece of evidence to be taken into account. After characterizing "intemperate" enjoyment of food and drink as purely a matter of touch, Aristotle distinguishes intemperate pleasure from "more refined" tactile enjoyments, giving as an instance of the latter the enjoyment of a warming massage in the gymnasium. The ground of the distinction is that "the touch that the intemperate man enjoys does not involve the whole body, but certain parts only" (1118b4–8). (The "certain parts" are presumably the gullet, for food and drink, and the sex organs.) This might suggest that Aristotle accepts the second of the two pictures of sexual activity sketched above, according to which sexual activities such as stroking and kissing are valued only as means to the production of sensations located specifically in the sex organs. That may be what he meant, in which case he does indeed represent the intemperate as enjoying, not those activities themselves, but merely sexual sensations produced by them. That distinction cannot, however, apply to the enjoyment of sexual intercourse itself; the latter is an activity the enjoyment of which consists in part in the enjoyment of sensations occurring in the sex organs. In any case, Aristotle's words can be taken in another sense, which is perhaps somewhat more plausible. This is that what distinguishes sexual activity from other forms of activity, and consequently sexual pleasure from other forms of pleasure, is the specific parts of the body that it involves. Then to say that sexual enjoyment is all a matter of touch will not be to say that it is enjoyment of sensations and not activities, but merely to say that one enjoys the activities of touching and being touched not with respect to the whole body, but with respect to certain parts only. This, too, is pretty plainly false, especially given the restricted interpretation of "certain parts" assumed above; but the falsehood reflects inadequate observation (or possibly differences between ancient and modern sexual practices) rather than any conceptual error.

My conclusion, then, is that while Aristotle believes that the intemperate man goes in for his intemperate activities for the sake of bodily sensations, he does not say or imply that he enjoys only those sensations and not the activities themselves. Intemperate pleasures are important examples of a sort of enjoyment of activity that is itself constituted in part by the enjoyment of sensations. Hence in those cases it is a mistake to infer that someone who enjoys that sort of sensation does not enjoy the activities themselves. But that mistake, if committed by anyone, has been committed by Urmson, not by Aristotle. Where Aristotle goes wrong is in his very queer view of what it is that is enjoyable about "intemperate" activities, and in particular about the intemperate enjoyment of food and drink. He is also wrong, in my view, about sex, though less obviously and grotesquely so. Specifically, he is wrong to classify all these forms of enjoyment as consisting purely in the enjoyment of tactile sensations. But, contra Urmson, he is right to think that the enjoyment of tactile sensations fits happily into his general account of pleasures as the enjoyment of activities, under the heading of enjoyment of the exercise of the senses. For the senses can be employed, and enjoyed, in the having of sensations as much as in active exploration and discrimination, and the passive enjoyment of tactile sensations is the paradigm instance of the former kind of enjoyment.

J. M. E. MORAVCSIK

The Perils of Friendship and Conceptions of the Self

According to Greek legend, the god Prometheus was banished to a lonely rock, with birds of prey gnawing at his insides, because he stole fire from heaven to save humanity. The Greeks thought of Prometheus' loneliness as a part of his punishment, on a par with his physical agony.[1] The same high value placed on friendship is exemplified by the legend of Philoctetes. His being without friends, rather than his physical tribulations on a deserted island, is presented as the worst part of his fate.[2]

We can see the recognition of the centrality of friendship in human experience not only in Greek literature but also in the philosophies of Plato and Aristotle. In recent philosophy friendship does not have this pivotal role. Yet the perennial human interest in this phenomenon suggests that the topic be taken up again.

There are many types of friendship. Some friendships result from a balance of relations of domination among humans. Others are based on mutual gratification or matters of mutual utility. Aristotle, however, pointed to the importance of friendship that transcends considerations of gratification or utility and is based on care and concern for another human being solely in virtue of the person he is.[3] This essay explores some of the salient features of such friendships. In solving a few puzzles concerning this phenomenon it indirectly defends the possibility of such a relationship and denies the thesis that all human relations must be based on self-interest.

The type of friendship under consideration is unconditional, in contrast with the other types that are conditional on continued gratification or utility. This unconditionality might be seen as providing the participants with safety. For it enables us to rely on the support of others even if we are no longer useful to them and do not satisfy their needs or desires. Safety, however, involves not only security but also the lack of vulnerability. Hence a tension arises between the desired safety and the resulting increased vulnerability.

Having friends increases vulnerability in two ways. Our care for a friend leads to involvement in his or her affairs, and the misfortunes of the friend become our burdens as well. A person who has friends has more to worry about. We suffer with our friends; to the vicissitudes of our own lives we add those of others. The other way in which vulnerability is increased has to do with the fragility of human relations. Relationships like friendship carry no guarantees; they can go sour even if the difficulty is nobody's fault. This leads to additional pain. Every friendship is a relation that can break up; and, thus, entering upon such relationships increases our vulnerability. We can be helped by a friend and also hurt by a friend in ways in which a person without friends would not be hurt.

We should explore now how the tension between the safety promised by membership in a community of friends and the ensuing increased vulnerability can be resolved without our falling back on contingent and doubtful calculations of balance and trade-off.

Consistency and Loyalty

Plato's *Symposium* contains implicitly a conception of friendship that would give us a way out.[4] For, according to this view, a person at his or her best becomes friends with someone on account of some admirable characteristics that this person possesses. The possession of these characteristics becomes the sole basis for friendship. This conception construes friendship as similar to admiration. For when we admire someone we do so solely in virtue of some characteristics that this person possesses. Thus admiration is an attitude that requires consistency. If we admire someone with qualities $Q_1, Q_2, \ldots, Q_n$, then we should admire anyone with those qualities, provided that there are no countervailing factors and the characteristics are possessed by the other persons in the same combination. Given the alleged similarity, consistency becomes also the chief requirement for friendship. Friendships formed in the Platonic manner ultimately have the character rather than the individuals possessing it as their basis. Hence if one loses a friend, it does not matter much as long as the desired character traits are still possessed by many. Likewise, if something happens to the friendship, a new tie with another person with the same character can fill the role just as well. And, of course, nothing can really happen to the character traits themselves if these are construed within a Platonist ontology. Neither the fragility of human relations nor the vicissitudes of life can really harm friendships based on this orientation.

Some features of this account ring true. We expect a certain consistency from a person whose choice and maintenance of friendships we respect. This consistency has two aspects: consistency in character and in rational justification. Furthermore, it affects both the formation and the maintenance of friendships we respect. The consistency of character at issue here involves the maintenance of a steadfast attitude, both in the formation and in the sustaining of friendships, toward certain qualities and character traits. That is to say, a person with this consistency would be attracted to others as friends by a certain set of qualities; this set of qualities would not vary from time to time and from person to person. Paralleling this, we expect of such a person that in his explanations of why he formed or sustained his friendships he would regard certain qualities and character traits as good grounds for the valuing of a person as a friend. If a quality is valued in these contexts, we expect the person to value it both with regard to different persons and regardless of the passing of time. Needless to say, there are qualifications to this expectation of consistency; a ceteris paribus rider needs to accompany it, but for our purposes a detailed account of this is irrelevant. Finally, we expect a person to have the two aspects of this consistency in harmony. That is to say, the qualities that he regards as valuable in a friend should be the same as the ones that consistently attract him to individuals as friends.[5]

Nevertheless, if this were a complete account of friendship, it would lack an important element. For when we claim that we are friends with someone "no matter what," this rider refers not only to external conditions but also to some changes in personality and character. Furthermore, while my admiration for a person in virtue of qualities $Q_1, Q_2, \ldots, Q_n$ can be superseded by admiration for another person, met later, who possesses those qualities to an even greater extent, a genuine friendship will not be abandoned in favor of a new relationship on account of a newly met person possessing desired characteristics to a greater extent. Unlike admiration or approval, friendship requires not only consistency but also loyalty to the individual. A true friend cares for a friend even if certain changes in character and personality take place, or if the character is seen as not the best available. Loyalty is the perseverance with an attachment in the face of internal and external changes, even if a more virtuous person is met.[6]

Pondering these matters might lead us to suppose that loyalty ties us to a person regardless of his or her qualities. But such an interpretation leads to difficulties. We cannot take the "no matter what" rider quite literally, for we do not owe loyalty to an entity that has changed all of its qualities. For example, loyalty does not carry over what Aristotle would have called substantial changes—turning from prince to frog, from human to monster from another planet, etc.

Thus we arrive at the paradox of friendship. On one hand, the demands of consistency pull us in the direction of construing friendship as based solely on the qualitative nature of humans, in particular their desirable qualities and character traits. On the other hand, the demands of loyalty seem to force us to say that a loyal person will stay with his or her friend through quality changes as long as that friend remains a human being. On this conception the person viewed as a friend emerges as an almost qualityless entity, having only the minimal nature of falling under a natural kind, and a creature whose individuality is shrouded in mystery. Is the basis of friendship the qualitative nature of a human, or the individuality of a human as an "I know not what," the friend emerging in this way as an echo of what the novelist Robert Musil called "a human without characteristics"?

There are at least three ways of attempting to find a solution to this paradox. One of these posits for each person a unique essence, that is to say, a combination of qualities that is possessed uniquely only by that person. Such an essence would distinguish each such entity from all other actual and possible entities. This account, then, posits a one-to-one correspondence between persons and qualitative essences. Each person is unique in terms of internal qualities. This allows us—or so it would seem—to preserve both the elements of consistency and loyalty in friendship. Friendship, on this account, is oriented toward unique individuals; thus the account preserves loyalty. At the same time, it seems to preserve consistency, since it allows us to say that we are friends with someone on account of his or her qualitative nature. Do consistency and loyalty really flourish within this conception? Attractive as this proposal may seem, it faces at least two difficulties.

First, consistency requires that some general attributes that are shared among several persons, such as generosity, good humor, wisdom, etc., be valued in many persons, and not a unique individual essence. Thus this solution accounts for consistency only if we assume that the individual essences posited will share as constituents certain general attributes. This leaves, then, the burden of accounting for loyalty on the posited unique combinations of characteristics. It is not clear, however, that our loyalties to friends are linked to whatever unique essences they may have.[7]

The second difficulty is even more formidable. For it involves the metaphysical plausibility of the whole conception. There are no compelling reasons to posit individual essences, and it is easy to imagine two persons who, apart from spatial and temporal relations, have the same qualitative structure. Identical twins are usually not really identical, but it takes little imagination to envisage perfect twinship realized.[8]

A second solution emerges from the Christian religious literature. We find here a view that assigns to each human a personality structure or character ("psyche") and also a unique constituent, a spirit ("pneuma"), that links a human to God. This is a basic, undefinable element, which is different for each person. It is neither an individual essence nor a propertyless substratum. Within such a conception there is an element in each human in virtue of which we can be friends with him or her as an individual, and at the same time this element does not have to be construed as a purely qualitative structure. Once more, both loyalty and consistency have their basis in a conception of a person as a possible friend.

Though this may be a viable ontological and theological construction, as a solution to the paradox of friendship it faces two difficulties. First, even if accepted it accounts only for spiritual friendship and not for the wide variety of non-utilitarian secular friendships. The second difficulty is the circular nature of the explanation that we would derive from this conception. For it would account for the appropriate object of loyalty and consistency by positing a unique, undefinable element. Thus it adds a new primitive to an explanatory framework; all we know about it is that it is supposed to solve the problem of personal uniqueness without committing us to individual essences or propertyless substrata. Unless we are told what it is about this new posit that explains loyalty and consistency, we do not have a non-vacuous explanation.

The first proposal interpreted the uniqueness of the friend in terms of qualitative structure, the second in terms of a theological primitive. The proposal to be offered as adequate in this paper construes the ground of loyalty to a friend in terms of certain causal interactions that specific persons have with each other. In order to present this proposal fully, let us step back and fill in the conceptual background.

An analysis of friendship must involve evaluative assessments in addition to conceptual descriptions. For a person can be good or not good at either forming or maintaining friendships. Thus, apart from the general issue of evaluating ideals for life that do or do not include having friendships, there is the evaluation of a person in terms of his choice of friends and his ability to maintain friendships. The latter assessments are parts of overall assessments of character and personality. They are not matters of obligation, for we do not have a duty to form and maintain the right kinds of friendships, nor are they matters of utility, since often these questions surface in non-utilitarian contexts.

An adequate account of friendship must distinguish the following three elements:

1. the causes of forming or maintaining a particular friendship;
2. the reasons for forming or maintaining a particular friendship;
3. obligations arising from specific bonds of friendship.

All three of these notions apply both to the formation and to the maintaining of friendships. The assessment of causes is partly a normative matter. We expect of people that they should be influenced in their friendships by factors such as character, shared aims, certain feelings, etc., and not have these relationships based on such superficial features as persuasive manner, economic wealth, good looks, etc.

The role of reasons should be stressed, for even though the forming and maintaining of a friendship is not simply a matter of decision, we assume that people who live a good life can explain and justify their choices of friends and the maintaining of certain bonds. One can expect to have answers to the question "Why have this friend?" or to inquiries about why we maintain certain friendships, and not all answers are equally adequate.

Finally, there are obligations that emerge out of our having certain friendships. We have duties to reciprocate in certain ways, or to give up some of our plans in order to accommodate a friend, or to offer help of a special kind that we do not owe to every human being. Having, however, distinguished this third element from the first and second, we shall leave it aside and will not deal with it during the remainder of this paper.

We will deal mainly with the first and second elements. Though these can be separated, they are also closely related in some contexts. For—as Donald Davidson has stressed repeatedly—reasons can also function as causes. With these conceptual points in mind we turn to the proposal of this paper, according to which both loyalty and consistency have roles within friendships without driving us into contradictions.

We spelled out already the consistency that is expected of a person with friends. This involves the person's having a character such that a given characteristic encountered in others functions consistently as either a positive or a negative factor in his forming and maintaining friendships. It also involves his assessing the same characteristic consistently as a positive or negative reason in explaining or justifying friendships. A person not meeting these conditions is regarded as unreliable. Being unreliable is not the same as being disloyal. Disloyalty involves abandoning friendships without adequate justification, while unreliability is merely having a character such that others' characteristics, whether common to different persons or proper to the same person at different times, do not always affect us causally or rationally in the same way. The unreliable person also tends to become disloyal, but the latter notion has many other roots as well.

Consistency does not require more than that. In particular it does not require that we should base our friendships solely on qualitative grounds. Consistency is, rather, a frame within which our friendships are to function. We can, then, place loyalty within this frame.

The basis for remaining loyal to a person as a friend will be a history of interactions such as enduring hard times, working for a common cause, sharing certain emotions, and similar contexts in which two or more persons share experiences. From the point of view of the person who pledges loyalty, such interactions individuate the friend; for it is this particular individual with whom he shared certain experiences. The indexical expression "this" within such a characterization is an ineliminable element that picks out an individual without having qualitative descriptions mediate such reference.

To say that loyalty is grounded in such interactions is not to say that every time we experience such interactions a ground is created for loyalty. If affection, caring, and other emotions pertaining to friendship evolve in the course of such interactions, then the interactions become the ground for loyalty. It is not a part of this enterprise to answer the question of when and how such interactions generate the emotional constituents of friendship. In fact, this paper leaves it open whether that question will ever be answered, or whether friendship will remain one of the mysteries of the human condition.

We see, then, that consistency does not demand a purely qualitative specification of the friend, and loyalty does not require us to take the "no matter what" rider in the specifications of genuine friendships literally. The demands of consistency delineate the class of persons within which our true friends will be found, and loyalty anchors our particular friendships to individuals in view of their unique life histories, including not only qualitative but also relational and geographical histories. The proposal, then, goes between the horns of the dilemma, and leaves room for both consistency and loyalty.

We must admit, however, that we are left with possible conflicts between consistency and loyalty. There may be cases in which the friend loses some of the qualities that play a key role in our specifications of the kind of friend we want to have. There is no general rule that can tell us for each case which factor should prevail. Furthermore, there may be some cases in which there is no right solution. Of such stuff are drama and tragedy made. We need the analogue of moral luck—a topic discussed elsewhere in this volume—in order to avoid such situations.

Many causal interactions are irrelevant as conditions of loyalty. These include casual encounters and relationships involved in ordinary business transactions. We deal with lawyers, businessmen, politicians, etc., regularly, but these interactions do not typically form the basis of the kind of relationships that spawn friendships. It would be impossible to give a full account of the relevant causal relationships within the confines of this paper, but a few conditions should be mentioned so as to indicate the outlines and direction that such an account will have to take. First, the relevant relationship is one of which one must be aware. I might owe feelings of gratitude to a parent whose identity I do not know; but an unknown benefactor is just that, and not a friend. Furthermore, the interaction must evoke both emotional reactions and some form of evaluation. If the interaction evokes no emotions, why should care, concern, and affection emerge from such experiences? Furthermore, mere suffering will not lead to a meaningful sharing of experiences; the suffering would have to be seen as undeserved, or as leading to a shared state that has value on its own. These conditions help to show why so often the shared interactions that form the basis for friendship and loyalty are experiences involving common goals or needed cooperation.

Causal interactions are not only the ground for loyalty; they are also the lifeline of the friendship itself. Friendship involves activity, and as such is subject to all of the contingencies and uncertainties that affect human activities. Still, within our resolution of the apparent conflict between loyalty and consistency, the key role of causal interactions is that of forming a basis for loyalty. This can be seen by considering hypotheticals. For if we consider a hypothetical situation in which the causal interactions did not take place between the prospective friends, then we lose the grounds for loyalty. Friendship and loyalty emerge as a result of certain shared experiences and common goals. Without the history of causal interactions the issue of loyalty cannot arise.

Considering these proposals enables us to place a variety of attitudes and bonds on a conceptual map. Some attitudes carry a heavy demand of consistency, and thus are oriented toward their objects solely on qualitative grounds. Other attitudes are tied to both loyalty and consistency and hence are grounded in both qualitative considerations and the history of causal interactions. Finally there are attitudes and bonds that have as their basis solely the history of causal interactions. In these cases only loyalty is linked to the attitudes; no demand for consistency arises.

Approval, admiration, and, in general, attitudes and bonds in which some form of evaluation plays a decisive role fall into the first category. For in these cases only consistency matters. Certain types of obligations and family relations fall into the third class. For example, the love that a parent has for a child is based on the history of causal interactions and need not carry with it any implication of the child's having admirable character traits. Friendship, love, and care fall into the second category, for both loyalty and consistency play roles within these relations. We form friendships with some of those persons whom we regard as having good or endearing qualities. The maintaining of the friendship with specific persons depends not on the persistence of these qualitative structures but on the history of causal interactions that develops between us and these persons.

The history of shared experiences that forms the basis for a friendship with a specific person is contingent and fragile. Its continuation depends on external and psychological conditions that cannot be guaranteed. A friendship can go sour or break up even if both sides have done their best to maintain it. One has to realize that even the bonds one most cares about might be destroyed. We see, then, that while focusing on the histories of causal interaction involved in friendships helps us out of the paradox, it brings us back, at the same time, to the tension between safety and vulnerability. We considered the purely qualitative, Platonistic account in order to escape from vulnerability. This led us to an inability to account for loyalty. Our subsequent reanalysis of the basis of friendship with an individual gave us a way out of the paradox, but it led us back to the tension between safety and peril. We need to take a fresh start in order to extricate ourselves from this conceptual prison.

Safety and Peril

As an introduction to the solution to be proposed, let us consider the famous literary example of friendship between Philoctetes and Neoptolemus. Neoptolemus, the son of Achilles, is a young warrior, anxious to discharge his duties but at the same time idealistic enough to be concerned when the Greek army orders him to carry out a task that involves being deceitful. Philoctetes, the old warrior, is abandoned by the Greeks on a deserted island because of misfortunes beyond his control that made him a liability for the army. He lives alone on the island, bearing a grudge against the Greeks who treated him unjustly. Philoctetes and Neoptolemus make up an odd couple if there ever was one. In terms of their respective needs and predicaments the two persons could not be more different. Nevertheless, in the course of attempting to carry out his mission, Neoptolemus comes to understand the basic elements of Philoctetes' predicament. He comes to appreciate the loneliness, the feeling of injustice, and the strength of the old man that helps him to survive. Their common concern for what is right, their respective isolation from people with whom they could talk over their problems, and their wrestling with their respective relations to the Greek army bring these two people together, and friendship develops. As Neoptolemus gains an understanding of Philoctetes' plight, he becomes involved—as we would say in modern parlance. The involvement and the friendship are not matters of duty or obligation. If Neoptolemus had simply carried out the instructions of the Greek army and not concerned himself with Philoctetes' plight, he would have met his obligations to the army and acted within the code of obligations imposed by his society. Nor is this a matter of utility. On the contrary, the friendship and the involvement threaten Neoptolemus' career and even his life, for the involvement leads him to disobey his orders, thus creating a conflict that could destroy him. The situation mirrors to some extent that of Prometheus, who becomes a friend to humans and is severely punished for it.

The friendship between Neoptolemus and Philoctetes undergoes changes. At times it flourishes, at times it verges on destruction. To trace the various reversals in detail would take us too far from our main concerns. At the end of the play the friendship is restored. The two friends join in what they take to be a worthy cause: they go off to help the Greeks against the Trojans. Thus various aspects of the perils of friendship are well illustrated by the drama.

One might try to adopt a stance of rational calculation and estimate the likelihood of the pain and suffering that the friendship might bring with it, and contrast this with the probability of enjoyment to be gained by the safety that friendship provides. As we saw, however, if we construe the friendship as ideal from an Aristotelian point of view, such calculations are quite inappropriate, since the relation is supposed to be non-utilitarian. And in fact, though Sophocles does not have Aristotle's theory of friendship up his sleeve, he is clear that Philoctetes and Neoptolemus are not calculating persons of this sort when it comes to friendship.[9]

One might, however, ask whether or not one should enter upon relationships of this ideal sort, and interpret this question as calling for a calculation of risk and probable gain. It is clear from the play that the dramatic figures are not meant to be persons raising such questions. For them this decision is fundamental; it concerns basic commitments to ideals, and questions of utility arise for them only relative to the conception of human flourishing that they implicitly subscribe to. But even if one wanted to calculate in a utilitarian way, one would have to face the question "Useful to whom? To what kind of person?" and the issue of choosing basic ideals for human well-being would arise once more.

Philoctetes bears a grudge against the Greeks on account of all of the sufferings they caused him, and does not want to leave the island to help them defeat Troy. How would one dissuade Philoctetes from adopting this attitude? One attempt might proceed along lines of moral reasoning. Even if rejoining former friends cannot be shown to be obligatory, one might try to present it as an act of supererogation. We could find a portrait of Philoctetes persuaded by such an argument admirable.[10] But this is not the portrait of Philoctetes presented in the Sophoclean drama. The play does not present him as sacrificing himself and rushing unselfishly to the aid of his comrades. Philoctetes is not a saint. Instead of contemplating altruism, he rethinks his life and basic commitments. He becomes the kind of person for whom overcoming resentment is not a matter of sacrifice but of fulfilling his own nature. He succeeds in seeing beyond his grudge and in seeing his own flourishing as involving the restoration and continuation of friendships even if these bonds were broken by others through their conscious doings.

Even if one were to interpret the rejoining of the army as an act of heroism, one could not construe Philoctetes' regaining friendships in this manner. One might rejoin an army out of a sense of duty, but one cannot become friends with someone out of a sense of duty. For friendship involves feelings, and, while duty can command action, it cannot command feeling. Furthermore, there is no moral claim on Philoctetes to renew friendship. Morality might command him not to take revenge, and declare him to be acting beyond the call of duty if he unselfishly sacrifices his own interests and helps his former comrades. Philoctetes' actions and thoughts are not along these lines. He becomes another kind of person. His joyful willingness to renew friendships is an expression of magnanimity that has its sources in Philoctetes' changed ideals and not in going altruistically and self-sacrificially beyond the call of duty.

Philoctetes' injury can be interpreted from different points of view. One can see it as a case of his losing some of his possessions and other goods. Viewed from this vantage point, it is similar to loss of property, and calls for redress or revenge. One can, however, view it also as an attack on a person by other humans that challenges or calls into question that person's worth and status. Subjecting someone to loss of prestige, shame, and loss of friendship and other bonds of loyalty are attacks of this kind. These attacks evoke—understandably—feelings of grudge and resentment. Such an interpretation and reaction would go hand in hand with a conception of a person according to which a human has as his parts mind, body, and potentialities but not any of even the more salient relational properties.

One could also view the self in a wider way, so as to have it encompass as some of its natural parts relational properties such as the friendships and loves that the person is involved in. On this view, damage to such parts as our rationality or emotional makeup calls for restoration and repair rather than resentment. Thus it is analogous to the case of damage to our health. Our main concern in these cases is cure. Issues of justice arise only in a secondary way. Given this analogy, one would want to repair damaged friendships and lost bonds of loyalty in the same way in which a person wants to restore health. In neither context is it rational to place high priority on grudge and resentment if we construe the self in the wider way.

In these reflections on *Philoctetes* we have gone far beyond the mere interpretation of Sophoclean texts. We have taken the drama as illustrating human predicaments and used it to suggest various philosophical solutions to the problems our heroes faced. We shall address these matters now in a more general and systematic way.

Conceptions of the Self

Philoctetes' condition is merely an extreme case of a kind of suffering that most humans endure at one time or another. Friendships break up, parents are hurt unjustly by children, and children are abandoned by parents without good cause. As the story of David and Absalom shows, the lost loyalty and suffering of a child can become the center of life for a father, and as Pasternak's *Dr. Zhivago* shows, a devoted couple sharing ideals, like Lara and her husband, can become estranged when they can no longer sustain this sharing. In various ways such experiences are common to all of us. Our reactions to these depend on the conception of the self and the ensuing attitudes that we adopt.

There are several aspects with regard to which conceptions of the self can differ. Since a conception of the self is a conception of a person, and there are many theories of what it is to be a person, two conceptions of the self may differ on account of having different conceptions of what it is to be a person underlying them. Secondly, a conception of a self is a conception of a human being. Hence conceptions of the self may differ on account of having different interpretations of what it is to be a human underlying them.

Finally, however, even apart from these underlying differences, there is an important way in which conceptions of the self differ. For different theories take different elements to be parts of the self. For example, bodily parts, mental structures, and certain human capacities are normally taken to be parts of a human. It is not easy to adjudicate between rival claims concerning other candidates for being parts. For the "part of" relation does not admit of a general definition; it has to be spelled out genus by genus. Criteria determining the parts of an animal are different from criteria determining the parts of a country or of a concert. Since the self is a notoriously controversial natural kind, agreement on its constituents is not easily reached. We shall concentrate on only one kind of candidate. As we saw, conceptions of the self can differ in terms of whether they take certain relational properties as parts of the self. On many accounts one can point to an exercise of intelligence, or a fine instance of self-control, and say "Yes, that is I." But on the account under consideration, one can do the same thing even in the case of a friendship and its episodes. This contrasts with the view according to which all relations and relational properties are external to the self. To be sure, it is implausible to construe all relations as parts of the self. One has relations to institutions, to workers in certain jobs, to colleagues, and to other members of society. Many of these would be odd as candidates for constituents of the self.

Relations like friendship, love, and other bonds involving trust can be viewed as constituents of the self. These relationships survive many changes, affect other parts of a person, evoke deep emotions, and affect evaluations of ourselves, and—as in the case of health—their deterioration can be seen as calling for repair and restoration.

The Aristotelian ideal of friendship can be linked to either a wider or a narrower conception of the self. But on one view the friendship is a part of the self, while on the other it is not.

The choice between narrower and wider conceptions of the self is not arbitrary. It is subject to rational argumentation and justification. The choice will be related to our conception of a flourishing human. Thus the choice is not in terms of duties and obligations, nor in terms of utility. The intuition that moves us toward the wider conception is captured in the vernacular by the saying that the person opting for the narrower conception is "missing something of life." To spell this out in philosophic terms would require a separate essay. These remarks are meant to show at least the direction that a justification of the wider conception would take. Such reflections are key parts of our need to reflect on human ideals prior to considerations of utility and independently of matters of obligation.[11]

The choice between conceptions of the self is not the only factor determining how we react to unjust treatment. One can also overcome resentment on the narrower conception of the self, in one of three ways: through an attitude of altruism, one of calculation, or just plain goodwill. If one has the narrower conception of the self, one might want to overcome resentment because of "saintly" attitudes that lead one to altruistic stances beyond the call of duty. Again, one might want to overcome resentment because of calculations of benefit. Finally, one might have an attitude of benevolence toward others that leads one not to react negatively to unjust treatment. In this last case, we face difficult decisions. For giving in and not reacting at any time to unjust treatment is not a good thing. It could lead to a person's becoming insufficiently assertive and to his actually encouraging others to continue their unjust practices.

To adopt the wider conception of the self is not to obviate the need to rise, on occasion, to heights of altruism, or to suspend benevolence. There will be contexts in which even on the wider conception a person is not given morally appropriate treatment, and then one must decide on a suitable reaction in terms other than cure and restoration. But the important feature of the wider conception—in our context—is that it enables us to view many conflicts not in any of the ways in which the person with the narrower conception views it, but in terms analogous to our wanting to restore health. Merely adopting the wider conception of the self does not automatically lead one to this enlightened attitude, but it provides the conceptual framework within which this additional way of overcoming resentment becomes possible for us.

On the narrower conception of the self, someone in a predicament similar to that of Philoctetes might feel called upon to forgive. Forgiveness is the surrendering of the opportunity to seek redress and the wiping out of the record of harm done. For the person with the wider conception of the self there will also be contexts in which forgiveness is called for. But in contexts resembling that of Philoctetes, such a person need not view things in this way. Rather, he or she can regard this occasion as calling for cure and restoration, thus enabling the other party as well to reconsider what human relations should be like, and to develop new ways of relating to others.

Adopting a wider conception of the self that construes our friendships as parts of ourselves helps to avoid the tension between safety and vulnerability. Vulnerability derived from having friendships has its source in the pain we feel either when friends or loved ones suffer misfortune, or when relations are damaged or destroyed. In the latter case, given the narrow conception of the self, one might take the loss to involve an attack by others on us, an attack that questions our worth or status. Given this construal, one is tempted to respond as Philoctetes might have, with resentment and hostility against the offenders.

Given, however, the conception that construes friendship as a part of the self, no less than those parts whose maintenance is involved in preserving our health, the primary reaction to Philoctetes' predicament, and our own predicaments resembling his, is an effort to heal and restore. On this conception vulnerability is not increased in kind. The vulnerability that comes via this type of ideal friendship is the same as that to which we are exposed in virtue of the desire to develop and maintain those constituents of ourselves that we deem to have real value. Everyone is subject to this kind of vulnerability simply in virtue of the fact that we are all forced to adopt, consciously or otherwise, some sort of human ideal: in connection with the realization of any ideal, things can go wrong. We could escape this kind of vulnerability only if we tried to live a life without adopting, even implicitly, any kind of ideal. Such efforts would be self-defeating.

The idea of friendship as a source of safety implies the narrow conception of the self. For it construes friendship as a relation between several separate persons, and—as we say in the vernacular—there is safety in numbers. The adoption of the wider conception of the self enables us to move away from the association of friendship with safety. For within this conception friendship makes the boundary between the affected persons less sharp. Hence friendship of the sort described involves neither "safety in numbers" nor a sharp separation of persons but a commitment to an ideal that focuses on the notion of a community. Within such a conception not only are genuine friendships parts of persons, but they also have lives of their own, and we develop special attachments to them.[12]

There is also the pain we experience when friends or loved ones suffer. This pain is not different in kind, however, from the pain and anguish we experience when we see, in general, other humans suffer. The choice we have to make is not between more or less pain but between conceptions of what a flourishing human being is. For if we take the task of avoiding pain of this sort seriously, we should arrive at a conception of the ideal human as the apathetic person—someone who does not have deep emotions or concern for others. Greek literature and philosophy have little regard for this kind of person. Once we decide that it is worthwhile to be a person with deep feelings, we cannot avoid the ensuing risk that love, care, and friendship might bring with them or the suffering caused by witnessing the trials and tribulations that humans from time to time have to undergo.

We have seen, then, how we can arrive at a conception of the basis of loyalty in friendship, a conception of the self, and an attitude toward the loss of friendship and esteem that will resolve the paradox of friendship and take us away from the tension between safety and peril. In the course of spelling out the required conceptions we have also uncovered the fact that we face a number of fundamental choices and commitments that make a great difference to what our ideals and values will be, and how we will interact with others. Yet these issues are not classifiable as mere matters either of obligation or of utility. These issues include the questions: Shall I have friendships of the sort Aristotle regards as ideal? Shall I take a view of myself that will include my friendships as parts? Shall I be the kind of person who bears grudges and resentment toward others when injured, or the kind who tries to overcome these feelings, even in contexts in which they seem justified, and strives toward a life in which friendship and other bonds of loyalty are seen as important parts of ourselves that need maintenance and restoration whenever possible? Pondering these questions helps us to understand why the Greeks construed ethics in a broad sense that went beyond theories of utility and obligation, and why such a broad conception is required by any theory that is to do justice to the fundamental questions that all humans must face about themselves and their relations to others.

Emerging from our solution to the paradox of friendship and

Friendship and the Self 151

the alleviation of the tension between safety and peril we see a certain kind of person. This person has an ideal that centers on the cooperative virtues, adopts the wider conception of the self, and succeeds in overcoming resentment by seeing this as part of an effort to heal and preserve the best in one's nature. This person can respond to injury as Philoctetes did. We saw, however, that even this solution leaves us fragile, for we must cultivate the emotional depth and concern for others that will enable us to sustain friendship. Our success in sustaining friendships depends partly on contingencies. Instead of providing a guarantee, it leads us to see that we need to rely on hope as we embark on this new journey. The attitude that allows us to leave behind what we may have become used to, to enter upon a new journey, and to rely on hope has its best expression in the noble lines that the poet puts into the mouth of Philoctetes at the end of the drama:

> Leaving this land, let me say goodbye,
> my cave, companion through sleepless hours,
> spirits of flowing streams and those of grassy glades,
> and you thunder of the sea, crashing against my rock;
> here the moist blows of the south wind
> often reached my head inside the cave,
> and the Hermean mount sent loud echoes
> of my groaning sounds as I lay alone,
> exposed to the wintry blasts of misery.
> But now at last I can depart,
> that for which I hardly dared to hope has come,
> so I am leaving you, springs of Lemnos and rivulets of this isle.
>
> Goodbye, sea-washed land of Lemnos,
> help me on my way,
> carried by Fate and friendly advice,
> and the might of the all-conquering one
> who saw that all these things be done.[13]

DAVID HEYD

Moral Subjects, Freedom, and Idiosyncrasy

Action beyond the call of duty raises some well-known problems for moral theory. In "Saints and Heroes," which has been one of Urmson's most influential works, saintly and heroic acts are described as supererogatory from an objective point of view yet as often subjectively binding.[1] Other philosophers note that we "ought" to perform these actions although they are not obligatory, or within our duty. This might mean that such actions are backed by moral reasons yet are not prescribed by moral rules. It is also claimed that unlike obligatory behavior, supererogatory action is optional, that is to say, chosen as a matter of personal discretion; however, this does not make it arbitrary or irrational, let alone devoid of moral value. One possible way of generalizing these difficulties is to formulate them in the language of reasons for action: How can supererogatory action be, on the one hand, beyond the scope of universalizable and universally binding reasons yet, on the other hand, still be based on morally good reasons? Or, how can moral reasons be only subjectively binding?

This essay is an attempt to explain away this seeming paradox by contrasting two types of moral reasons for action: those grounded in the concept of the moral subject and those originating in the contingent and idiosyncratic features of the individual agent. This contrast reflects two divergent conceptions of freedom, which may serve not only to illustrate further the distinction between the obligatory and the supererogatory but also to justify the special value usually accorded to the latter. Although the following discussion revolves mainly around the attempt to show how supererogation can be incorporated into a general moral theory, the argument has deeper and far-reaching implications regarding the role of idiosyncrasies in morality at large.

Models of the Moral Subject

When confronted with practical choices, human beings have to choose out of a plethora of reasons for action those reasons that, as a matter of fact, are to guide their decisions. This process of reason selection is especially manifest in *moral* choices, in which only some of the large number of the putative reasons are considered *relevant* to the choice in question. The selection of reasons for moral choice by means of a criterion of relevance is of a highly problematic nature, because it is typically theory-dependent. Reasons for moral action or choice can be regarded as relevant only *relative to* a theoretical concept of a moral subject or to a model of moral agency. Any ethical theory or system consists of a picture of what moral subjects are, and from this picture one infers what persons qua moral subjects ought to do. This picture, which we will refer to as "the model" (of a moral subject or of moral agency), is the key concept of an ethical theory and reflects its view of the fundamental purpose of morality, the means of justifying its principles, and the way it selects the relevant reasons for moral choice out of the many non-moral (and, as we shall see later, also "super-moral") reasons.

We call this notion of the moral subject "the model" because it is necessarily abstract and general as well as universal and immutable in its manifestation in human individuals. It is also called "the model" owing to its exemplary status, that is, its being an object of aspiration and imitation. Models of moral agency are logically necessary to any ethical theory because they introduce the element of uniformity into the infinite variety of individual character and circumstances that is typical of concrete human life. Without some kind of uniformity ethics cannot be guaranteed any prescriptive effectiveness, since individual beings can be subject to general prescriptions and norms only qua a certain *kind* of beings. Furthermore, if morality is to have a coordinative function, that is to say, the ability to harmonize heterogeneous desires and preferences, then it must establish a universal model of a moral subject. In other words, only by revealing *common* features in the boundless variety of individual persons can ethics formulate a notion of a moral *community*.

An obvious objection to the above analysis would refer to the central role of rules and principles in determining the morally relevant reasons for action. Thus, the reasons for not stealing or for helping the poor are derived from the respective rules formulated by the moral theory or code. However, this objection fails to note that the moral rules can only be ultimately justified within any theory in terms of its conception of persons (or persons as moral agents). The deeper level of agent-morality is therefore the justifying ground for all principles of moral reasoning.[2]

The history of ethics provides a wide variety of models of a moral subject. There are metaphysical or ideal models, as in Plato, Aristotle, and Kant. There are quasi-empirical models, such as Hobbes's, Bentham's, and Mill's; or fully empirical ones, such as Jean Piaget's and Lawrence Kohlberg's. And there are "political" models such as that suggested by John Rawls.[3] The moral subject can be conceived as the *phronimos* (prudent person), or the self-legislating practical reason, or a pleasure-seeking sentient being, or a rational contractor under a veil of ignorance, or again as the obedient servant of God. But what is common to all of these conceptions is their *thinness*, their being abstractions of certain features deemed to be significant, whether as empirical truths of human nature, as metaphysical ideals, or as pragmatic means for establishing universally agreed principles for social life.

The model implies a criterion for selecting the relevant reasons for action in moral choices. Any ethical theory strives through the thin and abstract model to supply a relevance criterion of reasons for action that would be sufficient for a decision procedure in *moral* choices. Thus, for a Kantian, only those reasons that apply to us as rational beings are considered relevant in making moral decisions, whereas for a hedonist, only those reasons that motivate us as pleasure-seeking beings have a role in our moral deliberations. By dismissing all other reasons as irrelevant, ethical theories can tell us what we ought to do, at least *as* moral subjects.

Obviously, however, individual human beings are not just moral agents: they have particular attributes that can never be captured by any abstract model. They act in a constantly changing world, out of personal preferences, and in a context-dependent manner. They often make their choices in the light of non-moral reasons, and indeed—as we shall see—can also change their minds concerning the valid criterion of relevance in their selection of reasons for action. In other words, persons are unique individuals, acting unpredictably in a contingently changing world. Whereas moral subjects are abstract beings representing the general, universal, necessary, and unchanging features of persons, individual human beings are concrete persons, exemplifying an infinite richness of particular contingent and idiosyncratic features.

Acting on non-moral reasons does not pose a special problem for ethical theory. Theory may regard such action as either immoral or as morally neutral (indifferent). But what is the status of the reasons for choosing to act on moral reasons? Are they themselves moral? And if not, can they be regarded as indifferent (for immoral they surely are not)? Supererogatory action also raises a theoretical problem, since it is often based on reasons that on the one hand are not directly derived from the model, yet on the other hand are of a particularly moral value. In supererogatory choices, as well as in the very adoption of the moral point of view, the idiosyncratic element in the process of reason selection gains recognition as morally relevant, despite its deviation from the model or its independence from it. How is that possible?

Types of Moral Idiosyncrasy

Reasons for action can be idiosyncratic in many ways, as we shall presently see. But idiosyncrasy itself is a *relative* concept. A feature of human agents can never be said to be idiosyncratic in itself, but only relative to a model of human agency, a model that is typically theoretical in nature. Thus, reasons based on want satisfaction are idiosyncratic for a Kantian moral theory; so are those based on an assessment of one's own contingent position in the world for a Rawlsian theorist, or those based on a sudden and changing mood for the Aristotelian. However, idiosyncrasy does not mean irrationality or arbitrariness. Idiosyncratic reasons, though not derived from the model, may still be considered rational in the light of a plan, a scheme, or a project that is part of the person's life and identity. This is because the model of a moral subject is not identical to that of a rational subject, the latter being logically weaker, since it consists of fewer constraints. Only extreme rationalistic theories would refuse to give the title of reasons to all morally idiosyncratic motives for action, since for them the model of rationality and that of moral agency completely coincide. All other ethical theories treat such motives as reasons, that is, as rational grounds for action, though overridden by the stronger, relevant, moral reasons. Throughout the following discussion "idiosyncratic" should be understood as relative to a concept or a model of a moral subject rather than as relative to a model of rational agency.

Naturally it is hard to outline a full taxonomy of idiosyncratic reasons for action, and we should focus only on those related to contexts in which a decision of a moral nature is to be made. Three general types of idiosyncrasy may illustrate the interesting role of idiosyncratic reasons in moral conduct.

The first consists of reasons that determine the particular way or manner in which a morally prescribed action is actually performed. We may repay a $20 debt in cash or by check, as the worn-out example goes, but the reasons for selecting either mode of repayment are idiosyncratic, since they are not grounded in the concept of a moral subject or in the conception of what a person qua a moral agent ought to do in such a situation. Still, they are definitely reasons that are logically related to interests, preferences, and other choices of the agent. The timing and object of actions discharging imperfect obligations (in the Kantian sense) are also idiosyncratic in our sense, although not irrational or arbitrary. Contributing today to a hunger-relief agency or next week to a group fighting cancer may be a matter of weighing various reasons, although both courses of action may equally fulfill the imperfect duty of helping people in distress, or equally reflect the ideal of a generous character. We may generalize these examples by asserting that *any* moral choice is necessarily accompanied by choices of a non-moral nature, namely, the particular way in which the moral reasons are to be applied in practice. So although this type of idiosyncrasy is of no moral significance in itself, it should be recognized as an essential factor in any moral reasoning.[4]

The second type of idiosyncratic reason is relevant to morality not only as a necessary complementary feature of moral choice, but also as a basis for its very meaning and value. It consists of reasons for choosing to act on the model of a moral subject, that is, to adopt the moral point of view. These are, by definition, idiosyncratic reasons, since they cannot be derived from the model, which itself is open for selection as a criterion of relevance of reasons for action. What the reasons are for such a choice and how persons do in fact come to decide to act on moral reasons are hard questions to which controversial answers have been offered for a long time. We will discuss below Kant's view of "negative freedom" and its special value for morality. Here it suffices to note that for many theories a choice made immorally or egoistically or out of inclination cannot be automatically dismissed as irrational in the sense of being unsupported by reasons (for sometimes such choices are supported by good reasons). So it is perfectly plausible that the reasons—such as fear of punishment, the sense of fairness, religious belief, etc.—for choosing to adopt the model of moral agency as the criterion of relevance of reasons for action are idiosyncratic too. In other words, the answer to the question "Why be moral?" may refer to all sorts of idiosyncratic reasons relating to social pressure, individual upbringing, faith, or egoistic considerations, and not necessarily to moral reasons derived from the model (a justification of which would anyway be circular).[5]

Finally there is a third type of idiosyncratic reasons which is less controversially relevant to moral choice than the previous one. It comprises reasons for the agent to *transcend* the original model of a moral subject and thereby adopt a supererogatory course of action. This type of idiosyncrasy merits special theoretical attention because it touches upon the seemingly paradoxical nature of supererogatory behavior. Action beyond the call of duty is personal and non-universalizable, yet morally good and rational (backed by reasons).

In supererogatory action the agent chooses to re-draw the demarcation line between reasons that have a hold on him as a moral subject and those that do not. The agent creates his own personal model, which is in some respects *richer* than the thin model he adopts in his usual moral reasoning. That is to say, some idiosyncratic features of either the agent's character or his circumstances and situation in the world become, at least temporarily, regarded as morally relevant and reason generating. The agent of a supererogatory act sees himself as bound by certain reasons that are not thought of as binding on others, because he chooses to detach himself from the criteria of relevant similarities between moral agents (as determined by the model) in favor of stricter criteria. These make him either part of a smaller, "elitist" group or a totally unique moral agent.[6]

Some supererogatory actions are motivated by reasons that are idiosyncratic in the sense that they apply only to a small group of people with certain, often rare, features that reflect a permanent trait of character. These are the well-known saints and heroes who consistently display a special degree of courage, humility, generosity, or readiness to sacrifice. But supererogatory behavior can also be momentary, ad hoc, and idiosyncratic not only relative to any abstract model of a moral subject but also relative to the small group or to the character and personality of the agent himself. Thus we find some dramatic heroic acts, such as a sudden decision to sacrifice one's life to save another life, performed by ordinary, inconspicuous types of persons. The idiosyncratic reason is given a dominant role just on that particular occasion. Some of those actions look almost whimsical, but may still be produced by rational deliberation or grounded in reasons.

Idiosyncrasy of reasons for supererogatory action can be related to the particular *context* of action as well. The king who declares a general amnesty for criminals on the occasion of a military victory or an anniversary is acting on a reason that is, although impersonal, nonetheless typically idiosyncratic, in that it arises only out of a contingent state of affairs that is neither captured by any moral rule nor based on the model.

However, the idiosyncratic element in supererogation usually expresses a shift from the impersonal considerations derived from the abstract model to personal reasons, that is, reasons that take into account the particular identity and character either of the agent or of the beneficiary of the action (or of both). Personal contingencies are necessarily considered as idiosyncratic from the point of view of standard moral theories, for logically they *can* never be captured by any model, however rich. But it is usually this personal dimension that lends supererogatory behavior its special worth, which shows why personal contingencies also *should* never be integrated into the model.

The particular identity of the agent is, for example, important in determining the relevant reasons for supererogatory acts of beneficence. The agent's self-image as a moral subject is "more demanding" than that of the universal model. It may involve individual preferences, personal inclinations and tastes, higher sensitivity, certain emotions, attitudes, and ideals. These features constitute the *creative* aspect of the formation of a moral personality and self-image. It is exemplified both in the dramatic manifestations of supererogation, such as beneficence and heroism, and in the more trivial cases of considerateness, tact, and small favors.

Some supererogatory actions are motivated by a special regard for a particular recipient. Unlike the impersonal act of legal pardon or amnesty (which, as we saw, is usually related to certain objective circumstances), forgiveness and mercy are often shown to persons who display certain individual features and traits of character that appeal to the agent. We may forgive a friend without binding ourselves to forgive an enemy; we are permitted to have personal biases in selecting the beneficiaries of our supererogatory conduct. The reasons for giving blood (assuming it is a supererogatory act) can either be related to the way a person sees himself or to a particular personal way in which he regards the recipient in need. In the first case the donation is anonymous; in the second it is selective (made either to a particular person or to persons belonging to a special group). The same can of course be said of acts of beneficence, forgiveness, and other acts beyond the call of duty.

Finally, there is a theoretically interesting type of reasons for action that may serve as the limiting case of idiosyncrasy. Some forms of supererogatory action are motivated by their quasi-indexical character: the fact that it is *I* who actually perform the action is of a special importance to me. This is the most extreme type of idiosyncrasy, since it is based purely on the indexical nature of agent identity rather than on a set of character features—whether of the agent or of the recipient. It is usually displayed in acts of volunteering, in which the agent insists that *he*—rather than someone else equally or even better situated and able—do the good act. This kind of reasons for action is of course alien to moral reasons involved in obligatory action, for those are indifferent to the identity of the agent unless some features in his character, history, or circumstances can be shown to be relevant. Moreover, the appeal to such quasi-indexical idiosyncratic reasons for action is sometimes condemned as reflecting moral self-indulgence, which is intrinsically bad and also may (as Kant noted) lead to moral fanaticism. Volunteering may also endanger the effectiveness of the moral system, for instance when *my* insistence on doing the required act does not tally with the general impersonal considerations that may find another person more suitable for carrying it out.

For some ethical theories, such as existentialism, Nietzscheanism, or egoism, the model of a moral subject is itself inherently "idiosyncratic" (unique, indexical), and thus results in the following paradoxical implication: it is he who acts on reasons derived from an allegedly universal model that is acting in bad faith or inauthentically. But these ethical theories have hardly any coordinative effectiveness and can hardly establish *social* morality. They of course also allow no room for supererogation.

Before concluding this section on idiosyncratic reasons a general remark about the universality of reasons is called for. Reasons for action, unlike desires and preferences, are universalizable, that is, they apply equally to relevantly similar cases. Idiosyncratic reasons are no exception. They are, by definition, never irrational or purely arbitrary. This means that they also have universal application (to relevantly similar agents and circumstances). However, the very criterion of relevant similarities is shown by cases such as supererogation to be a matter of free choice rather than something fixed by an objective model. Idiosyncratic reasons are those that morally bind all, but only, those who *choose* to treat them as relevant, as derivable from a richer model. This should explain why, in the eyes of the supererogatory agent, the idiosyncratic reasons for his action are considered as good—even overriding—reasons, yet not as applying to most other people (sometimes not even to the agent's own future selves). It also clarifies the problematic status of "indexical" reasons (egoism and volunteering), which are indeed a limiting case and perhaps even beyond the realm of practical reasons in the strict sense.

Equity and Discretionary Powers

There is another important area in ethics in which idiosyncrasy adds a dimension of complexity to moral reasoning. This is the realm of equity and the contexts calling for the exercise of judgment and discretionary powers. Unlike the choice to *adopt* the moral model (the second type of idiosyncrasy) and the choice to *transcend* it (the third type), this kind of idiosyncrasy is displayed in the way in which decisions are made *within* the model of moral reasoning. But unlike the idiosyncratic choice of the means by which the moral action is to be carried out (the first type), which is morally indifferent, this area of idiosyncrasy is specifically moral in nature.

Equity is called for in circumstances in which the application of the rules of justice is either undetermined or directly opposed to what is conceived as a right and just outcome. Equity is a necessary complement to any system of justice because no system of general rules can ever be expected to cover the infinitely rich variety of circumstances that might arise.

This deficiency in the system of justice is not a matter of ignorance or lack of sophistication on the part of those who devised it, but rather a result of the tension between the generality of its rules and the particularity (uniqueness) of the states of affairs to which they are applied. As Aristotle states in his classical discussion of the subject, equity "corresponds to what the lawgiver himself would have said if he were present, and what he would have enacted if he had known [of this particular case]."[7] The only way to avoid that tension is by making the rules so specific and ad hoc as to rob them of the status of rules altogether. Equity is therefore a necessary feature of any non-intuitionistic system, that is, one based on general rules and principles.[8] In the legal system the judge is given discretionary powers to decide cases to which the rules of law are either not directly applicable or in which such application would yield an unjust or a morally undesirable outcome.

Decisions based on the concept of equity are typically sensitive to idiosyncrasies. But unlike the reasoning of the supererogatory agent, in which the idiosyncratic elements are relative to a model of a moral agent, equity is concerned with idiosyncrasies of the circumstances. For that reason equity is not strictly speaking based on what we called idiosyncratic reasons. The same model of a moral subject guides the reason-selection of the equitable judge (or agent) as guides that of the "just" judge (or agent). Equity is a virtue within the bounds of moral reasoning and justice.

Thus the relation between equity and supererogation is just that of an analogy.[9] Neither can ever be governed by rules; they are thus of an ad hoc or discretionary nature; yet they are backed by reasons and are never arbitrary. In both we find an extension of the area of relevant reasons, the extrapolation of the standard moral reasoning procedure, in a way that is consistent with that procedure and even considered an improvement of it. Yet the crucial difference between the two is that while equitable reasoning is *corrective* and hence obligatory, the supererogatory transcendence of duty is only *ameliorative* and hence optional. Equity ensures that the moral system (based on the model) works well; supererogation offers (by the enrichment of the model) a way to act that is better than the way required by the system. Equity is required and universally binding, although its specific exercise can never be governed by rules. Supererogation is purely optional because it does not arise out of any deficiency, either in the system of moral rules or in the conception of the moral subject. Equity, again in Aristotle's words, belongs to the same genus as justice, yet it is better than justice. Supererogation, on the other hand, is beyond justice, although it belongs to the more general genus of the morally good.[10]

In "Saints and Heroes" Urmson implicitly pushes that analogy one step too far. He suggests as one of the justifications for regarding supererogation as a distinct category in ethics the fact that not all morally good actions can be prescribed by general rules. The domain of moral action is too complex for that.[11] But by this sort of justification Urmson seems to attribute a "corrective" function to supererogation, indistinguishable from that of equity. For reasons that I have elaborated elsewhere,[12] I believe this view of supererogation is wrong and does not do justice to the optional character (and the merit derived from it) of heroic, beneficent, and forgiving behavior. Urmson offers another justification for supererogation in terms of the moral illegitimacy of *demanding* heroic sacrifices as a matter of duty. This can be understood as pointing in the direction of an ameliorative rather than a corrective interpretation.[13]

Radical Freedom

At least one major concept of freedom in the history of ethics is directly related to or derived from the idea of a moral subject.

Moral Subjects, Freedom, and Idiosyncrasy 163

If freedom is defined in terms of the absence of *external* constraints, then the area of free action can be determined only by specifying a certain core in human personhood relative to which all considerations outside it are external. This is, in Isaiah Berlin's terminology, the concept of "positive liberty," which is typically displayed by rationalistic theories of morality. If reason is the genuine nucleus of a person, then acting on the basis of feelings, tastes, and instincts cannot be regarded as free; only acting on the model of the rational person (who in this case is also the moral subject) is totally unconstrained. This applies equally to Kantian practical reason, Aristotelian *phronesis*, or Spinozistic cognitive awareness of man's place in the world.

This rationalistic concept of freedom consists, then, in action according to reasons that are relevant from the point of view of a model of a moral subject. Being so, this concept of freedom cannot, by definition, reflect individual contingencies, idiosyncratic traits of character, special preferences, or personal tastes. It expresses the uniformity of human nature rather than its variety. It can thus serve to achieve unanimity (as in Rawls's original position) or communality (as in Kant's Kingdom of Ends), thus realizing the prescriptive and coordinative functions of morality.

A completely different concept of freedom is that of *liberum arbitrium*. This is the freedom involved in arbitrary choice, that is, in a choice that is not guided by reasons (except, maybe, for the second-order reason that calls for making *some* choice). It is the freedom to pick one of two or more alternatives that are fully symmetrical, or to act on either of two or more reasons that are equally weighty. This is the freedom of Buridan's ass, of the supermarket shopper arbitrarily picking a particular token of a desired type of goods, or of a Cartesian voluntaristic God in creating the world. Beyond the logical and metaphysical debate regarding the coherence of such a concept of freedom, one can safely claim that it has had only minor impact on ethical theory and was hardly used as a basis of moral action. Arbitrariness and irrationality (detachment from reasons) are alien to both the prescriptive and the coordinative functions of social morality. *Liberum arbitrium* is idiosyncratic in an *absolute* sense, that is, not relative to any model of a person.

A third concept of freedom lies in between the two previous ones and is of special importance for the theory of supererogation and indeed for understanding action motivated by idiosyncratic reasons in general. This is freedom in the sense of acting on reasons, yet not those related to the model. It is the freedom not only to *act* on morally relevant reasons, but also to *choose* the very criterion of relevance demarcating the line between the personally binding reasons and those that are not. It is thus a kind of freedom that is typically exhibited in circumstances involving the two morally relevant kinds of idiosyncratic reasons mentioned above: the decision to adopt the moral point of view and the choice of supererogatory action. It is also manifest in circumstances involving the other type of idiosyncratic reasons, which guides non-moral choices *within* moral reasoning; but in this context this type of freedom is not morally significant and is unproblematic from the point of view of ethical theory.

This idiosyncratic concept of freedom is more radical than the rationalistic one, as it is not restricted by an abstract universal and uniform model of human agency. It allows much more actual variety of choice—both interpersonally and intrapersonally. It is identical to individual autonomy in the liberal sense rather than in the Kantian sense (of acting on self-legislated laws of reason). It is related to a belief in human spontaneity in the everyday sense of the word and also to the Kantian meaning (the capacity to initiate a new causal series in the world). It leaves the agent with real options rather than with one necessary and uniquely rational solution. It is the freedom sometimes associated with the power of discretion, typically exercised by judges and referees but also by ordinary people in their everyday choices (choices that are not governed by closed systems of rules but by judgment).

Positive, rationalistic freedom can be exercised by following rules, obeying laws, or acting upon principles. But rules and laws can never completely define the manner of their application (idiosyncrasy of the first type); nor can they serve as grounds either for adopting them as action guiding (the second type of idiosyncrasy) or for determining their limit (the third type). So if there is indeed any element of choice in the idea of freedom (an element that Spinoza was willing to forgo), it seems that "radical" freedom is a necessary complement to the rationalistic concept.

Kant recognizes this, although he finds it hard to reconcile the two concepts of freedom in one theory. He implicitly, and sometimes inconsistently, introduces idiosyncratic elements of all three types into his moral doctrine. He assigns *judgment* a special role in the formation of moral choice, judgment being the power to apply general rules and principles to concrete circumstances. He is aware that there are no rules for the formulation of the maxims, which are the object of the universalization test. Then he specifically attributes to persons the irreducible freedom to choose between acting on the moral law and acting out of inclination. This is a kind of radical freedom, since the two alternatives are completely incommensurable ("antagonistic" in his own terminology). Human beings are not only rational beings but also sensuous, and they are free to decide not to act on the model. This concept of "negative" freedom is particularly important to Kant, for it endows moral behavior with its distinct human value. Without it persons would have acted like moral automata, being motivated by rational necessity, having in effect no responsibility over their acts, and deserving no merit.[14] Persons have freedom of choice, embodied in the power of *Willkür*, which they exercise spontaneously and independently of rational as well as natural laws (negative freedom)—both when they adopt the moral law (positive freedom) *and* when they choose to act on inclination.[15] The grounds for the free choice lie in "a rule made by the will for the use of its freedom,"[16] and it can either be governed by the moral law, or run contrary to it (and we may add that it can also be governed by a supererogatory ideal). Such grounds are subjective in Kant's words, or idiosyncratic in our own. And as this negative freedom is not governed by either the laws of reason or the laws of nature, it is non-universal, inscrutable, and beyond theoretical analysis.

It is only Kant's rigid deontology that made it hard for him to extend this notion of freedom to the third type of idiosyncrasy, namely, to the realm of supererogation.[17] But as we shall see below, the same kind of justification and value is attached to supererogatory choice as to the very adoption of the moral point of view.

But radical freedom is not necessarily inscrutable and beyond rationality, for contrary to Kant, we have shown that it can have reasons, although of an idiosyncratic nature. This freedom is distinct from *liberum arbitrium*. It is not capricious, since it is backed by reasons; it is not arbitrary or "blind," since it is not indifferent as to which of the alternative courses of action is chosen. Although it is idiosyncratically exercised (i.e., in relation to the model), it is not absolutely ad hoc. It is rational in the sense that it is exercised within the framework of a personal project or self-image. Although it allows for more room for choice than does positive freedom, it is not totally unconstrained. It is in that respect an intermediate concept between the two extreme concepts of freedom, which are, indeed, artifacts of philosophical theorizing more than of intuitive belief.

Liberalism is based exactly on a model of the moral subject in which *all* possible inclinations and preferences, tastes and powers are taken to be part of the core of personhood. But then, if the model depicts persons as beings who in their essential nature act on a variety of uniquely personal reasons, how can we draw the very distinction between moral and idiosyncratic reasons for action? Can idiosyncrasy be introduced into morality as the sole standard of what it is to act qua moral subject? Strict application of our definition of idiosyncrasy as a deviation from the model seems to yield a paradox. Liberalism is, however, different from egoism and existentialism, which were shown to generate that same paradox. The liberal model of the moral subject as an autonomous individual ("idiosyncratically" motivated) can serve as a basis only for a limited theory of morality and moral reasons for action. For it is essentially negative, stating only the limits of the freedom to intervene in the affairs of others. Such a liberal theory does not positively set any relevance criterion for reason-selection in moral choice, and is therefore a political theory rather than a moral one. We thus see that negative freedom in Kant's sense is closely related to negative freedom in Berlin's liberal sense. Both are kinds of radical freedom.

The Value of Supererogatory Action

Sensitivity to the central role of idiosyncrasy in moral reasoning and to the concept of radical freedom involved in choice and operation of moral reasons may throw light on the special value usually ascribed to supererogation. Part of the value of action beyond the call of duty is formal, that is, related to the way in which it is motivated, the way in which the agent is led to choose it. Another part of the value of supererogation is substantive, namely, the consequences it has for the world. The two sources of value cannot always be easily separated in our admiration for a particular act, but we could think of some acts of forgiveness as typically manifesting the first, and of acts of heroism or extreme beneficence as illustrating the second. The formal justification of supererogation is associated on the one hand with the good intention of the agent and on the other hand with the radical freedom that motivates it. The distinction between the supererogatory and the obligatory is based on grounds similar to those that reject the legal enforcement of morals.[18] The value of gratitude and truthfulness (let's assume they are morally obligatory) would be voided if they were made legally binding. In the same way, the value of volunteering and pardoning would be nullified if they were made morally obligatory.

Supererogation is valuable because it expresses individual variation—because it recognizes the central role of idiosyncratic reasons both in the way a person defines and expresses himself and in the way he establishes personal relations with his fellow beings. The abhorrence of moral automata, which leads Kant to introduce a radical concept of freedom in the choice of morality, is not very different from what we would feel toward a community of moral subjects who always stuck to the impersonal and universal standards of behavior derived from their being moral subjects, and never expressed other (personal) features of their character and preferences. It is hard to offer a theoretical justification of radical freedom; to most of us it seems to be intrinsically good. It may just reflect our preference for a richer world, for variety, and for room for creative choice, and our aversion to uniformity, total predictability, and regularity beyond that required to achieve the prescriptive and coordinative purpose of the moral system. The three kinds of idiosyncratic reasons reflect that basic preference: the first displays the personal style in which a person carries out his duties, the second blocks the possibility of moral automata, and the third shows that agents can freely choose to extend morality beyond the limits of its model.[19]

But in what sense can we say that supererogatory action is an *extension* of the moral sphere, an enrichment of the model of the moral subject? There must be continuity between the supererogatory and the obligatory for the former to be of *moral* value. Otherwise, the only value of the deviation from the model would consist in its being grounded in a radically free choice (a choice that could be morally indifferent or even plainly immoral). The continuity requirement introduces non-formal considerations of a consequential nature. The outcome of supererogatory behavior must be morally good, that is, good on the same scale of values as standard obligatory action. To state the point in terms of the enrichment of the model itself, the extra features in the self-image of the moral agent must be morally good in the sense of tending to promote the good (beyond the level required for the minimal conditions of social life). However, the value of supererogation lies also in its being a free choice to engage in an optional course of action, that is to say, it is of *intrinsic* value.

In this context it is interesting to examine R. M. Hare's views of idiosyncrasy and his analysis of supererogation. On the one hand he seems to recognize the legitimacy of some forms of idiosyncratic preferences. He says that "prima facie principles requiring partiality have in some cases a high acceptance-utility even when judged from an impartial critical standpoint."[20] Although he refers here to "particular loyalties," the same can be said of supererogatory (biased) acts. On the other hand, he insists that moral judgments must be "unbiased," "impersonal," and "made from an impersonal standpoint." They are objective exactly in ignoring, as irrelevant, the identity of the agent and recipient of the moral act.[21] Hare would of course deny that there is any contradiction involved in these two claims, appealing to his distinction between the two levels of moral thinking—the intuitive and the critical. Yet by that distinction he misses the intrinsic, non-utilitarian value of supererogation (and also, in my view, of loyalty, which is another excellent example of the personal dimension of morality based on idiosyncratic reasons).

It is not surprising that Hare treats supererogation as binding only on those few who have a special vocation or strong character (saints and heroes).[22] I have criticized such a "qualified"—that is, capacity-based, utilitarian—view of supererogation elsewhere. But I would emphasize again that utilitarian justifications of supererogation incur the negative results of making it a duty: they not only miss the intrinsic and often emotionally moving value of saintly and heroic acts, but also fail to cover the less dramatic forms of supererogatory conduct, for which no particular capacity is required.

Since Hare believes in a purely formal definition of morality, his view of the critical level of moral thinking allows only for *im-*

partial reasons, excluding all idiosyncrasy (which is legitimized only indirectly on the intuitive level). The alternative view presented here justifies supererogation also in substantive terms, that is, those pertaining to the kind of value achieved by supererogatory acts. Morality itself (on the critical level) should recognize *some* partial and idiosyncratic elements, as long as they satisfy the continuity condition.

Freedom is considered intrinsically valuable. But it can be ordered in a hierarchy: the value of political freedom in a democratic society (the obedience to laws made by the citizens themselves); the value of positive moral freedom (the obedience to the self-legislated moral law); the value of radical freedom (choosing the moral point of view and the supererogatory); and possibly, as a limiting case, the value of *liberum arbitrium* (the total absence of reasons for action—either moral or idiosyncratic). These correspond to political autonomy, moral autonomy, individual autonomy, and absolute autonomy or self-determination with no reference to any given *nomos* or reason. Ethics must recognize the moral value of both the common, universal, and immutable in human life and the personal, individual, and unique.

JONATHAN DANCY

Supererogation and Moral Realism

Moral realists take it that moral properties of actions are real properties. That an action is tactful or cowardly, charitable or cruel, is as much a fact about the action as the length of time it took to do it. This is moral realism about the ground-level moral properties, which contribute to our overall moral view of the action. Such properties have been called "thick" or prima facie right-making properties. But what are we to say about the properties of rightness and goodness, properties we attempt to discern when we say whether one action is overall better than another, or right, or a duty, or what we ought to do? What form of realism, if any, should we adopt about these "thin" properties?[1] David Wiggins seems to abandon realism with respect to these properties, on the grounds that they lack what he calls "regular truth." And there is indeed a temptation to say that our use of these thin concepts is more in the nature of a decision than a discovery. If we yield to this temptation, we say that in calling one alternative right we do not disclose a further property, but merely mark our adoption of that action, an adoption guided by its thick moral properties. But this is not the line I prefer. I have not the space to argue the point here, but the most consistent form of moral realism seems to me to be the extreme one, the one that treats the thin properties more or less as it treats the thick ones. On this approach we say that our adoption of the action seems to be guided by our recognition of a thin property of the action, perhaps that of being better than any alternative. Moral realists should, then, be thinking of these thin properties as further, equally real properties of actions, in response to our recognition of which we adopt or reject alternative courses of action.

I admit, however, that there is a strain on our intuitions here. It seems hard to think of there being action-related properties such as those of being right, being the action one ought to do, or being the best, *as well as* all the thick properties that guide our choices. What is more—and here is the problem this paper is really about—we might perhaps allow an action to have one such property, but can we really allow it to have several? Wouldn't the admission that there have to be several distinct thin action-guiding properties show that the realist has stretched our intuitions far beyond the breaking point?

It may help in describing the moral realist's difficulty to give an example of a realist account of thin properties that is vulnerable to the complaint that it can only make sense of there being *one* such property. The account that tempts me takes its start from a case in which I am not yet sure how I should act. Suppose, for instance, that I am driving to the railway station in order to meet my wife's train. It is 10:30 P.M., but I am alert, my car is in good order, and the street lighting is adequate. I am also late, and the station is not a very healthy place for unaccompanied women at night. Would I be justified in exceeding the speed limit? So far, perhaps, I would. But at that time of night large numbers of less than sober people are leaving pubs and other sources of liquid refreshment. They may behave unpredictably, and of course the street lighting could always be improved. Should I increase the chances of running one of them over as they stumble out from behind parked cars, by driving faster than the legal limit?

The problem here does not seem to be a question of fact, except at the outer limit. I am not in a quandary about any fact, except the putative fact of how I ought to act. What I am in doubt about, according to me, is the correct *shape* to give those facts, which to see as *salient* and which to see as recessive.[2] One possibility is that I see as most salient the fact that my wife is alone in insalubrious surroundings. Another is that the fact that the streets are filling up with unsteady persons springs into prominence. My problem is how to see the moral facts I already have, what shape or profile to give them. But this does not mean that I should treat in other than a realist way the question what the correct shape is.

The relevance of this account for present purposes is that the second-level question what I ought to do in this situation is treated as the question what shape my action's thick moral properties are to be seen in. And this raises the question how there can be more than one thin moral property, for how can a given set of thick properties have more than one shape? It looks as if it is going to be difficult for the realist, on my showing, to draw distinctions between different sorts of shapes, more than one of which an action's moral properties can possess at one time. This would leave the realist unable to draw any distinction between different thin properties.

I do not mean to say that this problem is obviously insuperable. The uncashed metaphor of shapes may be misleading; we will have to face the question whether the distinction between different thin moral properties is at all like the distinction between different shapes. Of course in one sense an object can have more than one shape at one time; it can be square and rectilinear. More of this below. At the moment my problem has only the status of a threat or a worry. And of course as a problem it bugs more moral theories than just moral realism. In the heyday of ethical intuitionism it would have been described as the problem whether we might intuit more than one thin property in an action. And presumably there was, or should have been, a way of putting the question to emotivism. The problem is bound to arise once we adopt a form of ethical pluralism, which has seemed to many to be the acceptable face of intuitionism.[3] For with pluralism we lose the hope that the attempt to determine the thin moral properties of an action is essentially a question of the operation of some monistic calculus. Even when we know all the different thick properties of the action, we still have a problem how to bring this knowledge to bear on an overall decision.

It is not just that there *might* be more than one thin moral property of a given action. It has been common for moral theorists to distinguish explicitly between two: rightness and goodness. But this distinction is only an instance of a more general distinction between two classes of thin moral concepts, the *deontic* notions of the *right*, our *duty*, and most generally what we *ought* to do, and the *evaluative* notions of the bad, the praiseworthy, and the good. My strategy, in seeking to determine what sort of difference there is between the thin properties of being right and being best, is to ask more generally what sort of difference we must admit between deontic and evaluative properties. To do this I turn my attention to the phenomenon that is, I think, held to be the main reason for drawing an interesting distinction between the two, namely, the existence or at least the possibility of supererogatory action. After establishing as best I may what sort of distinction is required to make sense of supererogation, I return to the question whether this result is one that the moral realist can easily assimilate.

Supererogatory actions are those that, though they have merit or value, still lie beyond the call of duty. At the limit, these are the actions of saints and heroes, actions that, though of supreme merit, cannot be said to have been the agent's duty. There are also supererogatory actions of less exceptional value; quite ordinary actions can exceed the demands of duty, while still attracting approval.

Expressed in this traditional way, the supererogatory imposes a contrast between actions that have high value and those that have the special deontic property of being a duty. But in fact supererogationists (those who accept that there are such things as supererogatory acts) have been happy to extend the contrast,[4] since they claim that heroic actions of self-sacrifice are in no sense actions that we can say the agent *ought* to have done. We could not require such actions of anyone, and this means that the contrast at issue is really between the most general evaluative and deontic concepts, those of being good and of being something that one ought to do. (Occasionally, however, the concentration in the literature on the notion of duty to the exclusion of other deontic concepts will lead me to resort to the special contrast between duty and the supererogatory.)

So the possibility of supererogation is used to force us to distinguish between deontic and evaluative properties. On the one side, it leads us to think that an action can have a high-grade evaluative property without having any deontic property at all. But, on the other side, can an action have a deontic property without having an evaluative property? Supererogationists are divided on this question. Some—and I suspect that J. O. Urmson, who was responsible for bringing the notion of supererogation back to the attention of moral theorists, is among them—hold that whether an action is a duty or has any other deontic property is independent of the question how much value it has or would have, so that there is room for actions that we ought to do but that are evaluatively quite indifferent. Of course, an action may derive value from being done from the motive of duty; but this epicycle is irrelevant. The extreme position I am outlining here maintains only that some actions that are duties, say, are so not because of any value that they have, or even despite their lack of value. A more moderate position would hold that an action can only be a duty if it has an evaluative property from which the property of being a duty somehow emerges.

Now the relevance of this distinction between extreme and moderate positions lies in the question how extreme the differences are between deontic and evaluative properties. The point of this question can be brought out by considering the analogy between shape and thin properties that I introduced earlier. If there is to be a difficulty for the moral realist here, it derives from the feeling that an action's properties cannot have two shapes at the same time. For this feeling to be true, as it were, we must be employing a sense of shape in which no object can have two shapes at once. An object can, however, be both rectilinear and triangular; indeed any object that is triangular is rectilinear, though an object can be rectilinear without being triangular. Is the relation between deontic and evaluative properties anything like this? On the moderate position, it is. An object can have an evaluative property without having a deontic one, but it cannot have a deontic property without having an evaluative one. But this does not yet determine exactly which of several possible relations the deontic properties bear to the evaluative properties.

Our task, then, is to pin down the exact relation between the deontic and the evaluative. This will enable us, crucially, to see whether we should say that when an action has both deontic and evaluative properties there is no more difference between these properties in the action than there is between the two relevant properties of a triangle. This would help the realist who is worrying about the possibility of two shapes at once. On the extreme position, however, no such move is available. The two properties are entirely distinct when co-present, as is shown by the fact that each could be present without the other.

Moral realism seems then to be threatened more severely by the extreme position than by the moderate one. Whether this is so, however, depends on the exact sense that the moderate position gives to the relation between deontic and evaluative. We cannot prejudge that question here; it is answered in our final section.

Two propositions have now emerged:
1. Every deontic property of an action results from an evaluative property.
2. Every evaluative property of an action results in a deontic property.[5]

The extreme and moderate positions differ about proposition 1. But what about proposition 2? Traditionally, supererogationists have denied proposition 2, since they hold that an action can have great value but not be a duty or have any other deontic property. This is what we might call the strong form of supererogationism. But there is a weaker position ("weak supererogationism") that sees the supererogatory act not as an act that is not our duty despite its value, but as an act that, despite being our duty, or at least being one we ought to do, is one whose nonperformance does not attract sanction, disapproval, or penalty. The weak supererogationist holds that we ought to do these actions because of their value, but that nobody is going to blame us if we don't; and that therefore proposition 2 is true.

We now have two distinctions at work, extreme/moderate and strong/weak. The first concerns proposition 1, the second proposition 2; this is how to tell them apart. They generate four possible positions; we have to determine which is the most attractive and then show how this result affects the prospects of moral realism. The natural thought is that a moderate and weak supererogationism is preferable for the moral realist, because that combination yields the best prospects of a systematic relation between the deontic and the evaluative. I start, then, by examining the respective merits of strong and weak supererogationism. From that examination we will derive an initial account of the relations between deontic and evaluative properties, which we will be able to use to determine our choice between extreme and moderate positions.

The first move in the strong supererogationists' defense of their position is normally to argue that it is a good thing that not every action having value should be considered as a duty or as an action that ought to be done. That is to say, we are offered moral reasons (an example of which will be considered below) for drawing some sort of a line between duty, etc., and the supererogatory, and the reasons provided will tell us more or less where that line is to be drawn. This is obviously important, but its weakness, as we shall see, is that though this sort of moral justification tells us where to draw the line, it does not itself tell us exactly how to conceive of the acts that fall on either side. What this means is that there is a good chance that all its points can be absorbed and indeed adopted by the weak supererogationist, who also wants to draw some sort of a line or at least introduce a distinction of degree between acts that are supererogatory and acts that are not. So strong supererogationists need to add to their moral reasons some more philosophical reasons why the weak supererogationist cannot simply take over their distinction and rewrite it in his own terms. We need to be told how to conceive of the actions falling on either side of the line, and we need an argument that this is the right way to conceive of them, not just a possible way; and all this should be done in a way compatible with the moral reasons offered at the outset.

The main difficulty that the second, more philosophical half of the strong supererogationists' story faces is what David Heyd calls the "good-ought" tie-up. This is the resilient intuition that if an action is good, this gives us a reason to do it, and if it is the best available, we have more reason to do it than to do anything else and so ought to do it. If this intuition is sound, the best available action will always be the right one, the one that one ought to do. So the good-ought tie-up flatly contradicts the claims of the strong supererogationist, and constitutes the main reason for adopting the weak position. Strong supererogationists need, then, a philosophical reason for abandoning the good-ought tie-up. They need to say how we can make good sense of the possibility that an action might be the best available without being the one that one ought therefore to do.

If you are not persuaded already that there need to be two stages in the defense of strong supererogationism, I hope to convince you now by examining one moral reason commonly offered in its favor.

According to Michael Clark, any theory of supererogation

needs to answer two questions.⁶ The first is, What gives us the moral right to refrain from supererogatory actions? The second is, Why is it nonetheless virtuous to perform them? An example of a strong supererogationist answer to the first question is that it is unrealistic to consider every action that has value to be one we ought to do; to do so would bring the notions of duty and obligation into disrepute since people would increasingly recognize that the fulfillment of duty and obligation was beyond their reach. But if there is this sort of moral value in refusing to consider every valuable act a duty, it seems to be effectively duplicated by the weak supererogationist's refusing to disapprove of non-performance in the same way or to the same extent. Thus there is nothing in the strong answer that the weak supererogationist need disagree with; this particular moral reason does not argue for the strong position rather than the weak one.

The prevalent answer to Clark's first question focuses more promisingly on the individual agent's autonomy. David Heyd's view, for instance, is that the value of the autonomy of the individual provides a natural limit to the demands of public duty. He argues that our duty is restricted to those actions that can be required of us in the public interest, that is, to secure a minimum basis for social coexistence. This is why he can think of all duty as public duty. Urmson also slips into speaking of duty as "basic duty," which is unfortunate since it suggests that there may be such a thing as non-basic duty, and (incompatibly) that all duty is of this basic, that is, restricted, type. However this may be, the idea common to Heyd and Urmson is that there is a value in the individual's not being always at the beck and call of duty, and having the right to pursue her or his own projects and generally to live her or his own life. This value is to be set against, and exists as a limit to, the value of getting people to act in the interests of others. We all know the example of the clergyman who dedicates himself entirely to the interests of others. The feeling here is that it is possible to go too far in this direction, and this possibility is highlighted by the value of reserving some of one's time and resources for oneself.

I think all parties can agree on the general thrust of this approach. The questions I want to raise concern only the nature and role of this appeal to autonomy. As an answer to Clark's first question, how does it work to provide a moral reason for strong supererogation? (Heyd calls these considerations the negative justification of supererogation, since they aim to explain how there can be a limit to the demands of duty.) The first point to make is that the weak supererogationist can at least make an attempt to talk in similar terms. Any pluralist, for instance, is used to the idea that there are competing claims on one, which need to be somewhat precariously balanced against each other. In the present case it may be that the best way to balance the claims of self and of others is to veer now more to one side and now more to the other. This does not in itself mean that the claims of others are to count as duties, and one's own claims as justifiable self-indulgence. A pluralist of this sort may even go so far as to talk of one's having a duty not to neglect oneself, and this not in the purely material sense of remembering to wash behind one's ears. So the mere mention of autonomy is not sufficient to make out a negative justification of strong supererogationism.

But perhaps the point is that autonomy enters the scale as a *value*, one that cannot be reduced to duty or any other purely deontic notion. Although there is a conflict here, as the pluralist saw, it is not between one duty (a prima facie duty, of course) and another, but between one's duty to others and something that is not a duty but enjoys a value of a different sort. If this is the point, however, it seems to me that it does not itself advance us very far in the direction of strong supererogationism. As things stand, the appeal to autonomy amounts in this context simply to the production of a purported example of a non-deontic value, which may or may not be found convincing. Either way, as such an example it is vulnerable to the resurgence of the good-ought tie-up in another form. For we would have to ask why it is that considerations of autonomy don't enter the scale simply as being or at least as generating further reasons for action (or reasons against devoting yet another evening to collecting for charity). On this view of autonomy, it is still the case that the action that is best in the circumstances is the one that one has most reason to do and therefore the one that one ought to do. This is the question that the weak supererogationist would press, and considerations of autonomy in themselves provide no answer.

So I think that if the appeal to autonomy were intended as a complete justification for strong supererogationism, it would amount to begging the question because it assumes the very distinction between duty and value, or more generally between the deontic and the evaluative, that it would be supposed to justify. The crucial point is that it fails to provide a justification for moving away from the talk of reasons for action that makes the good-ought tie-up so appealing. But really we knew in advance that this must be so. Moral reasons for strong supererogationism need philosophical supplementation, without which the good-ought tie-up still threatens. The virtue of Heyd's approach to this topic is that, unlike Clark, he recognizes this point and makes an attempt to provide what is needed.

The good-ought tie-up, which generates the paradox of strong supererogationism, is at its strongest when expressed in terms of reasons for action. Joseph Raz, expressing it in this way,[7] seeks to escape from it by introducing a second level of reasons for action. He says that we can only make sense of supererogation by supposing that, in addition to the ordinary level of reasons for action, there is a higher level of reasons, exclusionary reasons, which can justify our doing something that on the lower level we do not have most reason to do. For instance, considerations of autonomy might act in this way, nullifying the normal tendencies of our lower-level reasons and justifying our pursuing our own projects when we could be promoting the welfare of others.

The problem with this attempt to escape the good-ought tie-up is that, even if we admitted that considerations of autonomy *might* have this nullifying power, it seems equally possible that considerations of the general good are the exclusionary reasons, nullifying the normal tendencies of reasons of human autonomy. What is needed is an argument that the nullifying goes one way rather than the other, and nothing available within the confines of Raz's approach looks very promising here. This is a point we have seen before. We need a philosophical reason to persuade us to use Raz's distinction between two levels of reason in the way Raz wants us to, and none is forthcoming. Heyd, who makes these points, concludes that the strong supererogationist had better seek his philosophical justification elsewhere than in the area of reasons for action.[8] So I now turn to Heyd's own account.

The difficulty faced by all attempts to escape the good-ought tie-up is that the tie-up tends to resurface in a new guise just as one thinks one has disposed of it. This is effectively what happened to Raz, and another example is given by Heyd's first attempt at the philosophical justification of strong supererogationism.[9] He suggests that the problem of the good-ought tie-up is to be resolved by recognizing that there are two senses of "ought," one evaluative (according to which "is best" implies "ought to be done") and one prescriptive (according to which "ought to be done" implies "is one's duty"). But this distinction between two senses of "ought" seems to be a mere restatement of the problem, which resurfaces as the question how an evaluative "ought" could fail to be prescriptive too. In fact the problem of supererogation just is the problem how moral thought can be evaluative without being prescriptive. Now Heyd has an answer to this question, and this answer amounts to the remainder of his argument for strong supererogationism.[10]

The answer takes its start from the idea that the evaluative predicate "good" is an impersonal predicate; we can call an action good irrespective of any relation to any agent. In particular, we can say that some possible action would be a good one, even though there is no one in the offing as a potential agent. In such a case, Heyd wants to say that there is no one who ought to do that action or who has a duty to do it even though it would be good if someone did it. And this provides just what the strong supererogationist is looking for: an action that has an evaluative property but no deontic property.

This idea comes from H. A. Prichard. He wrote, "In order to think of some change as one which *we* ought to cause, we must think of the change as in some special way related to ourselves, even if that way consists in its affecting someone other than ourselves."[11] From this he concluded that Moore was wrong to say that if a man's happiness is good, everyone has an equal reason to pursue it. Duties, obligations, and such things only arise when there exists some special relationship between potential action and potential agent, no matter how great the value of the action. Value alone, therefore, does not constitute a reason for action for anybody.

It is worth stressing the conclusion here. Prichard is arguing against the moral theory that holds that an action is a duty or ought to be done if and only if it has a good effect. His position is that the goodness of the effect may be necessary, but it is not sufficient. The goodness of the effect alone creates no claim on anybody (is no reason for anybody to act) who does not stand in some special relation to the proposed act. Of course if there is such a person, the goodness of the effect does count as a reason for that person to act. Prichard could not object if we expressed his position as the claim that if an action is good (has a good effect) it is a duty for anyone who is in a position to act. For *opportunity* is a special relation, and it seems to be one that meets Prichard's point. (This at least is the way Heyd sees the matter.)

How will this serve to defend strong supererogationism? Heyd, acknowledging Prichard's point, tries to use it as follows:

It cannot be the case, therefore, that any valuable state of affairs in itself constitutes a reason for action for an individual person.

Moral reasons for action prescribing what one ought to do arise, then, not from the desirability of states of affairs, but from a certain *relationship* between the agent and the beneficiary of the action. . . . It is not true that one ought always to do whatever is good (or best) because one's *own* good may have priority in one's practical reasoning—even if it is less good than that achieved by an alternative action.[12]

And with this thought he swings into the defense of strong supererogation, thus tying his philosophical argument in perfectly with the central moral reason for his position, namely, the notion of autonomy, which we have already examined.

But there are all sorts of things wrong with this passage. First, according to Prichard the relationship that is required is not between agent and beneficiary, but between agent and action. Second, Prichard's position is not that value cannot count as a reason for action, as Heyd's second sentence suggests, but that value *alone* cannot provide such a reason. Heyd has missed the point, being misled by the ambiguity of the phrase "in itself." This can either mean "alone" or "in its own right"; Prichard takes it in the first sense, Heyd in the second. Third, and more important, the last sentence is misconceived. It pretends to consider the value of autonomy entirely in consequentialist terms, and to suggest against this background that we are somehow justified in pursuing our own projects even when doing so is worse than not doing so. But surely autonomy is at least partly a non-consequentialist value, and one's own good may have priority in one's reasoning just because of the value of autonomy. And then one is left saying that one ought always to choose the best available course of action (here we see the relation of opportunity), and that since it is sometimes best to pursue one's own projects rather than to shelve them for the sake of others, this is what one sometimes ought to do. But this thought is something that the weak supererogationist will happily grant; it is no argument for strong supererogationism.

There is also an unfortunate slide in the passage. Heyd starts with the thought he got from Prichard, that it is not true that everyone ought equally to do what is best, because "oughts" of this type emerge not just from value but require also a special relation between action and agent. He moves from this to the thought that it is not true that everyone ought equally to do what is best because everyone has a right to ignore what is best (sometimes) in favor of her or his own projects. But the latter thought in no way springs from the former. Prichard's point was not that the existence of the special relation has a value that enables it to convert something valueless into something valuable, or that justifies our performing the relevant action when some other action would be better. However, the instance of a special relation that Heyd seeks to introduce (hinging on the notion of the agent's autonomy) only plays its part because of those features. This seems to mean that Heyd's more philosophical argument fails to fit his moral reasons in the way he hopes. Indeed, the claim that one's own good may reasonably have priority in one's practical reasoning seems to leave us holding that we *ought* sometimes to pursue our own projects, for we surely find here, if anywhere, the desirable combination of value and special relation that on Prichard's view generates a duty. But to count this as a duty or even just as something we ought to do is dubiously compatible with the non-deontic value ascribed to autonomy as a moral reason.

It seems then that Heyd's philosophical arguments are unsuccessful, and that the good-ought tie-up still lives. Nothing in Prichard's point, even if we accept it, forces or even entices us to express the value of autonomy otherwise than in the language of reasons for action, the language that gives the tie-up its strength.

But we have not yet considered the answer to Clark's second question. Why is it virtuous to perform supererogatory acts when one has a perfect right to refrain from them? I think that the discussion so far has given us reason to suppose that the answer to this question is not going to mend matters as far as the strong supererogationist is concerned. But one never knows; we might still find here something sufficiently distinctive about the supererogatory to tempt us away from weak supererogationism.

Clark and Heyd give similar answers to this question; Heyd calls his answer the "positive justification," because it tells us what is good about the supererogatory. Both answers revolve around the notion of an action that acquires value from its being optional for its agent. Clark holds that a supererogatory action is virtuous because it involves an optional sacrifice, made from altruistic motives. Of course many duties involve sacrifices made from altruistic motives. It is the optionality that is crucial.

The first question to ask here concerns the difference between the value of autonomy and that of optionality. Are we clear that these are different, or is this answer to the second question simply a disguised version of the answer to the first? Neither of these authors is very explicit about the nature of the optionality on which he is relying. But I want to suggest that either it is not in the end distinct from autonomy, or it is a valuable feature of all moral action, in no way available to serve as the distinctive mark of supererogatory value.

There are two possible senses of the notion of optionality. In the first, we claim that an optional action is one that forms part of an agent's personal projects, as opposed to his contribution to the general climate of social cooperation. (Actually I'm not sure why my projects should not include or at least ought not to include the furthering of that contribution. And if they do, what would the strong supererogationist say about it? Wouldn't he have to say that in such a case it was no longer my duty to do my duty, or that my doing my duty has the supererogatory value attached to any exercise of autonomy?) In this first sense, there is no real gap between optionality and the exercise of autonomy, and I have already argued that the claims of autonomy as a value can be handled perfectly by a weak supererogationism. In the second sense, we can claim that an optional action is one that the agent may or may not perform, without sanction or penalty for either choice. Now the real point of introducing the notion of optionality into the discussion is to bring out an implied contrast between our duty, or more generally those actions that somehow we have to do, and the supererogatory actions that, lying beyond them, are a matter of personal choice (optional); we don't have to do them, but it would be a good thing if we did them nonetheless. But to the extent that the value of the optional derives from the fact that we don't have to perform an action if it is optional, there seems to me in the end to be no relevant difference of type between the supererogatory and the non-supererogatory.

First, if there is a sanction on the non-performance of one's duty there is also one on the non-performance of the optional supererogatory action. It may not be so severe a sanction, but in calling an action supererogatory we are clearly saying that it is better than mere duty and thereby evincing approval of it and even recommending or commending it. But this is just the sort of sanction there is on the non-performance of duty. It is an illusion to suggest that disapproval begins and ends with duty. There are some actions that lie beyond duty, at least as Heyd conceives of it, but that I am happy to commend forcibly to others and myself, and that very commendation introduces a weak sanction.

Second, there may be a feeling in the air that an action is the better if done willingly rather than as the grudging performance of an externally imposed duty. But this feeling fails to discriminate between the supererogatory and mere duty. Actions that are duties are the better for being performed willingly. They are also the better if they would have been performed whether they were duties or not. So there is nothing here to comfort the strong supererogationist. Heyd recognizes this, I think, and says that "the morality of supererogation is based on freedom and voluntariness in a more radical sense than that of freedom and voluntariness in the morality of duty. The decision to act beyond what is required is free not only from legal and physical compulsion, but also from informal pressure, the threat of moral sanctions, or inner feelings of guilt. It is purely optional."[13] But the trouble with this is that the very commendation that the notion of the supererogatory involves is a form of moral pressure, which only too easily creates feelings of guilt. The only thing one can say is that it involves less pressure and less guilt. But this plays into the hands of the weak supererogationist.

Beyond the two senses of optionality noted above, there is a third way in which we might use the notion to answer Clark's question. It is to say that optionality creates a special value when it is relevant to the agent's motive. The idea here is that what distinguishes the supererogatory is that the agent chooses it in the light of its optionality; the fact that it is optional explains the favorable light in which the agent saw it. In making this remark we are, I think, distinguishing between the value of the action and that of the motive in a way that we might later come to regret. But, letting that ride for the moment, there are two things wrong with this suggestion. First, it seems hard to make very good sense of the idea that one might choose an action on the grounds that it is optional. Second, many supererogatory actions are considered by their agents to be duties; the agents are perhaps misguided in this, but their mistake surely does not detract from the distinctive value of their actions as supererogatory.

Surely whatever value the supererogatory possesses is ordinary value. The fact, if it is a fact, that supererogatory actions are optional may perhaps add to their value. But it does not contribute to the explanation of why they are not duties (this role was played by the notion of autonomy), and whatever value is added by optionality is surely insufficient to justify the high place we assign to the supererogatory. Supererogatory actions are good for the same sort of reasons as other actions are: because of their effect on others, for instance. They may have surpassing quantities of this sort of value, but this is nothing to the point. Perhaps it was a mistake to think that the only way to answer Clark's second question was to find an entirely distinctive form of value, restricted to the supererogatory. But if it is a mistake, it is one endemic only to strong supererogationists. The weak supererogationist sees no reason to seek a distinction of type between supererogatory actions and those that are mere duties.

So where have we got to after all this? There are two propositions with which we have been centrally concerned:
1. Every deontic property of an action results from an evaluative one.
2. Every evaluative property of an action results in a deontic property.

The purpose of emphasizing the good-ought tie-up, or of insisting that evaluative properties either are or at least generate reasons for action, was to fortify proposition 2, against the claims of strong supererogationists. We have not accepted proposition 2 directly, but have seen nothing wrong with a version of it, culled from Prichard:

2'. Every evaluative property of an action is one from which, where there is a special relation between agent and action, a deontic property results.

This proposition was, surprisingly, the one on which Heyd relied. It was no help there, because the standard examples of supererogatory actions are just ones in which there is the required combination of evaluative property and special relation. It depends, of course, on just how special is special. But we could not require that the relation between agent and action needed for the generation of a duty be more special than that between the action and any other potential agent. The recruit who, in Urmson's example, throws himself on a grenade to save the lives of his fellows has admittedly no more of a duty to do so than has any of the fellows. But there still exists a sufficiently special relation between agent and action to enable the value of the action to count as a reason for our hero to act. In the case of supererogatory action there will always be a special relation between agent and action, if only that of opportunity.

According to Prichard's position, summed up in proposition 2', the deontic shadows the evaluative. Wherever there is an evaluative property and a special relation, a deontic property results. This gives us a distinction between deontic and evaluative, though not one that is any comfort to the strong supererogationist. Though the good-ought tie-up has not survived in exactly the form originally intended, as expressed in proposition 2, its successor, proposition 2', has more or less the same effect as far as supererogation is concerned.

We now emerge with the basics of a general account of the relation between deontic and evaluative properties. These properties are not identical, nor can we hope to define the members of one class in terms of members of the other. But there is a systematic relation between the two, which we expressed in proposition 2' in terms of the notion of resultance. The relation between the two is not one of entailment, nor merely the contingent one of possible coexistence. Resultance as usual offers us a middle road between these two extremes.[14] And the systematic relation that it offers seems to be one that the moral realist can cope with. On the account contained in proposition 2', the evaluative properties result from properties other than those concerned with the existence or otherwise of a suitable relation between agent and action. As such, they do not yet stand as reasons for any agent to act. They only become such reasons when there is added to them a relation of the sort required. The whole then counts as the agent's perception of the situation confronting him, which stands as his (total) reason for acting.

We are now in a position to deal with proposition 1, which concerns the choice between the extreme and the moderate positions outlined in the third section of this essay. It is worth stressing that the mere fact that we have rejected strong supererogationism does not in itself direct us toward the extreme or toward the moderate position. It is the particular account of the relation between deontic and evaluative that led to that rejection that now leads us to accept proposition 1, against the extreme position.

On this account it seems to me that though we can still use the metaphor of shape introduced in the opening section of this essay, the metaphor no longer threatens to make it hard to understand how there can be more than one thin moral property. We now have the vestiges of a theory of how there can be two distinct classes of moral properties, which does not seem to contain this threat. It is accompanied by a theory of supererogation according to which evaluative properties are not themselves deontic, without this meaning that there can be supererogatory actions that we cannot say the agent ought to have done.

The way to move forward now seems to me to be to start making distinctions between different deontic properties. One of the strengths of strong supererogationism was its insistence that supererogatory actions are nobody's *duty*. We could admit this if we held that being a duty is a rather special deontic property, which only covers a small range of the deontic. To go with this, we could discern other restricted deontic properties, such as that of being an obligation or a commitment. These three and others are ways of being an action that one ought to do; what is needed is a detailed account of the differences between them and how they fit together to provide a network of practical concepts that makes all the distinctions we need. Among the decisions to be made is whether there can be an action with the most general deontic property of being an action that we ought to do but that has none of the more restricted properties such as that of being a duty. Such a decision would, it seems to me, help to combat the apparent emptiness of the position we have ended up with, which holds that there are some actions that we ought to do but that nobody is going to say anything much about if we don't.

One of the merits of the account offered here is that we can lose our sense that the notion of duty, for example, is a radically distinctive notion giving life to a distinct and restricted area of moral thought, the deontic. Instead, with a general understanding of the relations between deontic and evaluative, we can make room for this separable (but now less distinct) notion of duty if we want. But we might equally decide that it doesn't really offer us anything interesting, or even that it has undesirable connotations, and drop it altogether.

BERNARD WILLIAMS

What Does Intuitionism Imply?

Intuitionism in ethics is nowadays usually treated as a methodological doctrine. In the sense that John Rawls gives to the term in *A Theory of Justice,* an ethical view is intuitionist if it admits a plurality of first principles that may conflict, and, moreover, it has no explicit method or priority rules for resolving such conflicts.[1]

The use of the term to stand for this kind of view represents a change from the practice of the 1950's and 1960's, when it was taken for granted that intuitionism in ethics was an epistemological doctrine, a view about the way in which ethical propositions were grasped or known—the kind of view held, for instance, by W. D. Ross and H. A. Prichard. As such, intuitionism was much criticized at that time, to considerable effect.[2]

It seems to be mainly the influence of Rawls that has brought about this change in the understanding of the term. Interestingly, the change restored an earlier state of affairs. J. O. Urmson[3] tells us that when he was an undergraduate and attended Prichard's classes, it was assumed that intuitionism was to be understood as a methodological position: it was opposed, necessarily, to utilitarianism, and Moore (for instance) was not regarded as an intuitionist.

Rawls seems to regard the epistemological doctrine as an addition to the methodological, and sees intuitionists as a methodological genus of which the notorious epistemological intuitionists are a species. I shall be concerned with the relations between methodological intuitionism (MI), on the one hand, and, on the other, two different epistemological doctrines that may be called "intuitionist" (EI). However, I do not want to follow Rawls's practice and treat EI only as a species of MI. The reason for this is well illustrated by the case of Henry Sidgwick, who insistently rejected MI, but famously claimed that the supreme principles of his utilitarianism were grasped by intuition. In saying this, he precisely wanted to indicate an area of agreement between himself and the traditional anti-utilitarian intuitionists. Again, someone could accept a *rationalized pluralism*, with explicit priority rules, and so not accept MI, but yet take an E-intuitionist view on the question how the rules were grasped. The classes of positions associated with MI and with EI merely intersect.

This does not mean that the questions raised by the two sorts of position are entirely distinct. In particular, those who accept MI, such as Urmson and myself, should consider whether it has any particular epistemological consequences. In his brief article "A Defence of Intuitionism," Urmson confines himself in effect to the claim that MI correctly describes our experience. That seems to me importantly true, but it is not enough for a defense; apart from the question what that tells us about our experience, there is the issue, raised by many opponents of MI, whether our experience should be left in that state. Their challenge can be fully met only by considering what antecedent warrant there is for the demand that we should rationalize our ethical beliefs, and what conceptions of rationality are being deployed in that demand. This is particularly significant because a charge of unreflective conservatism is often applied to MI. It is a mistake to think that in order to take a critical view of our ethical beliefs, we have to systematize them in a theoretical style. Indeed, the theoretical stance may not even encourage a critical view. Some systematizations are themselves very conservative, and the rhetoric of radical rationality conceals how conservative they are. The picture of rationality for ethics expressed in terms of theory and system is inadequate. Moreover, we do not have to think that what is principally wrong with our ethical life and our understanding of it is that they are insufficiently rational: they may be, for instance, insufficiently honest. The valid objections to uncritical conservatism can be represented within MI itself.

Here I am concerned more narrowly with the relations between MI and EI. I shall consider EI in two different versions. One version, the view to which the title "intuitionism" was traditionally most often applied, rested on the idea that there was some instructive analogy between ethical propositions and truths of mathematics, particularly truths of mathematics that were supposedly self-evident. The criticisms of this are well known, and surely sound. It is hard to find ethical propositions with any content for which the required self-evidence can be invoked in the first place (Sidgwick's own fundamental intuition is illustrative in this respect.) Even if such propositions were available, it is not clear how far we should have got, since it is not clear how much is done by the notion of intuition even for mathematical truths. C. D. Parsons has made the interesting suggestion that it does some work only if "intuition that" is linked to "intuition of," and that is not going to be available in any helpful way for the ethical case, however it may be with mathematics.[4]

Why should anyone want to associate MI with an EI that is conceived in the mathematical style? On the face of it, it is an improbable connection. If the epistemology of ethics is to be mathematical, so (one might expect) should be its development and presentation. One would look for an ethical theory that would be axiomatized or organized in a deductive form. That aspiration, which few since Locke[5] have entertained, stands at the opposite pole to MI. So why should the mathematical analogy encourage any association with MI?

The answer presumably lies in the fact that the mathematical analogy did not go beyond considering ethical convictions individually. It was enough that they seemed to display immediate non-empirical certainty, which encouraged an analogy with the grasp of very simple mathematical relations, rather than with any model of mathematical discovery. All that the analogy could do in the heuristic direction was to exclude any process of empirical discovery. It offered no distinctive picture of the discovery of ethical truths except the intuition of such truths one by one. If the propositions that were supposedly intuited were very general and few in number (as in Sidgwick's case), empirical facts could be applied and subsumptive arguments used, and the way would be open to systematization. But if the intuitions were numerous (at the limit, particular in content and indefinitely many, as in Prichard's case), the absence of any model of how they might be associated could lead to MI, and in this case, the alleged certainty of these various ethical convictions, the absence of any ways in which they might in principle be corrected or rejected, indeed grounded the utilitarian objection that intuitionism was conservative.

The supposed analogy between ethical and mathematical propositions was encouraged by the fact that the ethical concepts appearing in these propositions were very abstract and general. E-intuitionists in the mathematical style have been, to use Susan Hurley's term, "centralists,"[6] believing that very general concepts were logically prior to more specific ones; and the truths that were supposedly intuited used very general concepts such as *good* and *right*.

If we look away from these very general notions to more specific or "thick"[7] ethical concepts, such as *treachery* or *cowardice* or *promise*, we may be encouraged to accept a different style of EI, one in terms of an analogy to sense perception. Such a view has been advanced by John McDowell.[8] The point of calling this an (E-)intuitionist theory (though I do not know that McDowell calls it that himself) is that it presents a range of particular ethical convictions that are immediate and claim to perceive something objective. McDowell regards their claim as justified, once an important distinction has been made between two senses of objectivity. In one sense, a quality is objective only if it can be characterized without any reference to experience at all. In another sense, it is objective if "it is there to be experienced, as opposed to being a mere figment of the subjective state that purports to be an experience of it."[9] In the first sense, values (as the objects of these intuitions may be called) are not objective, but neither are secondary qualities; in the second sense, they have as good a claim to objectivity as secondary qualities have.

McDowell considers the objection that value qualities play no real role in the explanation of value experience, whereas secondary qualities do play a role in the explanation of (say) visual experience. His answer to this is as follows. The right test with regard to explanation "is not whether something pulls its own weight in the favoured explanation (it may fail to do so without thereby being explained away), but whether the explainer can consistently deny its reality."[10] It is this test that admits secondary qualities. By this same test, values can figure in explanations, and this is all the more clear because the explanations are different from those appropriate to secondary qualities. McDowell illustrates this point by reference to something that is not itself a value: "We make sense of fear by seeing it as a response to objects that *merit* such a response. . . . For an object to merit fear just is for it to be fearful. So explanations of fear that manifest our capacity to understand ourselves in this region of our lives will simply not cohere with the claim that reality contains nothing in the way of fearfulness."[11]

Before considering the relation of this kind of EI to MI (a question on which McDowell has something to say), I shall make some remarks about the epistemological view itself; they are not intended as a fully argued criticism of it. The crucial word in the passage I have just quoted (as so often in discussions of objectivity) is "our." Consider a people who are filled with terror, perhaps of a rather special, numinous kind, by certain features of their environment. They have a word to pick out things to which they react in this way. It is not a blankly causal, still less a merely individual, reaction, and children are instructed in what does and what does not merit it. We—the ethnographers—come to understand these reactions, and the word that picks out things in terms of that reaction. We do not share the reaction, except to the extent that we imaginatively enter into their view of things: for instance, we do not share beliefs and attitudes that make this reaction intelligible. Is the quality for which they have this term "there to be perceived"? It is part of their world; it is not part of our world. Is it part of *the* world? Or—we may put it another way—is it part of our world, when "our" relates to a *we* for which there are no others?[12]

We can distinguish at least three different levels in the understanding of situations like this. There is, first, a *shared practice*, in particular a linguistic one: people in this society have a word that they can apply to new situations, teach to their children and so on. That raises a *psychological* question: there must be some explanation of how they can go on from one situation to another in using this term, and why one thing rather than another elicits from them the related reaction. Then there is the question of *objectivity*, whether "there is something there to be perceived"; the answer to this is of course connected with the nature of the explanation that answers the psychological question.

In the case of secondary qualities, if we give a positive answer to the last question, this hangs together coherently with what we want to say about the shared practice and its psychological explanation. The reason for this is that if we find a group whose recognitional and classificatory practice differs from ours, we have an explanation of this that indeed refers to objective qualities; it is a matter of their and our capacities to perceive what is there. An important element in this is the fact that we can fit together what they can perceive with what we can perceive, in the sense that we can form a picture of one world, differently perceived, and that picture can contain these qualities. With the example of fear, and equally with what are clearly values, this is not so. We again have the phenomenon of a shared practice that requires psychological explanation. But here we can do nothing with the claim of objectivity, because here the explanation of why things are like that for them *and not so for us* does not bring in that quality. We could not, as in the case of secondary qualities, fit together into one world the qualities that they are supposedly perceiving and those that we are supposedly perceiving, let alone all the qualities demanded by the various value systems that there are or might be.

Nevertheless, the nature of the shared practice shows that it is world guided, and explanation will hope to show how that can be. What the explanation exactly may be, is to be seen: but we know now that a vital part of it will lie in the desires, attitudes, and needs that we and they have differently acquired from our different ways of being brought into a social world. The explanation will show how, in relation to those differences, the world can indeed guide our and their reactions. "The world" in that explanation will assuredly not be characterized merely in terms of primary qualities; the account of it will need to mention, no doubt, both secondary qualities and straightforwardly psychological items. But it will not contain value qualities corresponding to their experience, or to ours. There is no room for all those qualities, and even if there were, there would be no coherent explanation of why we are able to perceive some of them, and they others. For what we already have good reason to believe about such explanations—that they must refer to different styles of socialization, for instance—would demand a model of a selective perceptual filter, culturally tuned, which is barely intelligible.

If we or they had an explanation of how the world guides the application of thick value concepts, it would not follow that we or they could take from the explanation some non-value concepts, combine them with a very general value term, and succeed in continuing the practice: that is to say, it would not reinstate centralism. Centralism is a doctrine about language and linguistic practice, and there is no reason at all to think that people could substitute for a linguistic practice the terms in which that practice was psychologically or sociologically explained.

These questions are directly relevant to ways in which McDowell's picture may bear on MI. McDowell thinks that if a "projectivist" picture were correct, as opposed to the kind of picture he offers, "having one's ethical or aesthetic reactions rationally suited to their objects would be a matter of having the relevant processing mechanism functioning acceptably. . . . The upshot is that the search for an evaluative attitude that one can endorse as rational becomes, virtually irresistibly, a search for . . . a set of principles: a search for a *theory* of beauty or goodness."[13] Such a theory would be opposed to MI, to which McDowell himself is attracted.

This seems to me a non sequitur. Even though there is no doubt more to "projectivism" than there is to a minimal alternative to McDowell's objectivist picture, the point at issue is a quite general one. A theory of value is something that we are supposed to use in determining what is valuable, worth pursuing, and so on. Why should anything of that sort follow from or be contained in the correct explanation of how people share a practice and go from one case to another? McDowell's conclusion seems to be based on the idea that, if his picture is correct, then we have an account of rationality (based on objectivity) that is compatible with MI: thus we can compare one case with another, appeal to a shared sense of resemblance, and so on. But if his picture is not correct, then the only rationality there can be will be that of theory.

Such an argument rests on two unsound assumptions. One is that case-by-case comparison and appeals to a shared sense of resemblance are not available unless his picture is correct. That is not true. The possibility lies in the shared practice, not in McDowell's objectivist explanation of the shared practice, and when such a practice exists, such methods are available. To the extent that such practices do not exist—when, in particular, two groups use different thick concepts—the possibility of course does not exist; but then it does not, and McDowell's account is not going to bring it into being, particularly since that account contains no practicable theory of error or account of how each party fails to perceive things that other parties perceive.

A second assumption of the argument is that, without McDowell's picture, theory (as opposed to MI) provides the only rational way of discussing ethical convictions. (A form of this assumption is of course shared by the ethical theorists who oppose MI.) This is also not true. To mention only one possibility, we can ask what understandings of human nature, society, and history are presupposed by a given shared practice, such as the use of some thick concepts rather than others, and those understandings may be open to criticism.

McDowell's objectivism is not necessary for a rational MI. Indeed, one may wonder why his picture should not lead in the opposite direction. Surely the world cannot simply contain a jumble of value qualities, perceptible to various differently trained observers? If there are such qualities, one would hope and expect that, as with secondary qualities, they had some discoverable theoretical structure. That McDowell's picture is not sufficient for MI (not that he claims it to be so) is suggested in an interesting way by the views of Hurley, some of which I have already mentioned. Her picture of the application of thick ethical concepts seems to be entirely compatible with McDowell's. However, she considers a further question, how a decision of what it is right to do can emerge when several such concepts apply in a situation and pull in different directions. Here she appeals to theory. Indeed, she adopts the very surprising claim that "when we say that a particular alternative would be right, *it is part of what we mean* that there is some theory which is the best theory about the specific values that apply to the alternatives at hand and that this theory favours a particular alternative."[14] It is not clear how much the term "theory" is meant to imply (indeed it is hard to find a sense of the word weak enough to make this particular claim in the least plausible). But there is certainly nothing here to exclude, and much to encourage, the idea that on the basis of an intuitive application of thick concepts there needs to be erected a structure of ethical theory, of the kind that MI opposes.

The upshot of this discussion seems to be that EI and MI have no very close relations to one another. The closest association has been in the case of the EI in the mathematical style that accepted a large number of separate intuitions; and there the outcome itself gave some reason to distrust the epistemological model.

However, those E-intuitionists were not wrong in thinking that there is a large number of unobvious particular judgments to be made, and that fact is the starting point of MI. No one supposes that all judgments of value, or judgments of right action involving value, are intuitively to be arrived at in isolation from one another. The question of MI's credentials is a question of how far we should expect all the values that we respect, and all the considerations that bear on decisions of right action, to be ordered in a systematic structure. That question arises at two levels, at least: we have to consider how far systematic connections and priorities can be set up between different values or principles at a general level, and also how straightforward the process is likely to be of applying them to particular cases.

There seem to me to be two very general kinds of consideration that should lead one to expect the kind of answer that MI gives to these questions. The first applies particularly to the general level, while the second applies to both the general and the particular levels. The first has some epistemological implications, or at least favors some tendencies over others in that area; the second should have some force whatever one's epistemological views.

The first consideration is to be found in a fact often neglected by ethical theorists, that our ethical ideas consist of a very complex historical deposit. When we consider that fact, and the relations that this deposit has to our public discourse and our private lives, there seems no reason at all to expect it to take, in any considerable measure, the shape of a theory. How compelling one finds this consideration certainly depends to some degree on one's epistemological assumptions. If one thinks that there is no other place to start ethical reflection than the life we actually have, it will seem compelling; the more independent leverage on that life one supposes possible, the less one will be impressed. But even those who believe in the independent leverage must find it hard to explain how, as ethical theorists seem often to assume, the theoretical structure is *already there* in our ethical thought and responses. How did it get there?

The second consideration, it seems to me, should have weight whatever one's epistemological assumptions. It rests on the fact that judgment is constantly required, and that judgment is overwhelmingly concerned with questions of what considerations, in a particular case or more generally, are more important than others. These need not necessarily be practical judgments, though practical judgments provide the central cases, and the weighing of ethical considerations in other connections is often closely relevant to possible practical judgments. Importance is of various types: something may be important to the agent, to others involved, to people in general, or, at the limit, it may be simply important.

The following points seem to me obviously true. Judgments of importance are ubiquitous, and are central to practical life and to reflection at a more general level about the considerations that go into practical decision. Moreover, judgments of importance indeed require judgment. There are certainly reasons why some considerations are more important than others, in any of the previous senses, but judgment is still needed to determine how far those reasons can take you. It may be obvious that in general one kind of consideration is more important than another (for instance, one kind of ethical consideration is more important than another), but it is a matter of judgment whether in a particular set of circumstances that priority is preserved: other factors alter the balance, or it may be a very weak example of the consideration that generally wins. Last, there is no reason to believe that there is one currency in terms of which all relations of comparative importance can be represented. On the contrary, any such currency (satisfaction of desires, for instance) consists of some consideration about which it will make sense to ask whether, on a given occasion or more generally, it is more important than something else.

Philosophy needs a better account of importance than it has at present, and such an account might display any of several epistemological inclinations. But whatever form it took, it would surely be a test of its adequacy that it preserved these banal truths; and any account that does preserve them is bound to leave a good deal of room for methodological intuitionism.

PART III
Aesthetic Values and Valuations

BRUCE VERMAZEN

Aesthetic Satisfaction

Much water has been sprinkled, and not a small amount of fertilizer spread, on the garden of philosophical aesthetics since J. O. Urmson wrote his well-known essay "What Makes a Situation Aesthetic?"[1] Although the essay stimulated and continues to stimulate inquiry into the boundary between the aesthetic and the non-aesthetic, no universally appealing solution has yet been worked out. The plot that Urmson dug over has yielded its share of turnips, but we still await the strawberries.

In the following pages, I want to look closely at Urmson's essay to try to grasp at least some of what it accomplished, to point out some difficulties one would encounter in trying to carry out his recommendations for aesthetic inquiry, and to uncover the source of those difficulties.

Despite its title, the essay concerns not situations but, through most of the text, "reactions and judgments" and, in the summary, "evaluations."[2] Often, especially at the beginning, satisfactions, aesthetic and otherwise, are offered as examples of reactions. Perhaps the essay was to have been entitled "What Makes (e.g.) a Satisfaction Aesthetic?" Urmson's project is to separate aesthetic reactions and judgments from reactions and judgments that are personal, moral, economic, and intellectual (and so on), and so, ultimately, to provide a general idea when it is appropriate to use "aesthetic" as an adjective, for example in characterizing "thrills, satisfactions, toleration, disgust," "delight," "disappointment," "admiration," "appraisal," "evaluation," "appreciation," "consideration," and "purposes" as aesthetic.[3] It seems to me that except for the last item, these all plausibly are or involve evaluations (this accounts for Urmson's use of that term in the summary) and certainly all except the last two are reactions, in the very broad sense that they all come about in a person as a result of that person's coming to have a belief about some present object. But they are not all reactions in the sense that they are emotional or cognitive states resulting from the new belief; satisfactions in particular are not such reactions, as I shall argue below.

First, I will remark briefly on the two items that are clearly not reactions. "Consideration" seems in context to mean something like "the activity of perceiving or setting out to understand an object as an object of kind K," so that aesthetic consideration will be setting out to understand an object as one of the aesthetic kind, and this in its turn is setting out to see how well the object meets specifically aesthetic criteria. The notion of an aesthetic "purpose," the second of the two items, is neither so easy to understand nor so easy to relate to evaluation. Perhaps one has an aesthetic purpose when one's purpose in looking at, reading, listening to, or otherwise taking in an object is to scrutinize the object for those properties that would make it meet one's aesthetic criteria. Urmson uses the phrase "aesthetic purposes" only once, and since it plays no substantial role in the essay, we can leave it aside.

Next, I will try to make a case for my claim that it is a mistake on Urmson's part to treat satisfaction as an emotional or psychological reaction. It is more plausible to treat satisfaction as at bottom a logical state of a person. What I mean by calling satisfaction a logical state is that although satisfaction is constituted by a relation between two psychological states of the person satisfied, it is not itself a psychological state, for the subject is satisfied no matter what feelings he is experiencing. Some psychological state—say, a feeling of well-being—associated with this logical state might also be referred to as satisfaction, but I suggest that it is so referred to because of the logical state, and not so referred to in the absence of the logical state.

The logical state of satisfaction comes in several varieties, which, at first glance, have nothing in common beyond the name. We speak of satisfying wants, desires, and cravings. We speak of satisfying our expectations and suspicions. We speak of satisfying our curiosity. Finally, we speak of satisfying ourselves that such and such is the case. In all these cases, we may speak of our satisfaction, and in some cases characterize it as aesthetic, moral, personal, intellectual, economic, and so on. But it is not the psychological reaction that constitutes the satisfaction. It is instead a relationship between the subject's antecedent psychological state (desire, expectation, suspicion, curiosity, wanting to reach a settled belief) and a true belief that he acquires.

Basic to the satisfaction of the subject in all the cases except satisfying curiosity and satisfying oneself that p is the satisfaction of some antecedent psychological state of the subject. But the satisfaction of the subject's want, desire, craving, expectation, or suspicion does not warrant calling the *subject* satisfied with respect to them. For that, we need also to know that the subject believes that the object satisfying the psychological state is his or that the relevant state of affairs obtains. My *desire* that a favorite lad have a certain income may be satisfied after my death, but that won't satisfy *me*, for I will be cut off (or so I think) from acquiring the pertinent belief.[4] A want (desire, craving) of mine is satisfied if I want (desire, crave) some individual x or any individual of kind K or that p be the case and subsequently I come to have x or a K, or p becomes true. For example, if I want a cup of coffee and get a cup of coffee, my want has been satisfied, no matter how I feel about the matter. My expectation is satisfied if I expect that p and subsequently p becomes true. My suspicion is satisfied if I suspect that p and p is the case.

Satisfying one's curiosity and satisfying oneself that p seem different from the others, in that they involve no underlying satisfaction, of which the person satisfied may have remained ignorant. One's curiosity is not satisfied just in virtue of the existence of some state of affairs not involving oneself, and nothing counts as satisfying oneself that p unless one comes to believe that p. Curiosity can be satisfied in a number of ways, corresponding to the aspects of a situation about which one can be curious: "Who did it?" curiosity is satisfied by arriving at a true belief about who did it; "Where is it?" curiosity is satisfied by arriving at a true belief about where it is; and so on. Satisfying oneself that p seems at first even less allied with the rest than they are among themselves, but it has a deep affinity with the first group of cases (wants, desires, and cravings). The process leading up to satisfying oneself that p seems to be gathering evidence for and against p, or perhaps better, for p and also for some competitors with p, and then deciding that the preponderance of evidence favors p, or perhaps something stronger, such as that p has no plausible competitors given the evidence. The logical state that constitutes this variety of satisfaction that p seems to be a relation between wanting to have a settled belief on a certain topic and having later reached such a belief, so the case is similar to the cases of wanting, desiring, and craving.

In summary, for the first set of cases, what is satisfied in the first instance is some psychological state of the person. The satisfaction of the person follows if the person has a true belief that the satisfier of the psychological state is his (in case it is an individual) or obtains (in case it is a state of affairs). The person is satisfied even if there are no accompanying bodily sensations, or only disagreeable ones. The satisfaction of the person is a *logical* state in that it is constituted by this relation between the person's antecedent psychological state and his relevant acquired belief; the satisfaction is not a further psychological state. For the second set of cases (satisfying one's curiosity and satisfying oneself that something is the case), the subject's satisfaction is even more clearly a logical state of the person constituted by a certain relationship between an antecedent psychological state and a subsequently acquired belief.

If that is the right way to look at the matter, we might naturally go on to suppose that what makes a satisfaction aesthetic is that the want, expectation, suspicion, or other psychological state that got satisfied was itself aesthetic. Such a position appears to be just a special case of Urmson's general principle that a reaction or judgment is aesthetic just in case its explanation (in the case of the reaction) or grounds (in the case of the judgment) are provided by adducing members of that subset of the criteria of value (for the thing being reacted to or judged) that counts as aesthetic. It must be admitted that this principle sounds much better as an explanation of aesthetic *evaluation* than it does as an explanation of aesthetic reactions in general. Perhaps Urmson's underlying view is that all reactions contain an evaluation as one component; thus, in explaining how an evaluation is aesthetic, he would also be explaining how any "reaction" with that evaluative component is aesthetic. It looks as if what gets satisfied in the aesthetic case is always a want or desire, never curiosity or a suspicion or an expectation. Further, what gets satisfied isn't the kind of want involved in satisfying oneself that p. It is a want or desire to experience something satisfying the aesthetic criteria of value. (Such a want was also involved in my earlier guess at what Urmson meant by "aesthetic purposes.")

Thinking of satisfactions in the way I recommend gives us a different way from Urmson's of answering his question whether moral, economic, and aesthetic satisfactions are all species of a single genus.[5] He thinks the question will be settled by answering the subsidiary question whether a single person can be simultaneously the locus of all three sorts of satisfaction with respect to a single object that brings about the satisfaction. His answer to the subsidiary question is yes, since he apparently conceives of "general satisfaction" as a psychological state that may have "a moral and an aesthetic [etc.] component."[6]

The correct subsidiary question to ask, I suggest, is whether a single satisfaction can have all three characters. The locus of these satisfactions is no more relevant than if he had asked instead whether three persons could be in the same room when one of them was morally, another economically, and a third aesthetically satisfied. The answer to my subsidiary question, in light of my thesis that satisfaction is a logical state of a person, seems to be no. For the desire whose satisfaction underlies the person's aesthetic satisfaction is a desire to experience something satisfying criteria of aesthetic value, while the desires or other psychological states that underlie the other satisfactions, whatever those states may be, are presumably not the desire to experience something satisfying criteria of aesthetic value. As a guess, a desire to be economically well-off underlies economic satisfaction, and a desire that events should conform to one's view of what is right underlies moral satisfaction. The distinctness of the desires guarantees the distinctness of the satisfactions. Thus moral, economic, and aesthetic satisfactions are all species of a single genus.

Urmson's first statement of his solution to the problem what makes a satisfaction, reaction, or judgment aesthetic is cast in terms of "appraisals": "I wish to suggest that the moral, the aesthetic, the economic, the intellectual, the religious and other special appraisals should all be understood as being appraisals distinguished by their concentration on some special sub-set of criteria of value." The philosophical aesthetician will first try to discover which subset is the aesthetic one and then "clarify the principles on which we select the special set . . . properly to be counted as relevant to aesthetic judgment."[7] This final part of the task, in the sequel, turns out to be not that of clarifying the *methodological* principles by following which we discovered the aesthetic subset, but that of clarifying the principle underlying the set discovered, that is, finding a reason why these criteria, which as a matter of fact are grouped together by critics, *are* grouped together—a principle of unity for the set. A satisfaction is not an appraisal, of course, especially if "satisfaction" is explained as a logical state in my sense. Nor does every satisfaction involve an appraisal. But satisfactions and appraisals are related in an intelligible way, so that Urmson's claim about appraisals can be applied to the question what makes a satisfaction aesthetic. If a desire is satisfied, then if the subject were to appraise the satisfying object (the object the satisfying belief is about) using the criteria involved in the desire, he would be appraising it aesthetically, morally, personally, and so on, according to whether the criteria were aesthetic, moral, personal, and so on. If I call this hypothetical appraisal "the corresponding appraisal," a satisfaction is aesthetic if and only if the corresponding appraisal is aesthetic according to Urmson's account.

A problematic aspect of the solution that Urmson mentions only in passing, although it is related to his earlier work in "On Grading," is his claim that the criteria of merit we use are "to be formulated in terms of the 'natural' features of things appraised."[8] That claim is not made directly in the earlier essay, but it is very much in the air. Fieldwork among critics will tell us which criteria are aesthetic criteria; but it seems also to tell us that criteria are frequently not formulated in terms of natural features. Which features are natural? The matter is notoriously unclear, but evaluative features like goodness and beauty and any features whose attribution involves an evaluation are excluded. Included are those features that people usually agree on and about which disputes can be more or less conclusively settled, like redness and roundness. When Urmson parodies intuitionism as an account of the use of grading labels, he says "it is not possible to see, hear, smell Extra Fanciness, so it must be a non-natural character."[9] Urmson's examples in "What Makes a Situation Aesthetic?" seem mostly to involve criteria that are not clearly natural. According

Aesthetic Satisfaction 207

to Urmson's reading of A. E. Housman, the poet excoriates as non-aesthetic criteria "the philosophical truth and moral loftiness of the content of the poetry" under discussion, but endorses "the thrilling utterance." Urmson quickly sketches an analysis of this last in apparently natural terms: "the sound, rhythm, and imagery of the words used."[10]

But I question both whether the non-aesthetic criteria can be analyzed into complexes of natural features of the object and whether Urmson's sketch for the aesthetic criteria can be filled in satisfactorily. Even if truth is a natural feature or analyzable in terms of natural features, moral loftiness is just the sort of property that Moore originally intended to class as non-natural when he devised the natural/non-natural distinction. A poem that is morally lofty (ignoring the ironic cast of the phrase) must contain the truth about some important moral subject—a correct claim about the goodness or badness of some central concern of human life; it is implausible that such a truth could be cashed out in terms of natural features. Even if the goodness or badness of (for example) certain kinds of behavior *depends* upon what natural features the behavior has—its effect, continuing the example, upon people's longevity and level of nutrition—its goodness or badness is not to be identified with these features. Thus, though a morally lofty poem contains the truth about something's moral bearing, that truth is not to be identified with the truth about the natural properties upon which the moral bearing depends.[11]

In another of the examples quoted from Housman, Urmson reports as non-aesthetic criteria the powers of a poem "to startle by novelty and amuse by ingenuity," and speaks of "inharmonious" verse as verse that fails to meet an aesthetic criterion.[12] Perhaps the non-aesthetic criterial features here are, or are reducible to, natural features of the verse, since it could be empirically established whether a certain poem did or did not startle or amuse, and perhaps being startled and being amused are natural features or properties reducible to natural features. But that a stretch of verse is harmonious seems not to be a natural feature of it; to say that it is harmonious is already to attribute some value to it, and it was to exclude value properties from the natural that Moore devised the natural/non-natural distinction. Further, it is doubtful whether there is any set of natural features such that harmonious verse and only harmonious verse displays the whole set.

In two other places in the essay, Urmson cites criteria of value that seem intractably non-natural: the first is his statement that "in evaluating great works of art the reasons proximately given will almost inevitably already be at a high level of generality and themselves evaluative—we will refer to masterly style, subtle characterization, inevitability of the action and so on." The second is in a discussion of non-aesthetic criterial features allowed in as aesthetic "by courtesy" when the object being evaluated is a work of art; one such feature is "intellectual merit."[13] The phrase "proximately given" in the first passage hints that further investigation will reveal the natural features whose presence somehow amounts to masterly style and the rest. I suggest, however, that the relation between the natural features and the criteria is not that the features are somehow those cited in the final, careful statement of the criteria, but that the properties cited in the statement emerge from or supervene upon those natural features, and that the real criteria are exactly such properties as having a masterly style. Styles are just not like apples in this respect; accurate but unintelligent grading is not a possibility. Intellectual merit, again, is clearly an evaluative property and so not a natural one. And even if the properties that somehow give a work intellectual merit are themselves natural properties, it is the intellectual merit itself that figures in a partial criterion of aesthetic value (if only by courtesy), and not those natural properties.

Minus its commitment to natural properties as criterial features, Urmson's position becomes this: what makes a reaction or judgment aesthetic is its being grounded upon those features of the object reacted to or judged that meet criteria of aesthetic value (for objects of that sort). For the special case of satisfactions, supposing satisfactions to be logical states of the sort I outlined above, the position is this: a satisfaction is aesthetic if the psychological state satisfied by an acquired belief about some object is a desire, want, or craving to experience those features of an object that meet the criteria of aesthetic value for objects of that sort; and possibly also if the psychological state is an expectation of experiencing those features of an object that meet the criteria of aesthetic value for objects of that sort. There are some obvious and serious problems here, both in the general position and in the more specific one. The most serious one dwells in the phrase "for objects of that sort." Any object belongs to more than one sort; what is crucial in the case of aesthetic satisfaction, reaction, and their fellows is that sort that the judge thinks of the object as a member of. So that calls for an amendment.

A second problem is that a psychological state might be satisfied in part by a belief that the object beheld has property P, and P may in fact (that is, on the judge's system of judging) figure in the criterion of aesthetic value, but P may also figure in the criterion of some other kind of value, and it may be as meeting the latter criterion that it satisfies the desires or expectations of the judge. For example, the judge may detect a certain color harmony in a painting (this is the criterial property) that figures both in her aesthetic criteria and in her criteria for successful interior decoration. If what she wants at the moment is to experience something under the aspect of interior design, and if her want is satisfied by an acquired belief about this painting (the belief that it has the criterial property), then her satisfaction is not aesthetic, but interior-designish. In such a case, the reaction would not be aesthetic. So more needs to be said about the judge's antecedent psychological state. If her reaction is aesthetic, she is not just desiring or expecting that some object possess properties from some list; she is desiring that the object possess properties from the aesthetic list. Her desire or expectation is itself aesthetic, and that is what makes her reaction aesthetic.

What is it to possess properties from the aesthetic list? Urmson suggests that we can find out by doing fieldwork: looking at the writings of critics to see which properties they count as meeting aesthetic criteria and which not. We should not expect to find complete agreement, he says,[14] although we should expect to find very extensive agreement. But he hardly sketches the way in which such fieldwork should go. Do we, for example, go around looking for critics to say things as explicit as "This is an aesthetic criterion, that not"? Evidently not, since the examples he cites are of Housman's talk about "poetical delight" and the distinction between admiring "the poetry of the passage" and "something which they [the admirers] like better than poetry."[15] Urmson has silently extrapolated from a distinction between poetic and non-poetic reactions to one between aesthetic and non-aesthetic reactions. The evident principle involved in the extrapolation is that a reaction to the poetry in a poem is a reaction to the aesthetic side of the poem. We will need a whole array of such principles to extrapolate from the remarks of critics, who seldom explicitly make distinctions between aesthetic and non-aesthetic criteria, to what those same critics think about the distinction. And what will be the ground of those principles? We may guess that when a critic says "This is (or is not) a criterion for the merit of music as music" or "of painting as painting" or "of dance as dance," she means to draw a part of the line that Urmson wants to draw between aesthetic and non-aesthetic criteria. But what is the principle involved? Does it extend to the remarks of a critic of nature who says "This is a criterion for the merit of a sunset as a sunset"? Or of one who says "This is not a criterion for the merit of a building as a building"?

There seems to be a common element in the less controversial principles of extrapolation, namely, those governing such cases as the criteria for poetry as poetry, the criteria for music as music, or the criteria for art as art. The common element is that the substituends for "x" in "x as x" are expressions for the familiar varieties of works of art. These "x as x" locutions seem to depend on the idea that there is an essence of works of art, or of pieces of music, or of painting; "as x" invites one to strip away those features of the work that are irrelevant to its being an x, and the features that are left are essential features, the ones shared by every instance of x. In these cases, at any rate, our fieldwork could lead us to the conclusion that when a critic draws a line between criteria for the merit of some instance of x as x and criteria for the merit of that same thing as a member of some other kind, the critic is drawing part of the line she *would* draw between aesthetic and non-aesthetic criteria. If any criteria are aesthetic, the criteria for the merit of things as products of the commonly recognized arts are. The cases of criteria of merit for a sunset as a sunset or a building as a building would be left over as problem cases, to be settled by some other principle. Unfortunately for this proposal, the idea that art or music or painting has an essence is doubtful, since the items in the extension of "x" vary from age to age in a way that stymies the discovery of common and peculiar properties.

Yet, as Urmson's work presupposes, in critical practice there seems to be a boundary between grounds for a judgment that an object is a good painting (or piece of music or sonnet or performance) and grounds for other judgments of value about the object, for example, its monetary, historical, or curiosity value. Following Urmson's proposal for fieldwork, one could begin by sketching this boundary in terms of characteristic cases falling on both sides of it and then rationalizing the apparently disparate grounds that fall on the painting-music-sonnet-performance side. The general, rationalized grounding thus discovered would merit the label "aesthetic criteria" or "aesthetic grounds for judgments of value," and we would have a principled way of distinguishing judgments of aesthetic value from judgments of other sorts of value, aesthetic from non-aesthetic satisfactions, and so on. But this picture of the task is too hopeful. Against it, I suggest that the boundary in question is somewhat fluid, and that it has been drawn in different places by different surveyors and on grounds that will not yield to rationalization.

The fluidity of the boundary between aesthetic and non-aesthetic grounds or criteria stems from the historical process by which it is drawn. One element in the process is the drawing of boundaries between what is and what is not *art*, a process that also results in a boundary that cannot be rationalized. I will refer to the familiar thesis that art has no essence, that there is no set of properties common and peculiar to all works of art, as the thesis of the anarchy of art. Paul Kristeller[16] has argued persuasively that the idea of grouping the fine arts together, that is, the pursuits we now call the fine arts, and thus also their products, became current only in the early eighteenth century. The idea came with both a rationale and a corpus of art works. The rationale was the imitation theory: that works of art in whatever medium are imitations of nature. That rationale was not adequate to the corpus of art even as it existed at that time, architecture being only the least assimilable case. And as time passed and artists tried new approaches to music, painting, literature, and the rest, it became ever more evident that the rationale was inadequate. New rationales were advanced, but the concurrent changes in art gave the lie to theory after theory. Morris Weitz[17] suggests that attention to the mode of growth of the corpus of art shows that it will continue to defeat theory; the theory of art always involves prediction of the future course of both the arts and the decisions the language community (an ill-defined group, to complicate the problem) will make about what it will call "art," and it is unlikely that any very detailed prediction of those matters will be true. Even if it were true, we would have no strong reason to think it true, and so to accept the theory and let it guide us in our use of "art."

The mode of growth of the corpus of art is roughly this: "art" as a term designating products or performances (and not, for example, the capacity or mental activity of the makers) gets applied to whatever resembles already accepted designata of "art," or some preferred subset of designata; and both the preferred subset and the criterion of resemblance shift from age to age, or within an age from influential critic to influential critic. At the same time, nothing much is done to expel incumbent designata that don't meet the new criterion. If that were done, we might get a stable and coherent corpus, at least for a time. That is, given a clear set of paradigm art works, a clear criterion of resemblance to the paradigms, and the power to exclude from the corpus of art all those objects, no matter how widely counted as art, that were among neither the paradigms nor the objects meeting the criterion, one would get a corpus of art that might yield to a rationalization even deeper than the rationalization that merely cited the paradigms and the criterion: a set of intrinsic properties common and peculiar to all members of the corpus. But such an ideal situation is very remote from the actual one. And so the corpus is various and unrationalizable.

A parallel story can be told for the mode of growth of corpora within the corpus of art: that of music, of painting, of dance, and so on. Each such process only adds to the anarchy of art, since one of the regulative beliefs involved in the growth of art as a whole is that if an object belongs in one of the smaller corpora, it also belongs in the comprehensive one. If, for example, a work is music, it is also art.

Old designata sometimes get expelled from the corpus. Landscape gardening was a fine art for Kant,[18] but not for us. The position of clothing design is currently unclear. It too was a fine art for Kant, but a century later it had been demoted to a merely decorative art, and it is only now perhaps edging back into the corpus, aided by Diana Vreeland's exhibits at New York's Metropolitan Museum (of *Art*). The polemicists who advocate the new preferred subset and criterion of resemblance regularly advocate the expulsion of old designata. But the campaign that succeeds in admitting the new rarely succeeds also in expelling the old. Clive Bell[19] seems to have advocated excluding Raphael's paintings from the company of art, and certainly advocated the exclusion of numerous *"littérateurs* of the brush" (Roger Fry's phrase)[20] whose products still hang in museums of art. Language is too conservative to respond to such advocacy. Perhaps we have much less to lose in admitting new objects into the extension of an old term than in throwing old ones out. Stretching the extension saves us the trouble of adding a term to our vocabulary, and downs the prospect of adding indefinitely many new terms on similar grounds in the future. Purging the extension would involve not only coining or finding a new general term for the items purged (supposing we still wanted to group them together), but also doing (or giving us reasons to do) lots of extralinguistic tasks, like purging the museums and art books and curricula. Instead of going to such trouble, we cheerfully welcome Christo or Kandinsky to the company of artists and allow the product- and image-oriented incumbents to remain seated.

One important relationship between the anarchy of art and the impossibility of rationalizing criteria of aesthetic value is that very often, maybe even always, the criteria of resemblance I have been discussing, which are criteria of admission into the extension of "art," "music," "painting," and so on carry with them criteria of evaluation, however indefinite. Kant, for example, thought that fine art was the presentation of an aesthetical idea.[21] This criterion suggests that good art presents the idea in such a way that an observer of the usual degree of sophistication gets it without too much trouble (for example, without having to use a dictionary of symbols or to investigate the maker's private associations of ideas). Perhaps, together with the rest of what Kant says, it also suggests that good art presents aesthetical ideas that put the "cognitive powers" into a relatively high degree of "free play." Bell and Fry[22] thought that art was significant form, and this suggests that good art (here, most clearly, painting) eschews "narration" or "psychology" and makes its forms distinct and uniquely readable. That is, this view of art's essence suggested this standard of value *to* Bell and Fry. As a final example, and clearest of all, if art is defined in terms of some purpose (as Tolstoy defined it in terms of the communication of feeling),[23] its distinctively aesthetic value will result from its accomplishing that purpose. Tolstoy offered as the criterion of aesthetic value a function (or perhaps just an unreduced binary score) of the goodness of the feeling communicated and the efficiency with which it is communicated. The latter component is a strict consequence of assigning a purpose to art as art.

Thus many campaigns to stretch the extension of art to accommodate new members (or in Tolstoy's case, to draw new lines between centrally important art and peripheral art) bring with them, however loosely, criteria of evaluation that fit the new members and the preferred subset of the old extension well. That is, on the new criteria, the new members and the members of the preferred subset turn out to be good art. Some of the old members come out bad on the new criteria of evaluation, and some turn out not even to be works of art, so that the new criteria don't properly apply to them. This last situation arises especially clearly in cases in which the new requirement for admission is suggested to its advocate by a single art, like painting, but is supposed by him somehow to fit all the arts. Bell, for example, came by his notion that art is significant form from his experience with plastic art. Fry accepted this notion, in a somewhat modified form, but attempted to apply it also to literature. If the essence of literature (or literature as art) is significant form, the valuable aspect of a work of literature must be its shape (in some sense), not (for example) the lesson it imparts or its capacity to entertain the reader (except as the reader is entertained by shapes). Here is Fry on the present topic:

M. [Charles] Mauron suggests that we should, for literature, transpose the idea of volumes from the domain of space to the domain of spirit and conceive the literary artist as creating "psychological volumes." . . . It may be no more than an analogy, but it enables us for the first time dimly to grasp what it is of which the relations are felt by us when we apprehend aesthetically a work of literature.[24]

The ordinary reader (who, in the mass, owns the language and so determines what shall be art) doesn't have to accept Bell and Fry's theory along with their candidates for admission to the corpus of art, and so is not stuck with the unfamiliar task of judging literature by its plastic volumes. He can cheerfully admit Bell's protégés into the extension of "art" but keep literature, conceived otherwise than Bell and Fry conceive it, in the extension as well; and he can judge the new painting by Bell and Fry's criterion and literature by whatever he is accustomed to judging it by. The ordinary reader is not inconsistent in this, for the ties between essence and value are usually less than logical (except when essence includes function). Even in cases in which the ties are logical, the reader is inconsistent only under the assumption that Bell and Fry's *general* theory of art is correct, and that is not an assumption he must make. He can read Bell and Fry as Weitz and W. E. Kennick do,[25] not as seriously advancing a philosophical thesis about art, but as advocating a certain kind of art and telling us what is valuable about it. Of course, such a reading is more plausible for Bell and Fry than it is for Kant or Hegel, but it is possible even for them. We ordinary readers can take them to be pointing out that we can consider in a certain light some of what already counts as art, and that this consideration reveals or at least highlights something valuable about it that we may have missed before; and further that some new objects or performances, looked at in this same light, have these same valuable characteristics, so that they, too, should count as art. Any more general theses advanced by art theorists we can interpret as hyperbole intended to make more compelling what they are pointing out.

Just as old designata of "art" accumulate, unrationalized by the currently held views of the essence of art or current enthusiasms for this or that kind of art, so the values—the properties employed as criteria of merit—that people formerly found in art accumulate, fitting badly or not at all with the values attending current views and enthusiasms. It is true that values tend to languish and die more easily than the designata, the artifacts, just because the artifacts physically exist, while the values depend upon people's systems of belief and desire for their existence. But consistency tends to be a virtue of the enthusiast rather than the ordinary consumer or even the connoisseur. Strict adherence to a definition of art and its consequences for criteria of aesthetic merit is rare. An exactly similar argument can be constructed concerning the definitions of music, dance, pure painting, and the other arts and their consequences for criteria of musical, terpsichorean, and painterly merit.

Where does this historical process leave the philosophical aesthetician who wants to "clarify the principles" according to which certain criteria of merit count as *aesthetic* criteria? One sort of generalization that one might make about aesthetic criteria follows from a claim about a sufficient condition for being part of a criterion of value for things of any sort at all: if a property is to be found only in objects of some kind K, then thinking an object valuable for having that property is (part of) thinking it valuable as a K. The consequence for the case of aesthetic criteria in art is that thinking an object valuable for having a property found only in art (or some subclass, such as music or literature) is thinking it valuable as art (or as music or literature), and that in turn is thinking it valuable on aesthetic grounds.

I would like to suggest also the plausibility of a weakened version of the generalization, namely, that if a property is best sought in objects of some kind K, then thinking an object valuable for having that property is (part of) thinking it valuable as a K. There are several situations that might result in a property's being best sought in a certain range of objects. The simplest situation is that in which those objects are the sole locus of the property; this case gives us the original criterion. Another is that in which those objects are the most *frequent* substrate of the properties. Monroe Beardsley, for example, counted perceptual unity as a criterion of aesthetic merit even though he conceded that this sort of unity was to be found in many non-art objects. He might have argued along the lines I am suggesting here that although perceptual unity is to be found elsewhere, it is found much more frequently in art. A third situation is that in which, even though the property is to be found elsewhere than in objects of kind K, it is easier to find it in K objects; it is somehow more accessible in them. Again, Beardsley might have argued that although perceptual unity is a property of most objects and events, it is easier to behold in works of art (probably because in most cases their makers were aiming at a product that would strike a beholder as perceptually unified).

The statement that some property is best sought in objects of kind K is a statement about the *kind*, not about the individual members of it, since some of the members may be found wanting. Beauty of melody, for example, is best sought in music, but don't listen for it in the "Ionisation" of Edgard Varèse. Since the statement is about the kind (musical composition, sonnet, basilica, and so on), it is a characteristic of the kind that it is a good source for the property. Thus, when we consider an individual as a member of the kind, we are considering it as, among other things, a thing likely to be a good source for the property; and thinking it valuable for having that property (if it turns out to have it) is part of thinking it valuable as a member of the kind. If the kind in question is art or music or the villanelle (or their numerous fellows), a valued property may figure in a criterion of aesthetic merit without being found exclusively in the products of one or other of the arts, or in all art.

But, although these generalizations may cover most of the properties we employ in criteria of aesthetic merit, they do not cover them all. The real explanation of why certain properties count as aesthetic criteria is both more powerful and less rational than either of my two generalizations: they are aesthetic criteria because they are among the valued properties that many people look for in works of art when they are treating the works according to established traditions for treating them as works of art. At some points in the history of our continuing effort to understand our reactions to art, there were compelling recommendations for attending, for example, to those properties nominated by Beardsley as the most general criteria of merit in art: the unity, intensity, and complexity of works of art.[26] So they became aesthetic criteria. Now, though the reasons may have evaporated, the slightly powdery criteria remain. One can guess where they came from. Unity and complexity are the residue of the eighteenth century's attempt to analyze *beauty*, which for Frances Hutcheson was unity amidst variety.[27] This guess is perhaps partly confirmed by a look at what Beardsley says about complexity: it is not complexity per se that is valuable, but complexity organized, brought into a unity. The value of emotional intensity is a residue of romanticism.

Beardsley claims to have arrived at his trio of highest values by doing exactly the sort of fieldwork recommended by Urmson: looking at actual critical remarks, weeding the lot a bit, and then discovering that the remaining ones all fit into one or another of the three categories. If that was his procedure, it is no wonder that he came up with the residue of the history of aesthetics, for he would have been generalizing over the practice of critics of all philosophical convictions (except hard-core "intentionalists") and some critics of no convictions at all.

Thus I agree with Urmson that fieldwork will clearly identify some criteria of value as criteria of aesthetic value, and that this identification will identify some satisfactions and reactions as aesthetic satisfactions and reactions. But outside the safe area, where criterial properties are singled out as contributing to the value of art as art, painting as painting, and so on, fieldwork will yield less clear results, except in the rare cases in which evaluators are willing to characterize their grounds explicitly as aesthetic or non-aesthetic. Thus the aesthetician's subsequent attempt to discover principles governing the fieldwork data will be frustrated. Lack of clarity about which particular criteria of value are aesthetic criteria will be reflected in an inability to generalize about aesthetic criteria.

I earlier put aside the case of aesthetic criteria in the evaluation of natural objects, with no intention of returning to it for serious discussion. It has often been suggested that aesthetic criteria for natural objects are adapted from those for works of art. Perhaps, for example, we appreciate the beauty of a vista because we have learned previously to appreciate the beauty of paintings of vistas. I think this is probably so for very many of our judgments concerning natural beauty, and if it is, a serious attempt to separate aesthetic from non-aesthetic criteria in the evaluation of natural objects will turn up a situation just as anarchical and indeterminate as the one in judging art.

PETER KIVY

Live Performances and Dead Composers: On the Ethics of Musical Interpretation

> If Bach were alive today, he would be rolling over in his grave.
> *Anonymous*

Early in his well-known and influential book *Aesthetics: Problems in the Philosophy of Criticism*, Monroe Beardsley reaches the conclusion that "intention . . . does not play any role in decisions about how scores . . . are to be performed."[1] And to the familiar belief that a primary function of the musical performer "consists in determining how the composer intended the music to sound . . . and then realizing that intention," Beardsley replies: "No doubt some performers operate upon this principle, but it can easily be shown that most of them do not."[2] It appears to me that this is false: that composers' intentions *do* play a substantial role in decisions about how scores are to be performed; that *most* performers, as well as musical scholars, *do* operate upon the principle of determining and being governed by the intentions of composers, although they labor under the expected quantity of self-deception about which intentions are the composers' and which their own. I propose to argue this case in what follows. In the first section of my paper I will counter what I take to be two distinct arguments that lead Beardsley to his conclusion about composers' intentions. In the second section, having urged that, Beardsley's arguments to the contrary notwithstanding, considerations of composers' intentions *do* play a major role in performers' realizations of scores, and, as a matter of fact, weigh very heavily in their decisions regarding them, I shall argue that there are rational grounds for this: that is to say, that intentions not only *do* play a major role but *ought to*. First, then, to Beardsley's arguments.

Beardsley's first main objection to composers' intentions as a criterion of correct or optimal performance—a special case of a more general argument advanced in his earlier article with W. K. Wimsatt—is that the composer's intentions are, for the most part, inaccessible to us and, therefore, *cannot* figure in the performer's decision procedures. He writes: "Since [the performer] must choose among possibilities left open by the score, the criterion he uses must be something besides intention, or in most music he would never be able to decide upon a way of performing it at all."[3] The claim seems to be something like this. Most of the decisions a performer must make regard just those places in the score where the composer has not made his intentions clear. Bach marked the third number of the *Magnificat in D* "adagio," and it is fair to assume that that is the tempo at which he intended it to be performed. But except for this and one other place, the work is (as is usual with Bach) completely devoid of tempo markings. The rest of the tempi, Beardsley would conclude, cannot, therefore, be determined on the basis of what Bach *intended*, for Bach did not make his intentions known in the score. Scores contain some such indications of composers' intentions, but not very many; and the performer's real work starts just where these few indications of intention leave off.

To this the performer and musical scholar would most likely reply that Beardsley has unduly restricted the sources of our knowledge of composers' intentions—particularly with regard to what Leonard Meyer has called the "secondary parameters"—to just those *direct* indications that are most obvious: tempo markings, phrasing, dynamics, and the few other directions such as "espressivo," "marcato," and the like, that occur with increasing frequency in scores of the nineteenth and twentieth centuries, and only rarely before that. But that hardly scratches the surface of our sources of knowledge of these secondary parameters and much else that is relevant to the intentions of composers. We possess now a vast and growing knowledge of the historical background, performance practice, and musical instruments of earlier periods, all of which together gives us a far wider and more substantial, albeit indirect, inferential knowledge of the composer's intentions than the obvious indications that Beardsley seems to suggest exhaust the possibilities. As an authority on the performance of "early" music has recently put the point:

The best performance of, say, a motet by Ockeghem, is only a representation of what someone, the director or the singers, thinks Ockeghem meant [i.e., intended], but any information that we have about how Ockeghem and his contemporaries sang, or in the case of later instrumental music, what the instruments were like and how they were played, cannot but help to make that representation clearer. To my mind this presents the performer with an absolute injunction to try to find out all that can be known about the performance traditions and the sound-world of any piece that is to be performed, and to try to duplicate these as faithfully as possible.⁴

Needless to say, Beardsley is not unaware of the historical research of the last hundred years or more on the performance practice of early music. But he insists that this does *not* constitute a revelation of composers' intentions.

To restore Bach's cantatas to the way they were heard when his singers and players performed them . . . we must investigate the techniques of performance, vocal and instrumental, that were used in his day. But in conducting these investigations, we are not seeking for the intentions . . . of Bach. We are asking what the music sounded like at a particular time, not what sounds the composer heard in his own mind. . . . [T]he customs of baroque performance were public conventions, historically discoverable, at least in principle; they did not depend upon the intentions of a particular individual.⁵

A number of points can be teased out of this passage, none, I think, conclusive against the relevance of the composer's intentions.

First, the performer and musicologist might well agree with Beardsley that one of the things we want to know, when we conduct research into the performance of Bach's cantatas, is how the music sounded in Bach's day. But how does this preclude the desire also to know Bach's intentions? And surely *one* of the ways we can find out how Bach intended his music to sound is to find out how in fact it sounded. We can reasonably, though not of course infallibly, infer how Bach intended the instrumental obbligato of the third number of the *Magnificat in D* to sound by finding out how the two- and three-keyed oboe d'amore of Bach's day sounded. Why we should perform it the way Bach intended is of course another question; and I shall get to that in the following section. But why we should perform it the way it sounded in Bach's day is also another question. And it is no more obvious that we should make a piece of music sound as it would have sounded in the composer's lifetime than that we should make it sound the way the composer intended, when there is a divergence, as sometimes there of course is. (Berlioz complained that most European orchestras of his day played out of tune: that is obviously not the way he intended his music to be played.)

Second, Beardsley seems to think that to know what the composer intended, we must know what sounds the composer heard in his head, and that in doing historical research "we are asking what the music sounded like at a particular time, not what sounds the composer heard in his own mind." Beardsley is correct in believing that there is a connection between finding out what sounds the composer heard in his head and what sounds he intended to be heard. But again, I do not see how the desire to know "what the music sounded like at a particular time" precludes the desire to know "what the composer heard in his own mind." Indeed, as before, the one is a means to the other. If a composer hears a piece of keyboard music in his head in E major, what he hears will be different if the keyboard instruments he is used to are given a mean-tone rather than a well-tempered tuning; and we are helping ourselves to know, therefore, what sounds the composer heard in his head when we do historical research into the tuning of keyboard instruments of the seventeenth century. Likewise, the oboe sound Bach heard in his head was doubtless the oboe sound of the instruments he customarily heard. So if we want to know what Bach heard in his head when he composed and orchestrated the third number of the *Magnificat in D*, we had better know what the two- and three-keyed oboe d'amore of Bach's time sounded like. Of course a composer may have an "ideal" sound in his head that exceeds the capabilities of the instruments of his day in certain respects; and that is what encourages instrument makers to improve their products. No doubt Bach would have preferred better intonation from his oboes than he got. But in general, the orchestral sounds Bach heard in his head were those of the instruments he heard in his world. So, clearly, when we do research into the way the instruments of Bach's orchestra sounded, we are, at the same time, doing research into the way music sounded in Bach's head; and, to generalize from the special case, when we "ask what music sounded like at a particular time," we are, ipso facto, asking what the composers of that time heard in their heads.

Finally, Beardsley here, as in "The Intentional Fallacy" and elsewhere, seems much concerned about the "privacy" of intentions, for he contrasts them unfavorably with the public, "discoverable" nature of past performance practice, which, he insists, "did not depend upon the intentions of a particular individual." But for a third time Beardsley seems to be representing as incompatibles things that are quite comfortable with one another. There is nothing necessarily private about an intention: we can, after all, make our intentions known. And the public conventions of baroque performance practice *are* the products of individual intentions of composers, performers, and audiences. Of course baroque performance practice is not just the product of J. S. Bach. Nor, however, are Bach's intentions unconnected with the conventions of baroque performance practice. Bach acquiesced in a great deal of the performance practice of his day. Indeed, he made a substantial contribution to it; it was in fact part of his artistic life's blood. He did not acquiesce in *all* of it, and he did not leave it unchanged. But taken as a whole, it is part of the public documentation of Bach's intentions, just as what I write in this paper, and where I publish it, are public documentation of mine. And just as one can make reasonable, if not infallible, inferences about my intentions by reading this paper, one can make reasonable, if not infallible, inferences about Bach's intentions by examining the historical artifacts of his day, both the written ones and the others. Intentions are revealed amply by what the intenders leave behind.

The second main objection that Beardsley makes to the relevance of composers' intentions is that we frequently decide *first* how the music is to be performed, and then infer the composer's intentions from *that*. Thus, for instance, in deciding where the accents should be placed in the scherzo of Beethoven's Fifth Symphony, Beardsley writes, "There can be no appeal to Beethoven; the conductor is after the intensification of some quality, a blend of playfulness and sinisterness, which it seems to him is best brought out in one way or the other." His conclusion from this and other instances is that "we don't decide what should be done after deciding what Beethoven wished, but the other way around."[6] That is to say, first we decide what the best or right or proper way is to perform a piece, on internal, musical grounds, and then we infer that *that* is what the composer's intention was.

Now as a matter of actual practice, performers do often, at least when they can, determine the composer's intentions about how a piece is to be played, and then comply with them. Often, that is to say, we go *from* intentions *to* performance. But Beardsley is quite right that often—perhaps more often—things go the other way around. We may then ask, in the latter kind of case, what role the composer's intentions play in the process. The obvious answer is none at all. But I am not sure the obvious answer is correct.

Anyone who, as either an amateur or professional, has taken an active part in a practical discussion of how a passage is to be rendered, will recall the following kind of comment's being made: "At measure 49 you must bring out the triplet figure in the bass so that it can be recognized as an echo of the main theme. If you don't, the movement just won't hang together. Surely Beethoven must have intended the triplet figure to be played forte, and the right hand somewhat subdued." What I am trying to suggest is that performers generally operate on some kind of principle of "charity" to the effect that the best way is the intended way. But the question is, What finally determines how the music is to be played: that it is the best way or that it is the composer's way? Such comments as the one just fabricated at least *suggest*—although I admit that is *all* they do—that it is the latter. If it were not, then the reference to Beethoven's intentions would be superfluous.

A test case would, of course, be a case in which the composer's intentions and the best way to play the piece diverged. In such a case, what would be decisive, the best way or the composer's way? Common sense would say, perhaps, the best way. But the answer is not so clear. To begin with, performers and musicologists have an almost unconquerable aversion to admitting that the best way could possibly not be the composer's way. No one performs Beethoven's symphonies at the tempi that *Beethoven's* own metronome markings indicate, because they are impossibly bad tempi. But no one is likely to admit, without a fight, that those really are the tempi Beethoven intended—some explanation is always invented of how the markings got fouled up. Thus it is hard to get a real case where "best" and "intended" are believed by musicians to diverge. All we can do is conjecture. But anyone who knows the way performers and musical scholars talk and behave will not find my own conjecture beyond belief: it is that the composer's way would more often than not win out; and even if it did not, it would nevertheless not be easily overridden.

To sum up, it seems to me that nothing Beardsley has said, in arguing against the claim that composers' intentions play a major role in decisions about how music is to be performed, has really dislodged the claim. Further, it seems a palpable fact that composers' intentions weigh heavily—perhaps even are decisive—in such decisions. The question I want now to ask is *what* justification, if any, there really is for this.

Let me begin with some distinctions, made recently by Randall R. Dipert, which I want to adopt. There are, Dipert points out, at least three kinds of intention that a composer might have. "His intentions concerning means of production of sound will be termed *low-level intentions*, which include the type of instrument, fingering, etc. *Middle-level intentions* are those that concern the intended *sound*, such as temperament, timbre, attack, pitch, and vibrato." Finally, we have "*high-level intentions*, which are the effects the composer intends to produce in the listener."[7]

Now as Dipert makes clear, it may well be impossible to realize *all* of a composer's intentions in any one performance, simply because his low-level, middle-level, and high-level intentions may have been, or may have become, incompatible. In such cases we will have to decide which of his intentions we are most anxious to realize; and, presumably, high-level intentions take precedence. Thus, Bach's low-level intention, in the third number of the *Magnificat in D*, was to have the instrumental obbligato played on the oboe d'amore of his day, to achieve a certain tone quality (middle-level intention) that, in turn, would have a certain expressive effect on his audience (high-level intention). But *that* tone quality and, hence, the effect Bach wanted, *might* be better achieved today, given the conditions of modern musical performance, by the modern French oboe d'amore, rather than the two- or three-keyed instrument of Bach's day. That being the case, we cannot serve Bach's middle- and high-level intentions most fully without going against his low-level ones. So when, from now on, I talk about the justification for taking intentions of the composer as decisive or powerful considerations in regard to manner of performance, this complication of the notion of composers' intentions, and its implications, should be borne in mind. They are assumed throughout.

It might also be well here to distinguish between a *strong* and a *weak* sense of what a composer does *not* intend, to be borne in mind in what follows. In the strong sense, Bach did *not* intend the instrumental obbligato in the third number of the *Magnificat in D* to be played on the flute or violin of his day; and in the weak sense, he did *not* intend it to be played on the modern French oboe d'amore. Perhaps we could make this clearer by saying that Bach intended the obbligato *not* to be played on the flute or violin of his day, but on the oboe d'amore; whereas he did not intend the obbligato to be played on the modern French oboe d'amore. I would call the former the *strong* sense and the latter the *weak* one, because Bach chose between the flute, violin, and oboe d'amore of his day, and rejected all but the oboe d'amore; whereas he was, of course, in no position to choose between the oboe d'amore of his own day and the modern French instrument. Bach positively did *not* want his obbligato played on the flute or violin; simply by default he did not intend it to be played on the modern French oboe d'amore. This complication, too, will be assumed wherever there is talk about what composers have and (especially) have *not* intended.

Dipert suggests that there are three possible answers to "the question of why we should want to play a piece the way a composer intended it to be played."

The first asserts that we have a moral obligation to the composer to play his music according to his intentions. The second holds that music, like other artifacts of a time and place, embodies the *Zeitgeist* of that period, and to understand the period properly, the historical artifact (in this case, a performance) must be correctly reconstructed. The third answer—and the one to which I am most sympathetic—claims *generally speaking* that we are likely to perform a piece of greater artistic merit if we follow the composer's intentions than if we do not.[8]

I shall have nothing to say here about the urge for historical accuracy per se; historical accuracy as an intrinsic value will appeal to few. The more compelling argument among performers, musicologists, and concert-goers alike is that historical accuracy, if a value at all, is an instrumental value merely, an avenue to the best performance of the music. Nor will I have anything to say about the argument that realizing the composer's intentions will usually result in a better performance. I too, like Dipert, am very sympathetic with this claim, and I believe it provides *one* very compelling reason for honoring the composer's intentions. Anyone who has ever heard Handel's oratorios or the *Mass in B Minor* performed something like the way they were intended to be will never again wish to hear them performed with booming contraltos, pious tempi, a choir of trombones, and a cast of thousands. But this defense, clearly, does not recognize composers' intentions as *decisive*. They are only sought for the purpose of gaining an optimal performance, on the assumption that, generally speaking, music sounds better when played the way the composer intended it to be. And if some piece sounded better performed in a way not intended by the composer, either in the weak or the strong sense, that would be decisive against the intention.[9] But, as I have said, I think there is a strong urge on the part of musicians to honor composers' intentions per se, an urge so strong that they will often, if not always, honor them over all considerations of musical aesthetics. And the conventionalist sulk, common among musicians, to the effect that "It can't be the composer's intention, because the other way sounds better," only reinforces the impression that there is an almost unconquerable urge to bring performance into compliance with intention, if not at the expense of aesthetics, then at the expense of logic. There is an almost missionary zeal here, something that can only be described as a moral imperative; and that, as well as the process of elimination, points of course to the only alternative left: a defense of honoring the composer's intentions on moral grounds. That, indeed, is the defense I want to give.

My model for this defense will be the familiar one of morals as, at least in part, a system of (perhaps conflicting) duties and obligations. I shall say, then, that along with such obvious duties as telling the truth, keeping promises, not causing unnecessary pain, and so on, we have an obligation to honor when possible the wishes and intentions of the dead, a special case of this last being the obligation to honor the performing intentions of dead composers.[10] We can think of the composer's score, in this regard, much as the dying words or written will of the deceased. That this is not such a bizarre suggestion can be seen from, among other things, the fact that we often refer to the body of a composer's work as his musical or artistic "testament." Just as we feel a strong obligation to honor the wishes of the dead, even when prudence and convenience recommend that we ignore them, and are quite convinced that the dead are beyond feeling the pain of disappointment that thwarted wishes and desires cause to the living, so we feel a strong obligation to honor the dead composer's intentions as to how his music is to be performed, whether indicated directly in his score or indirectly in some other way, even when musical prudence, in the form of a better way to perform it, might beckon us. At considerable expense and inconvenience to herself, a confirmed atheist, with no belief whatever in an afterlife or the immortality of the soul, will travel from Peking to Peoria with the corpse of a loved one to grant a dying request. And for what *other* reason than a strong moral commitment to honoring the wishes of the dead? It is no more surprising, I submit, that the same commitment might cause us to make a far less painful and costly sacrifice of an aesthetic kind to honor a composer's wish that his piece be played adagio, when a slightly quicker pace sounds right to us.

But at this point a serious objection to my argument is likely to be registered. Granted, it will be argued, that many (or perhaps most) of us do feel strong obligations to honor the wishes of the dead, this by no means implies that such obligations in fact exist. The belief that such obligations exist may, indeed, provide a psychological explanation of why the lady from Peking took all that trouble to get a corpse to Peoria, why a performer feels such reverence toward a composer's intentions that he might perform a piece adagio even though he really thinks it goes better a little bit on the andante side, or why I feel such outrage when one of the *Leonore* overtures is stuck in between the last two scenes of *Fidelio*, no matter how grand and moving it is. If, however, there is no justification for these moral beliefs, then the thing to do is not to continue to be governed by them, at considerable trouble to ourselves and to others; rather, we must give them up as basically misguided—relics of a superstitious belief that the dead watch over us. And, surely, the argument continues, there *is* no justification for them: we have no obligations to the dead, but only to the living (and perhaps to those who will be the living at some time in the future). In dismissing the moral defense for honoring dead composers' performing intentions pretty much out of hand, Dipert indeed relies heavily on what might appear to be the out-and-out absurdity of thinking that we can have very much of a duty, if any at all, to the dead, and refers us, in passing, to a passage in Aristotle.[11] It would be instructive here, as always, to see what he has to say.

In *Nicomachean Ethics* I.11, Aristotle writes: "That the fortunes of his descendants and of all those near and dear to him do not affect the happiness of a dead man at all, seems too unfeeling a view and contrary to the prevailing opinion." But he concludes that

> if any good or evil reaches them at all, it must be something weak and negligible . . . , or at least something too small and insignificant to make the unhappy happy or to deprive the happy of their bliss. The good as well as the bad fortunes of their friends seem, then, to have some effect upon the dead, but the nature and magnitude of the effect is such as not to make the happy unhappy or to produce any similar changes.[12]

Aristotle does not draw the expected moral conclusion from this, and for good reason, as we shall see in a moment; but surely we can do it for him. If the effects of our actions on the dead are vanishingly small, then so must be our duties and obligations to them. And if, as I and many others believe, our actions have no effect at all on the dead, who are beyond happiness or unhappiness, then how can we have any duties or obligations *at all* to them? How can good or evil reach them at all, if they can *experience* neither? I have duties to the living because they are in a position to experience the results of my moral observances and omissions. But what can be the moral or immoral cash value of a broken promise to the dead? What inconvenience can it cause? What disappointment arouse? Surely, just as the dead are beyond thinking and feeling, perception and pain, happiness and unhappiness, they are beyond wickedness as well.

As persuasive as this argument might seem, readers of the essay "Death," by Thomas Nagel, will have what seems to me to be an even more persuasive reply. For consider the assumption on which the argument is based. That we have no duties to the dead, because they cannot experience the results of our actions toward them, is simply a special case of the precept that "what you don't know can't hurt you." But think of what this means.

It means that even if a man is betrayed by his friends, ridiculed behind his back, and despised by people who treat him politely to his face, none of it can be counted as a misfortune for him so long as he does not suffer as a result. It means that a man is not injured if his wishes are ignored by the executor of his will, or if, after his death, the belief becomes current that all the literary works on which his fame rests were written by his brother, who died in Mexico at the age of 28.[13]

Or, we might add, if his oratorios are reorchestrated by every well-meaning composer and conductor entrusted with their performance.

But this cannot be right. Nor did Aristotle believe that it was, which is precisely why he did not draw the moral conclusion one might have expected him to draw from the passage in the *Nicomachean Ethics* quoted above. For in the preceding chapter, in fact, he had already expressed the view that "to some extent good and evil really exist for a dead man, just as they may exist for a man who lives without being conscious of them, for example, honors and disgraces, and generally the successes and failures of his children and descendants."[14] And that perhaps explains why, as Leibniz put it, "in man there is a certain concern for dignity and propriety which . . . leads us to look after our reputations, even beyond the point where this serves our needs and beyond the end of life."[15]

It is an injury to a man, then, to betray him, even if he never knows, and hence never experiences the pain of betrayal or its discovery. And it does not matter whether the betrayal is never known because his friends keep the secret during his lifetime, or because it is committed after his death. To quote Nagel again: "Someone who holds that all goods and evils must be temporarily assignable states of the person may of course try to bring difficult cases into line by pointing to the pleasure or pain that more complicated goods and evils cause. Loss, betrayal, deception, and ridicule are on this view bad because people suffer when they learn of them." But, Nagel points out, "the natural view is that the discovery of betrayal makes us unhappy because it is bad to be betrayed—not that betrayal is bad because its discovery makes us unhappy." Further, and much to the present purpose, "if this is correct, there is a simple account of what is wrong with breaking a deathbed promise. It is an injury to the dead man."[16] That the reason a man does not know, or therefore suffer, from the breaking of a promise to him is that he is *dead* is irrelevant. The broken promise is an injury to a living man, irrespective of his finding out or not. The inability of a dead man to know or suffer from the breaking of a promise cannot, therefore, make it benign. And if we can injure the dead, then we surely have the obligation to refrain from doing so when we can.

That the concept of obligation to the dead may still seem paradoxical, in spite of these considerations, is only to be expected; and perhaps the most paradoxical part of all arises from the difficulty in identifying just *who* it is we owe the obligation to, and *who* will be harmed by its nonfulfillment. For death is not just another state or condition that a person finds himself or herself in: it is no condition at all. Death is the total annihilation of the subject; no "person" remains after death for us to harm or have obligations to.

One way, perhaps, to get around this metaphysical problem of the lack of a subject, suggested by Joel Feinberg, "is to think of all harm done to men and women as convenient elliptical references to, and identification of, the interest that was thwarted or set back." Adopting this notion of harm: "Although *he* [the dead person] no longer exists, we can refer to his earlier goals (as a matter of identification) as *his* interests, and *they* were the interests directly harmed by his death," and, more relevantly, the interests that remain to be harmed or forwarded after his death by those who survive him. And so: "When death [or an event after death] thwarts an interest, the interest is harmed, and the harm can be ascribed to the man who is no more, just as his debts can be charged to his estate."[17]

Of course, not *all* of a person's interests survive his or her demise. "The interests that die with a person are those that can no longer be helped or harmed by posthumous events. These include most of his self-regarding interests, those based, for example, on desires for personal achievement and personal enjoyment." But Feinberg continues: "Because the objects of a person's interests are usually wanted or aimed-at events that occur outside of his immediate experience and at some future time, the area of a person's good or harm is necessarily wider than his subjective experience and his biological life." It is clear, then, that although some of a person's interests perish with that person, others endure. "These include his publicly oriented and other-regarding interests, and also those 'self-centered' interests in being thought of in a certain way. Posthumous harm occurs when the deceased's interest is thwarted at a time subsequent to his death." And Feinberg concludes, as do Aristotle, Nagel, and, I think, common moral sensibility, that for posthumous harm to a person's interests to occur, "the awareness of the subject is no more necessary than it is for harm to occur to certain of his interests at or before death."[18] It cannot, then, be an argument against the moral defense of honoring the dead composer's performance intentions that we cannot have obligations to the dead because the dead cannot suffer or rejoice, are, in fact, beyond all experience whatever. Thus, it seems to me, the most serious objection to the belief that we have an at least prima facie obligation to honor the dead composer's performance intentions is defeated.

But showing that we can and *do* have obligations to dead people does not, ipso facto, show that we have obligations to honor the intentions of dead composers concerning the way their works are to be performed. Perhaps we just don't in fact have such obligations to composers, for reasons other than that the composers are dead. I do not have the time here to canvass this proposal fully. I will conclude my defense, however, by briefly considering two further arguments by Dipert, each of which, I take it, is meant to be a reductio ad absurdum of the claim that we have duties or obligations to honor the intentions of dead composers. They are as follows. First, "there are many composers whose music we rarely or never play. Certainly they had intentions to have their music performed . . . , intentions which we guiltlessly ignore." And second, "there are intentions of even great composers which we have disobeyed, or would disobey if we could; for example, composers' often-expressed wishes to have scores destroyed."[19]

Now the answer to both of these supposed reductios is the same; and it is, in fact, the same answer one would give to the objection that we cannot have a prima facie obligation to tell the truth, since we would then have to tell Simon Legree that Eliza is hiding in the attic. The well-known answer is that duties can be overridden by other and stronger ones; but this does not show, even at the time they are overridden, that they are not real obligations. Let us look, in turn, at our obligation to perform the works of Johann Stamitz, as well as those of Joseph Haydn, and at our predecessors' obligations, if the respective stories are true, to destroy the manuscripts of Virgil's *Aeneid* and Mendelssohn's *Italian Symphony*. Johann Stamitz labored long and hard at the practice of musical composition. Were it not for his pioneering efforts toward the development of what we now think of as the classical style, Haydn could not have done all of the things that *he* did that we justly revere above the works of Stamitz the elder. Surely we *do* owe it to Stamitz to give his music a hearing from time to time, and we do the man an injury by ignoring him. There is nothing whatever absurd in the suggestion, as Dipert seems to think. But *of course* we are not obliged to perform his music as frequently as Haydn's, any more than we are obliged to spend as much time and money finding a cure for the common cold as on cancer research. A half hour of Stamitz is pleasurable and enlightening; three hours is a mind-deadening experience. On purely utilitarian grounds, if for no other reason, our obligation to Stamitz's intention to have his music played is overridden—but it exists as a real obligation nonetheless.

As for the alleged intentions of Virgil and Mendelssohn that the manuscripts of the *Aeneid* and the *Italian Symphony* be destroyed, our ancestors had an obligation to both of them to comply, as would anyone receiving a deathbed declaration concerning the disposition of the testator's property. But they had another obligation as well to refrain from injuring *us*, their posterity, by depriving us of those wonderful works, and to refrain from injuring Virgil and Mendelssohn by diminishing their reputations in ill-considered and irrevocable acts of vandalism. In short, the obligation to honor the intentions of dead composers is *defeasible*. But that should not be very surprising. So is the Sixth Commandment. I do not suggest, by claiming that we have an obligation to honor the performance intentions of dead composers, that we must honor them come what may. Handel intended many of the parts of his operas to be sung by castrated men, and they will never sound the way they should without the castrati. We quite rightly ignore Handel's intentions on moral grounds. Beethoven *apparently* intended his symphonies to go at "strange" tempi. There is some dispute about what Beethoven's metronome markings really mean—the device was, after all, in the early stages of its development. But if indeed it turns out that the numbers don't lie, and if those tempi really deprive us of truly enjoyable and musically satisfactory performances, then Beethoven's intentions are defeated on moral as well as on aesthetic grounds: on aesthetic grounds because the musical price we must pay to honor his intentions is too high; on moral grounds for the obvious reason that we owe *some* consideration, at least, to the maximization of musical pleasure in the auditors of these works.

Now it may seem to some that, in claiming our obligations to the intentions of dead composers are defeasible, I have given with one hand only to take away with the other. But that would only be the case if I permitted the overriding conditions to be so numerous and trivial as to render the obligations impotent. If I were to say that we have an obligation to refrain from doing x, but that that obligation could be defeated by, among other things, my simply feeling like doing x, then I have indeed completely emasculated, for practical if not theoretical purposes, the concept of obligation in this particular case. That is not my intent, however, in the present instance. I am *not* saying that our obligations to honor the performance intentions of dead composers are very easily overridden. Indeed, just because performers and musicologists believe they are not easily overridden, they resist the suggestion that the performance intentions of composers be overridden or ignored with a passion hard to explain if the *only* thing at stake were how the music will sound. It does not nullify our obligation to obey the Sixth Commandment to admit that it is defeated by our right to kill an assailant in protecting our lives or the lives of others. Likewise, it surely does not reduce to nothing our obligations to the performance intentions of dead composers to maintain that *sometimes*—how frequently and under what circumstances I will not venture to say—they are overridden by aesthetic considerations, or moral ones, or a combination of the two. As Ruth Barcan Marcus has forcefully argued, "Wherever circumstances are such that an obligation to do x and an obligation to do y cannot as a matter of circumstance be fulfilled, the obligations to do each are not erased, even though they are unfulfillable. Mitigating circumstances may provide an explanation, an excuse, or a defense, but . . . this is not the same as denying one of the obligations altogether."[20]

To sum up, then, I claim that we have a strong obligation to honor the performance intentions of dead composers. This is a special case of our obligation to comply, where we can, with the wishes and intentions of the dead; and this obligation has its source in our duty to refrain from injuring the interests of others. Arguments to the contrary notwithstanding, it *is* possible to injure the interests of the dead. Our obligation to honor the performance intentions of dead composers is defeasible; but, nonetheless, this obligation is usually strong enough to justify our honoring the performance intentions of dead composers even when doing so will make the music sound worse than if the intentions were ignored. Finally, the peculiar zeal with which performers pursue the performance intentions of dead composers even when the music may be the worse for it, as well as their extreme reluctance to admit the possibility of intention's diverging from optimal performance, can best be explained by their strong belief in an ethical calling vis-à-vis the performance intentions of the composers whose works they interpret.

I have said nothing so far about the very important and sticky question of how we are to interpret the wishes and intentions of the dead in light of posthumous contingencies that they cannot, of course, be aware of. It is frequently suggested that one fulfills one's obligations to the wishes and intentions of a dead person if one does what he or she *would have* wished or *would have* intended were he or she now alive and cognizant of present conditions. And this kind of argument is frequently appealed to by musical performers who take liberties, both small and great, with the musical text. Thus, conductors have insisted that they are indeed honoring Handel's wishes and intentions by reorchestrating the oratorios, because it is what Handel would have done himself had he been alive to know and appreciate modern musical instruments.

Such considerations are important, and open up areas of discussion that cannot be pursued here. It must suffice to point out that the form of the argument itself is perfectly consistent with what I have urged in the preceding pages. I have not suggested that we cannot reinterpret the wishes and intentions of dead composers in light of present musical conditions. On the contrary, I think that we have to do so, as in any other situation in which we feel an obligation to the dead, and must determine what exactly that obligation is, or how best to fulfill not just its letter but its spirit. The practical pitfall in such counterfactuals, I need hardly say, is that they can easily become irrefutable apologetics for doing anything you please. If the composer said p in 1720, who can prove that he wouldn't have said not-p in 1988? So if you want to play the *Art of the Fugue* with a quartet of kazoos, why not? Surely Bach *might have*—which easily slips into *would have*—intended his work for those instruments, had he only lived long enough to hear and fall in love with them. Nevertheless, that there are unscrupulous ways of applying a principle does not render the principle either useless or invalid; nor can we, I think, dispense with the present one without rendering the whole notion of honoring the wishes and intentions of dead composers (or anyone else) completely nonsensical. Bach could not have intended his *Art of the Fugue* to be played on a modern replica of a baroque organ; yet some of us do think we are carrying out the spirit of his intentions by doing so today.

In any event, what these considerations indicate—what I have been arguing all along—is how deeply entrenched in the interpreter's thinking composers' intentions really are: so much so that, no matter what route he or she takes to the right performance, we seem to arrive, either by logic or illogic, at the composer's intentions as a criterion of great, and sometimes decisive, significance.

And if we can, at least in principle, think of the composer's way and the best way as logically distinct, my conclusion is that sometimes we owe it to a dead composer to play his music as he intended, rather than in what we may think is the best way possible, because we have real obligations to the interests of the dead. Perhaps that conclusion may seem eccentric. Nevertheless, each time I hear the third movement of the *Magnificat in D* going even slightly more briskly than adagio, even though I have a nagging feeling that it sounds better that way, I see the stern visage of the Cantor of Leipzig before my mind's eye, and think to myself: "If Bach were alive today to hear *this*, he would be rolling over in his grave."

KENDALL L. WALTON

The Presentation and Portrayal of Sound Patterns

One of the most fundamental questions of musical aesthetics is this: Which is of primary musical importance, musical works (symphonies, songs, sonatas, etc.) or performances of musical works? Are works or performances the basic objects of musical attention, musical appreciation, and musical judgment?[1]

Like many fundamental questions, this one is not often confronted directly, or even clearly perceived. It is easy for the theorist to presuppose an answer to it of one sort or another without being fully aware of either the answer or the question. But work on other problems of musical aesthetics is likely to be colored significantly by one's attitudes concerning this question, and for the sake of clarity these attitudes need to be exposed and examined.

I will not address this fundamental issue immediately, however, but will delve first into several more commonly discussed problems of how particular performances are related to particular works. We can ask, of a particular performance, (1) what work it is a performance of, (2) whether it is a *correct* performance of that work, and (3) whether it is a *good* performance of it. I will focus on (1), but the discussion will lead me to some observations concerning (2) and (3) as well.

It will be illuminating at various points to compare the relation between musical works and their performances with relations between works of other kinds and *their* instances. I will discuss specifically how literary works are related to copies and (oral) readings of them, and how culinary dishes are related to their instances, the food that people eat on particular occasions.

Eventually I will return to the fundamental issue of the relative primacy of works and performances. I will sketch the position I propose to take on this issue, and show how my position opens the way for an illuminating theory of how performances are related to the works of which they are performances.

A rather exotic example will serve to introduce the problem of what determines which work a given performance is a performance of. Suppose that musical scores on Mars specify very different sorts of properties from those that our scores specify. Martian scores do not indicate what pitches a performer is to play, or for what durations. Instead they give detailed instructions concerning dynamics, tempos, articulations, vibrato, nuances of accent and timbre, etc.—instructions that are much more detailed than those provided by (traditional) scores in our society. The performer of a Martian work is free to decide what pitches to play and for what durations, but he is expected to play them with the dynamics, articulations, timbres, etc., indicated by the composer. Different performers playing from the same score will of course play different pitches and rhythms (and hence different harmonies and harmonic rhythms) in executing the composer's instructions, just as on Earth different performers play the notes (pitches with durations) specified by the composer with different dynamics, tempos, and articulations.

Now let us imagine that a Martian composer, one Ludwig van Marthoven, wrote a symphony, his sixth, and that the dynamics, tempos, articulations, accents, etc., called for in his score happen to be precisely those that characterized a certain performance by the Chicago Symphony Orchestra of Beethoven's Sixth Symphony. Imagine, further, that a certain performance by the Martian Philharmonic of Marthoven's symphony has, by coincidence, the notes called for in Beethoven's score. Suppose that, in these and all other respects, the two performances are acoustically indistinguishable.

This example might be treated in various ways. One way, which so far as I can see has little in its favor, is to say that there is but *one* musical work and that both orchestras performed this one work. However, Marthoven's score is radically different from Beethoven's; many performances that comply perfectly with one of them conflict drastically with the other. It would seem unreasonable not to recognize two different works corresponding to the different scores. Should we say that each performance is a performance of both of these works at once, that is, that the Chicago Orchestra inadvertently played Marthoven's Sixth Symphony while it was deliberately playing Beethoven's, and that the Martian Philharmonic inadvertently played Beethoven's while playing Marthoven's? This seems an awkward and unintuitive way of construing the example.

Another alternative would be to hold that something is a performance of a given work only *relative* to a "musical system,"[2] and that relative to our musical system both performances are of Beethoven's work and relative to the Martian system both are of Marthoven's. But this alternative still treats the two performances alike. I prefer to treat them differently.

The position I find most congenial is that the Chicago Orchestra performed Beethoven's symphony and *not* Marthoven's, and that the Martian Philharmonic played only Marthoven's. This means that which work a performance is a performance of depends at least partly on some non-acoustic properties of it, since the two performances are acoustically identical. What makes the Chicago Orchestra's performance a performance of Beethoven's symphony rather than Marthoven's is something about the context or setting in which it occurs: the musical tradition it is part of, or the intentions of the performers, or the fact that Beethoven's score played a certain causal role in bringing it about, or some combination of these circumstances.

Does it matter how we treat this case? Indeed, does it ever matter what work we say something is a performance of? It is obvious from much more mundane examples that our usual criteria for determining what is a performance of what are not at all precise. How horrendously can a student orchestra clobber Mozart's *Jupiter* Symphony and still be clobbering Mozart's *Jupiter* Symphony? If someone whistles a garbled conglomeration of *Carmen* and a Josquin Des Prés motet, is he thereby whistling either or both of these works, or parts of them? Is the "Dies Irae" a separate musical work that is performed every time a larger work (such as Berlioz's *Symphonie fantastique*) in which the appropriate notes are embedded is performed? How prominent must those notes be in the larger work? Must they have been put there intentionally? Should a performance of a four-hand piano transcription of a

Brahms symphony count as a performance of that symphony? These questions do not have clear answers. Is this because they do not much matter? Is it because it makes little difference what is regarded as a performance of what? We should not just assume that the performance-of relation is an important one, that it plays a significant role in the institution of music.

I contend, however, that this relation is very important, that what we take to be a performance of what can make a profound difference, that our criteria for assigning performances to works are a crucial part of the institution of music. But it will be clear why this is so only after I have given my account of what makes something a performance of a given work.

Let us say, tentatively, that a musical work is a *sound pattern*. It is important to avoid misunderstandings about my use of the term "pattern." A pattern is something that particular objects or events may fit or fail to fit (although the pattern itself is not a particular object or event). The American flag is a pattern of stars and stripes, which the flag flying above the post office in Decatur, Illinois, fits, as do many other similar objects. Something fits a given pattern by virtue of possessing certain properties. To fit the American flag pattern is to be a rectangular object (or surface) with fifty stars and thirteen horizontal bands of the right colors in the right relations. A piece of material has (fits) a checkered pattern just in case it consists of squares of alternating colors.

Whether something fits a given pattern is not a matter of how it is perceived, of how it is structured, organized, or parsed, in the perception of an observer. A checkered tablecloth might be seen as having white squares on a black background, or as having black squares on a white background, or simply as having alternate black and white squares. One might see in it the horizontal rows of alternately colored squares, or the comparable vertical columns, or the diagonal lines of similarly colored squares; the squares can be seen as diamonds rather than as squares. But how the tablecloth is seen does not alter the color and shape properties that it in fact possesses, and so does not affect what pattern or patterns it fits by virtue of its possession of these properties. The checkered pattern of the tablecloth may be structured in perception (or in thought) in any of many ways, but that the tablecloth has this pattern depends only on its actual colors and shapes.

There can be great differences among things that fit the same pattern. This is because (ordinarily) only some of a thing's properties determine whether it fits a given pattern. Checkered tablecloths can differ drastically in size, shape, material, and in the size and colors of their squares, since *these* properties do not affect whether something fits the checkered pattern.

Patterns are individuated by what must be true of particular things in order to fit them. Pattern P and pattern P' are the same just in case the properties something must have to fit one are exactly the same as the properties something must have to fit the other. So to specify a pattern is to specify what anything must be like in order to fit it. Musical scores specify patterns. A score indicates various performance features, thereby specifying the pattern such that whatever has those features fits it.

A pattern is a *sound* pattern if the properties required for fitting it are acoustic ones. A sound event (e.g., the succession of sounds produced by a particular performer on a particular occasion) fits or conflicts with a given sound pattern depending on qualities such as the pitches, durations, timbres, and volumes of the sound. The patterns that musical scores specify are primarily sound patterns.[3]

Assuming that musical works are sound patterns, which sound pattern is to be identified with a given work? A natural first answer is that a work is the pattern specified by its score. But some works do not have scores, and in oral musical traditions there are not even conventions for producing scores (conventions as to which performance features are to be notated and which not). Moreover, scores sometimes serve more than one purpose and their use for some jobs may interfere with their specification of the appropriate pattern. (I will explain this.)

I suggest, provisionally, that we think of a work as the pattern determined by the sound properties a performance must have to be a correct or flawless (not necessarily good) performance of it. (This suggestion will be modified later.) Assuming that P is a performance of work W, what sound properties must P have to be a correct performance of W? The answer enumerates the properties anything must possess to fit the pattern constituting W; it specifies what pattern W is.[4]

Scores in our musical tradition function primarily to lay down rules for correct performance. Discrepancies between a performance of a work and its score, if it has one, are usually what count as mistakes. Insofar as this is so the score specifies the pattern that constitutes the work. But some specifications in scores are better construed as advice about how to perform the work *well*, rather than as indications of what counts as a correct performance. György Ligeti's *Requiem* (ca. 1965–67) contains instructions such as: "change bow unobtrusively," "as though from afar," and "stop suddenly as though torn off." The score for William Kraft's *Momentum* (1966) instructs several players to "run amok" at the climax. Obviously composers *can* give advice about how to perform a work well, just as anyone can, and there is no reason why their advice should not be written on what we call "scores." The mentioned instructions of Ligeti and Kraft are plausibly regarded as this kind of advice. If a score is understood to go beyond indicating the conditions for correct performance, the pattern that it (taken as a whole) specifies is not to be identified with the work. The pattern constituting the work is (roughly) the one specified by the score *minus* whatever advice for good performance it contains.

The fact that many scores are thought of as having the dual function that I have described is, I think, a very important one. But for present purposes I will adopt (for now) the simplifying assumption that scores merely formulate conditions for correct performance, and hence that works that have scores are the patterns specified by their scores.

The distinction between correct and incorrect performances is not limited to works that have scores. We usually have a fairly clear idea of what counts as a correct performance of a work even if the conditions for correct performance have not been notated. Our conception of the conditions for correct performance amounts to our conception of the identity of the piece. Granted, not every question about what sound properties are required for correct performance has a definite answer. (This is true for scored as well as for unscored works.) Whatever uncertainties there are about such questions translate into uncertainties about what patterns works are.[5]

What is it for a performance to be a performance *of* a given work? One view is that it is to fit perfectly the work's pattern.[6] The perfect-fit theory, as I will call it, has the unsettling consequence that pieces cannot be performed incorrectly, that the slightest mistake in an attempted performance of Mozart's D Minor Piano Concerto, for example, aborts the attempt entirely; if the pianist slips and plays an A-flat where the score calls for an A he has not succeeded in performing Mozart's D Minor Concerto at all, and hence cannot even be said to have performed it incorrectly.

Moreover, I find the claim that fitting a work's pattern is a *sufficient* condition for being a performance of it just as questionable as the claim that it is a *necessary* condition. Is every performance that fits perfectly the pattern of Mozart's D Minor Concerto necessarily a performance of this work? If so, then we will have to say that, in the example described earlier, the Chicago Symphony Orchestra performed Marthoven's Sixth Symphony while it was performing Beethoven's Sixth Symphony. This seems to me an infelicitous consequence of the perfect-fit theory.

Developing a better theory requires consideration of the fundamental question that I raised at the outset.

Which are primary: works or performances; sound patterns or sound events? In this section I will indicate how one who holds to the primacy of performances might spell out his position. I do not agree with this position; I believe that it does not describe accurately the roles that performances and works actually have in our institution of music. But it is a tempting view that needs to be understood clearly.

The ultimate objective of composers and performers, according to this position, is the production of particular acoustic events that listeners are likely to find pleasing or fascinating or satisfying or in some way worth listening to. These sound events are the end products of the musical process. Ultimately they are all that matter musically. The composer's job is simply to give instructions to performers, to provide recipes for producing performances. Success or failure hinges entirely on how interesting or pleasing the resulting sound events are.[7]

We find it convenient to catalogue or classify musical sound events in many different ways. We distinguish between sound events in E minor and ones in the Phrygian mode, between polyphonic and monophonic sound events, between fugues and sonatas. We classify sound events according to how they were produced, whether by string instruments or by human voices or by electronic synthesizers. We order them chronologically by the dates on which they occur and by the dates on which scores that led to their occurrence were written. The notion of musical works constitutes just another way of classifying sound events (according to the view I am sketching). Some sound events are performances of one work, and others are performances of another one. The Martians I described can be regarded merely as classifying sound events differently than we do. (Their classifications are useful for them because of the kinds of scores their composers produce.) But such classifications are no more than conveniences. The sound events themselves are what matter musically, regardless of how they are sorted.

We do describe musical works, not just performances, as good or bad, delightful or profound, moving or sentimental. And we do speak of enjoying or appreciating works. But this can be explained away. What appear to be musical judgments of works are (one might contend) merely disguised generalizations about performances. To call a Bartók string quartet delightful or profound, for example, is simply to claim that all or most performances of that piece are delightful or profound, or perhaps that all or most correct, or good, performances of it are delightful or profound. An analogous case is the following: To assert that the North American Buffalo is a vegetarian is merely to advance the generalization that all or most animals that are North American buffaloes are vegetarians. It is not to describe some abstract object called "the North American Buffalo" as a vegetarian. Also, what we call appreciation of a musical work is merely appreciation of some performance of it plus anticipated appreciation of others. There is no such thing as appreciation simply of the work itself.

Wracking our brains about which performances are of which works would seem hardly worth our while, if performances are primary in the way described. We can listen to sound events, and we can judge and appreciate them musically, without ever wondering what they are performances of. And if we are interested we can investigate whether or not a given performance conforms to a given score, or to a manuscript copy of a score, or to the score as the composer meant it to be; we can investigate whether the performer was following, or meant to be following, a given score, or whether the sounds he produced were the ones he intended to produce; we can study the musical tradition to which the performance belongs—we can do all of this without worrying about what work the performance is a performance of. And what more is there to ask? Once we have collected as much of the above information about a sound event as we can, what else could we want to discover in going on to ask what work it is a performance of? The notion of musical works and that of sound events' being performances of musical works appear to be entirely inessential, ones we can easily do without.

The characterization sketched above of the roles of works and performances in the institution of music is, I believe, fundamentally mistaken, and I will shortly offer a better one. But it is worth pointing out here, for the sake of contrast, that culinary dishes and their instances are plausibly construed on the model of this false picture of musical works and performances. What is of gastronomic interest is simply the particular morsels of food that we eat, not the abstract culinary dishes of which what we eat are instances. Our concepts of culinary dishes merely amount to a convenient way of categorizing food. And judgments of a dish are just generalizations about its instances. To say that Devastatingly Rich Chocolate Cake is delicious is to say merely that all or most instances of it are delicious (or that all or most accurately prepared, or well-prepared, instances of it are delicious). What matters gastronomically is the taste of the food we eat, not how it is classified. Notions of abstract entities such as Devastatingly Rich Chocolate Cake are mere conveniences, ones we could do without and still say everything that needs to be said.

I propose an alternative picture of works and performances. I suggest that musical works—sound patterns rather than sound events—are objects of musical attention in their own right. Musical judgments of works are just that, musical judgments of *works*. To call the Bartók string quartet delightful or profound is to describe the Bartók string quartet itself, not merely to generalize about its performances. And appreciation of a quartet or cantata or sonata is appreciation of that work, not just actual or anticipated appreciation of performances of it.

This is not to denigrate performances. Performances are vehicles for presenting or conveying musical works to us. Sound events provide access to sound patterns. A performance is thus at least partly a means to an end rather than an end in itself. But it is an important means to that end, usually an indispensable one.

Literature is analogous to music in important ways. A copy of a novel is a vehicle for presenting a word pattern, which is literarily important. But there is an obvious difference between copies of novels and performances of music. Peculiarities of a copy of a novel such as the size, style, and color of the type, and the quality of the paper are irrelevant in a way in which peculiarities of a musical performance are not. One copy of a novel cannot be better or worse than another in the way that one performance of a sonata may be better or worse than another performance of it. Copies of a novel may of course vary in accuracy or legibility, but that is another matter.

Words can be spoken as well as written, and word patterns can be conveyed to us by vocal readings or recitations as well as by written copies. Copies are the usual vehicles for presenting the word patterns of novels, whereas vocalizations are often preferred in the case of poetry. A recitation of a poem is a performance, and is very much like a musical performance; nuances of intonation and inflection are important far beyond the requirements of accuracy and intelligibility. But I am interested in the differences between performances—musical or literary—and copies of literary works.

Part of the explanation for the fact that the details of a copy of a novel are irrelevant in a way in which those of a musical performance are not may be that whereas a copy of a novel serves *only* to present a pattern, a musical performance not only does that but is also an object of musical interest in its own right. The sound event and the pattern it presents are *both* musically significant. (This dual function is not unheard of in copies of literary works. The calligraphy of a manuscript may be admired in addition to the pattern it presents. Copies of "concrete" poems obviously serve both purposes.)

But performances are important in still another way, a way in which copies of novels are not. A performance not only presents a pattern, but portrays it in a certain light. It interprets, parses, organizes the pattern in some way or other, as well as indicating what it is. And how a pattern is portrayed or interpreted, as well as what it is, is musically significant.

A performance may, for example, emphasize certain analogies between parts of the pattern and obscure others. (One way to emphasize an analogy is to play the analogous parts with precisely the same nuances of timbre, phrasing, accent, etc.) One passage of a work may be portrayed as a restatement or variation or development or elaboration of another. A performance may bring out features of the pattern such as canons, strettos, melodic inversions, retrogrades, or augmentations; a different performance of the same work may make these features more subtle. A performer can choose to present an extended and complex section of the pattern as spun from, growing out of, a simple but pregnant motive. Or he might render a simple concluding passage as a "distillation of the essence" of the entire piece. A section may be portrayed as the beginning of a "new idea," or alternatively as a continuation of an old one. These are some of the ways in which performers interpret patterns.[8]

The organizing or interpreting of patterns by performances can be compared to the ordering of data by theories based on them. And good performances often have virtues analogous to those of good theories; they neatly accommodate all parts of the pattern and provide an elegant, simple, illuminating, theoretically satisfying view of them. The performance makes "sense" out of the pattern, and makes it easily grasped by the listener. Every detail seems "right"; there is a reason for everything. (I do not claim that these are the only virtues of good performances.)

A copy of a novel, by contrast, merely presents a pattern; it does not also provide a portrayal or interpretation of it. Different copies of a novel may differ greatly; they may range from a handdrawn parchment to a modern pulp paperback. But none of the copies provides an interpretation of the work that is more elegant or revealing or interesting or satisfying or obvious or subtle than others do. Each of the various copies (provided that it is legible and accurate) simply indicates what the relevant pattern of words is.

Vocal readings of a poem, performances of a play, and tellings of a story,[9] like musical performances, serve to interpret patterns as well as to present them. This is why their features—intonations, inflections, costumes, stagings, the words one chooses in telling a story—matter more than do the features of a copy of a novel that are not required for legibility and accuracy.

What about culinary dishes? We savor the most subtle tastes of our food. Virtually every tinge or hint of flavor in a piece of Devastatingly Rich Chocolate Cake is gastronomically significant. But this is not because the piece of cake interprets or organizes a pattern, as does a musical performance or a recitation of a poem. It is because the piece of cake does not serve to present a pattern at all; our interest is in the taste of the piece of cake itself. I do not claim that instances of food *could* not be understood as presenting or portraying patterns, but only that they usually are not so understood. We rarely if ever think of what we eat as indicating a pattern of taste features, and as organizing or interpreting it in a certain way, stressing analogies between certain aspects of it, etc., a way different from how another instance of the same dish might organize or interpret it.

The job, the purpose, of a performance is to present and portray a pattern; but *which* pattern? Any sound event conforms perfectly to many different patterns. The Chicago Symphony Orchestra's performance discussed earlier fits the pattern of pitches and durations that we call Beethoven's Sixth Symphony. But it also fits Marthoven's Sixth Symphony, a pattern of articulations, dynamics, accents, timbres; and it fits infinitely many other patterns as well. A single sound event can convey different patterns to different listeners. We hear the Beethoven pattern in the Chicago Orchestra's performance. Our musical experience has prepared us to discriminate and attend to patterns of notes rather than patterns of articulations, dynamics, accents, and timbres. Presumably a Martian listener would hear the Marthoven pattern in the same sound event, because of his different prior musical experience, and that is how he hears the performance by the Martian Philharmonic. So the same sound event, or acoustically indistinguishable ones, convey or present different sound patterns to Earthling listeners and to Martian listeners. On hearing indistinguishable performances the two audiences recognize and appreciate different musical works.

Most Earthling listeners are not of course explicitly or intellectually aware of the Beethoven pattern when listening to the performance; they are not capable of reconstructing Beethoven's score, an explicit specification of the pattern, from what they hear. But most of them could demonstrate in other ways some kind of awareness of the pattern. They may be able to sing parts of the pattern, that is, to produce vocal sound events that fit the pattern at least approximately, or they may be able to recognize other sound events as fitting the pattern, or parts of it. In fact, many listeners could without much difficulty produce vocal sound events that fit parts of the Beethoven pattern but differ drastically from the Chicago Orchestra's performance in other respects; they could sing melodies that they heard in the performance but with very different dynamics, tempos, articulations, accents, etc. Listeners who cannot produce such sound events may well be able at least to recognize them as melodies that the Chicago Orchestra played, despite the drastic differences between them and the sounds produced by the orchestra.

It would be enormously difficult for any of us to demonstrate awareness of the Marthoven pattern in any of these ways, to sing the pattern of articulations, dynamics, accents, etc., that characterizes the performance but with significantly different pitches and durations. Nor could we readily recognize sound events as fitting the Marthoven pattern if they differ substantially in other respects from the performance.

I am supposing that Martian listeners have the opposite abilities, that after hearing the performance they could produce or recognize other sound events that fit (parts of) the same pattern of dynamics, tempos, articulations, accents, but not ones that conform to the same note pattern. They hear the Marthoven pattern in the performance but not the Beethoven one.

The members of the Chicago Orchestra had the Beethoven pattern in mind, and it is the Beethoven pattern that they meant to convey to listeners. Moreover, the musical culture in which they performed is one in which the standard purpose of performances is to convey note patterns rather than patterns of dynamics, etc. Let us say that the function, the role, of the Chicago Orchestra's performance was to present the Beethoven pattern, and not the Marthoven pattern. This, I suggest, is what makes it a *performance of* Beethoven's work and not Marthoven's. In general, I propose that we consider a sound event a performance of a given work just in case its role, in the context in which it occurs, is to present the sound pattern identified with that work. It should be obvious that this way of understanding what it is to be a performance of a work makes the question of which performances are of which works much more than a matter, to be decided more or less arbitrarily, of how to catalogue or classify sound events.

Among the advantages of the theory I have just sketched is that it allows performances to be incorrect. A performance is incorrect if it doesn't perfectly fit the pattern it has the job of presenting. If in a performance of Mozart's D Minor Piano Concerto the pianist's finger slips, hitting an A-flat instead of an A-natural, the A-flat is a wrong note because the performance, in the context in which it occurs, has the job of presenting a pattern that calls for an A-natural at that point. (The pianist intended to play an A-natural; that is what the score he is playing from calls for; and the audience can be expected to regard the A-flat as out of place, "ungrammatical," and hence to assume that it was unintended.) The function of the performance is still to present the pattern with the A-natural, the pattern of the concerto, despite the slip. It is still a genuine performance of that concerto.

Wrong notes and other mistakes are to be distinguished sharply from bad (unsuccessful, ill-advised, unsatisfying) interpretations. These two sorts of performance defects *sound* very different (to the practiced listener), and our theory should explain why they do. To be unsuccessful interpretatively is not a matter of failing to fit the relevant pattern, but a matter of portraying or interpreting that pattern in an infelicitous way. An incorrect performance might be likened to a scientific theory that conflicts with its data; a correct performance whose interpretation is unsuccessful is more like a theory that is objectionable on other grounds—because it constitutes an inelegant or overly complex or unilluminating or otherwise unsatisfying ordering of the data.

We are now in a position to explain an intriguing difference between musical performances and copies of literary works. Typographical errors in a copy of a novel correspond to wrong notes in a musical performance. Typographical errors consist of a lack of correspondence between the copy and the word pattern it is designed to convey. But they are not nearly as upsetting or disturbing as wrong notes are. A typographical error is of little consequence if we can tell, somehow, how the text should have read; we simply take it as corrected and proceed. But wrong notes cannot be forgiven so easily. It is not enough merely to ascertain what note should have been played. An obviously wrong A-flat bothers us even if we are perfectly aware that what should have been played is an A-natural.

Why is this? At least part of the explanation lies in the fact that musical performances, unlike copies of novels, serve not merely to present patterns but also to interpret them. If the copy somehow gets across what the relevant pattern is, it has done its job. But even if a sound pattern is decipherable from an incorrect performance, the wrong notes are likely to disturb or destroy the performance's interpretation of the pattern. An A-flat where the pattern calls for an A-natural may well prevent the performance from portraying the passage containing the mistake as clearly parallel to or analogous to another passage with a corresponding A-natural.

The picture I have drawn so far is too simple in several respects. In the first place, a given musical performance may present to listeners not just one pattern but several or many. I do not mean merely that a performance may fit more than one pattern, of course, but that listeners may *hear* them in the performance. And it may be the *function* of a performance to present not just the pattern specified approximately by the composer's score but others as well. This means that, in many cases at least, a musical work is better identified with a set of patterns, often a hierarchically ordered series of them, than with a single pattern (though this too will turn out to be an oversimplification). Richly complex relations among the various patterns presented by a performance contribute importantly to the interest and excitement of listeners' experiences.

Exactly which patterns are to be heard in performances of a given piece is a subtle and delicate question demanding the utmost in musical sensitivity. Nor is it easy, even for the listener himself, to say which patterns he actually does hear on a particular occasion. No doubt questions of both sorts frequently lack definite answers. But we can see how things work by considering plausible conjectures.

Consider a performance of a Bach Chorale. I suggest that most listeners hear in it not only the note pattern indicated by Bach's score, but also the more inclusive pattern that a score in figured bass notation would indicate, the pattern that any sound event with the bass line and harmonic structure of the Chorale will fit, regardless of how the harmonies are realized in the upper voices. Evidence that we do hear this figured bass pattern is provided, again, by the fact that it is relatively easy for a person with a little musical training to sing or play variants of the Chorale in which the harmonies are realized very differently in the upper voices, and it is relatively easy for the practiced listener to recognize such variants. (Listeners may recognize the similarity between such a variant and a performance of the Chorale as Bach scored it even if they cannot say what the similarity consists in.) Notice that the figured bass pattern is more inclusive, more general than the note pattern in the sense that anything that fits the latter necessarily fits the former, but not vice versa.

I suggest, also, that listeners are likely to hear in the performance a third pattern intermediate between the note and figured bass patterns, namely, a pattern that would be indicated by figured bass notation with the upper parts written out, but in which it is understood that the performer is free to embellish and elaborate on the upper voices as he sees fit (within certain limits implicitly agreed upon).[10] To comply with this pattern a sound event must have the bass line and harmonic structure of the Chorale and also upper voices that conform in their general shape to what Bach indicated. But the upper voices needn't contain the particular embellishments that Bach wrote out. Bach's score (understood as requiring just the notes that are specifically indicated and allowing no others) spells out one of many ways of realizing this pattern.

Patterns of the three kinds discussed above are, I believe, to be found in much of the music of the "Common Practice Period."[11] But many works of this corpus, especially ones composed after Bach, probably involve patterns of still other sorts as well. A performance of a Brahms song, for instance, may well present to listeners and may have the function of presenting to them:

    1. a figured bass pattern;

    2. a figured bass pattern with restrictions on the general shape of the upper voices;

    3. a note pattern;
and in addition

    4. a pattern such that to fit it a sound event must not only contain certain notes and no others, but must also have certain dy-

namics, tempos, phrasings, accents, etc., that is, approximately the pattern indicated by Brahms's actual score.

Is there any limit to the number of patterns a performance might present? Not in principle. No doubt there are limits *to* how many patterns human listeners can hear at once in a given sound event, and even stricter limits on how many they can *attend* to at once. But I am inclined to think that listeners are commonly aware at least vaguely of more than four patterns in a given performance. In any case a performance may have the function of presenting more patterns than listeners can hear or attend to simultaneously; listeners may hear different combinations of the presented patterns on different occasions. This helps to account for the remarkable endurance of much music, its ability to withstand enormous repetition without losing listeners' interest.

Patterns 1–4 constitute a hierarchy of progressively more specific, less inclusive patterns. Any sound event that fits one pattern in the series will fit the preceding ones as well, but may not fit those following it. A note-perfect performance of the Brahms song that also has dynamics, phrasings, etc., within the ranges Brahms specified, that is, a performance fitting pattern 4, will automatically satisfy the conditions for fitting patterns 1–3, but a performance with the bass line and harmonic structure required by pattern 1 might not qualify as an instance of any of the other patterns.

The patterns presented by performances of a given work need not be hierarchically ordered. Among those that listeners hear in a performance of the Bach Chorale may be one instantiated by performances of different settings of the same chorale melody, a pattern requiring the notes of the chorale melody in the soprano but not much else—perhaps a certain harmonic structure or its outlines, perhaps not, and definitely not any particular melodic lines in the inner voices. This pattern is neither more nor less specific than the intermediate one consisting of the figured bass and its realization apart from embellishments, or (probably) the figured bass pattern. Each is such that some sound events that fit it would fail to fit the other.

But it *is* very common, it seems to me, for hierarchically ordered patterns to be presented by a performance. Patterns so ordered constitute levels reminiscent of Schenkerian theory.[12] The relations between the levels can be understood in terms of the relations I described earlier between performances and the patterns that I previously identified with works. Each pattern in the series corresponds to a particular way of portraying or interpreting its less specific neighbor. More precisely, any performance that fits one of the patterns thereby not only fits the pattern's less specific neighbor in the series but portrays it in a certain manner. To indicate what a given pattern in the series is, that is, to specify what a sound event must be like to fit it, is at the same time to indicate a way of organizing or interpreting the pattern on the next deeper level.

A performance of a work thus presents and portrays all of the patterns in the series at once. In presenting one it presents and portrays the next; in presenting this pattern it presents and portrays a still more general one; and so on. In fact, a performance— or rather, the very specific sound pattern that only a given performance and acoustically identical sound events fit—can be regarded as the shallowest level in the series, an extreme foreground, a surface structure lying in front of the scored pattern. The other patterns in the series correspond to different strata of deep structure, that is, to middleground, background, and intermediate levels.

It would seem arbitrary to identify a musical work with any single pattern, the pattern indicated by its score, for example, if its performances have the function of presenting other patterns as well.[13] Let's say (for now) that the piece is the *set* of patterns that it is the function of any performance of it to present. This will not include the entire set of patterns a given performance of the piece serves to present; it will exclude, for example, "performance patterns," ones instantiated only by sound events aurally indistinguishable from a given performance, for it is not the function of *all* performances of the piece to present any particular performance pattern. Works that have scores will be sets of patterns whose most specific member is, approximately, the pattern indicated by the score, though each of its performances may present one or more other patterns in addition to these.

But it may seem rather arbitrary, also, to make the score the indication of the cutoff point, or indeed to fix on any definite cutoff point at all. We should allow some flexibility here, admitting more and less strict notions of piece identity. Let's say that to be performances of the same piece, two performances must have the function of presenting all of the same patterns down to a certain level of specificity, leaving open what might be taken as an appropriate level of specificity.[14] This will accommodate nicely our hesitations about deciding some questions of piece identity. In playing a simplified version of Mozart's D Minor Piano Concerto, do a student pianist and a school orchestra perform the same piece that Rudolf Serkin performs with the Vienna Philharmonic? *Yes*, on a loose notion of piece identity; *no*, on a stricter notion requiring coincidence of patterns to a lower level of specificity. We can happily leave the matter right there.

But we cannot rest with the identification of musical works and sets of sound patterns.[15]

Most scores indicate to performers not only what sorts of sounds they are to produce, but also the manner in which they are to produce them. Composers usually specify the instruments to be used, and they sometimes give instructions about how the instruments are to be manipulated (*col legno, pizzicato, con sordino*, etc.).

If a musical work is a set of *sound* patterns and a correct performance is one that fits those patterns, the sound-making techniques employed by a performer will not affect the correctness of his performance, so long as they result in the right sounds. A Chopin Prelude could be performed just as correctly on an electronic sound synthesizer capable of mimicking the piano perfectly as it can on a piano. How then are we to understand Chopin's stipulation that the Prelude is for piano, and composers' indications of performance-means generally? Perhaps they serve merely to indicate, indirectly, the kinds of sounds required for correct performance (in specifying that a piano is to be used the composer indicates that sounds of the *kinds* pianos make are required for correct performance), and also to advise performers as to how such sounds can be achieved.

This conclusion is not a comfortable one. One cause for unease lies in the fact that the manner in which sounds are produced has a lot to do with their effects on listeners. A rendition of the Chopin Prelude on the piano may be brilliant, flashy, energetic, virtuosic; producing the same sounds electronically may constitute a relatively dull performance. In listening to the pianist our impression may be of a person and his instrument pushed to their limits, of enormous difficulties overcome by deep concentration and heroic effort. The synthesizer, in contrast, may seem merely a machine doing its job—matter-of-factly, competently, effortlessly, without emotion.[16] (I am assuming that the listener realizes in each case how the sounds are made.) In short, performances on the synthesizer and on the piano are likely to *sound* very different—even if they are aurally indistinguishable!

Since the Prelude was written for piano, we will want to describe *it*, not just the pianist's performance, as brilliant, energetic, heroic, virtuosic, etc. Surely there is something seriously wrong, then, with the duller, distinctly *un*virtuosic electronic performance. Shall we say that at least some of the patterns that constitute the piece are not pure *sound* patterns, but rather patterns such that to fit them a sound event must have been produced in a certain manner in addition to possessing certain acoustic properties?[17] If so, we can declare the synthesizer performance of the Chopin Prelude to be *incorrect* on the grounds that it fails to fit one or more of the relevant patterns.

But this proposal creates other difficulties. If the patterns constituting a piece are not sound patterns they are not *audible* in performances in the way that sound patterns are, and we will have to reconsider the sense in which performances can be said to present them to listeners. I will shortly suggest a different way of giving appropriate weight to the manner in which sounds are produced.

Musical works are not to be identified with any patterns or sets of patterns. We do need to recognize a set of patterns (*sound* patterns, I claim) corresponding to each work. But this set is best understood as only one component of the work.

A modulation that is daring in Mozart may be mundane in a twentieth- or late nineteenth-century composition. To indicate a given set of sound patterns in the eighteenth century may be to compose an imaginative, surprising, exciting piece of music; to specify the very same set of sound patterns in the nineteenth or twentieth century may be to compose a dull, clichéd work. The pieces are distinct, since they have different aesthetic properties, but the patterns are the same. So neither work is simply the set of patterns.

The difference between them lies in how their performances are to be heard, and that is determined in part by the circumstances in which they were composed. Very briefly: performances of the Mozart piece are to be heard as performances of an eighteenth-century work.[18] So heard, they sound exciting, and since they sound exciting when heard appropriately, the piece is an exciting one. Performances of the later work are to be heard as such. So heard they sound dull; hence the piece is dull.

We can identify the piece with the complex consisting of the set of sound patterns and whatever circumstances (such as the date of composition or the culture in which it was composed) go into determining how its performances are to be heard.[19]

The means by which sounds are produced enters into the latter rather than the former component of musical works. Performances of the Chopin Prelude are to be heard as *piano* performances—since Chopin wrote it for piano. This, together with the fact that when so heard they sound virtuosic, is (roughly) what makes the piece virtuosic. The use of a synthesizer in performing the Prelude forces or demands or encourages listeners to hear the performance otherwise. *This* is what is wrong with that performance. We needn't hold that the sounds produced fail to fit one of the patterns (partially) constitutive of the work, or one that its performances (qua performances of that piece) have the job of presenting. The defect is of a different kind. The patterns constitutive of the work are pure *sound* patterns, ones that are fully audible in its performances.

A musical work, I suggested, is a set of sound patterns plus the circumstances that go into determining how its performances are to be heard (in what "categories" they are to be heard). Among these circumstances are, in many cases, composers' designations of the instruments performers are to use and their instructions about the manner in which they are to use them.

TED COHEN

Sports and Art: Beginning Questions

This piece is a prelude, intended only to open a few questions about sports. I am interested mainly in questions of aesthetics, but I will also outline a point concerning ethics. In the first cases I want to advance a comparison of the appreciation of sports with the appreciation of art, and in the other case I will compare an attitude toward sports with a central moral attitude. An overall question, for another occasion, is how far these comparisons can be kept cogent.

Aesthetics

I am thinking of sports from the standpoint of the spectator, the critical appreciator. That is different from the position of a participant, but there is a connection. The connection is complex and unclear. It appears in various contexts, including ones involving the estimation of *difficulty*. I am thinking primarily of large-scale team games like baseball, basketball, and football, but it would do as well to consider individual competitions like tennis and ping-pong, or sports in which the participants do not vie against one another simultaneously, like golf and gymnastics. To appreciate the quality of play by some performer it is necessary, at least sometimes, to apprehend the difficulty of what is being done. This can count both ways, in favor of doing something difficult, and against failing to do something easy.

First consider the latter case, in which something easy or routine is bungled. This often seems to be the result of carelessness,

Sports and Art 259

thoughtlessness, or insufficient dedication to the main aim of the game.[1]

What does a spectator say or think about a thing like this? If it were polite enough to be quoted, it might well be something like "I could have done that" or "My mother could have done that" or "My eight-year-old child does that regularly," the first implication being that it is poor play to fail to do what *anyone* could do. Present in the background is the idea that it would not be especially good or even noteworthy to succeed in doing something anyone could do. Of all the kinds of negative appraisal of art I am aware of, none is more common or more intriguing than the complaint "I could make a painting like that" or "A child could make up music like that" or "A chimpanzee could make a sculpture you couldn't tell from this thing." Now we are not just yet concerned with whether these complaints—about sporting endeavors or works of art—are true. It may be harder to field a grounder, hit an overhead, or paint a likeness than you know, and we will look into these subtleties presently. For now let us assume that you are right: you could have done that. So what? When and why is it worthwhile or appreciable to do something only if it is a difficult thing to do, and when and why is it contemptible to fail at something that is not a difficult thing to do?

We must go slowly here, for some care is required in characterizing the difficulty of the thing you say you could have done. In the first place, it is relative in one respect but not in another. The difficulty is measured relative to what most people can do, or what an average person can do, or something like that. The difficulty is not, or may not be, measured relative to the player or the artist himself. If he is either extremely capable or very inept, then his experience of difficulty will be eccentric. It is, we may suppose, easy for Mozart to make up a tune, for Picasso to construct geometrically, for Chris Evert to hit deep, angled ground strokes; and yet this does not depreciate what they do, because these are *difficult things to do* independently of how difficult they are for these people. But often the difficulty experienced by inept artists and athletes will also be eccentric. It is hard for me to hit simple topspin backhands, for one-armed people to make routine plays in a softball infield, and for the very shy to perform supernumerary parts in amateur theater. (Our *doing them* is another matter. You may admire us very much for accomplishing what is so difficult for us, but this is not the same. You should fawn on me when I hit that backhand, but it is really a rather routine shot—my son has been able to make it since shortly after he learned to play tennis—and you would be wrong to shift your approbation from making the shot to the shot itself.) The difficulty in question, therefore, is a kind of absolute, for it seems to be measured against a norm independent of the peculiar capacities of the artist or player, and also independent of those of the spectator.

However the difficulty is measured, what kinds of difficulty matter? Not every kind. Certainly not every kind of difficult thing is a thing it is good to do, for a difficulty might be so radically out of place that its introduction is a blemish.[2] The player may have done something that almost no one in the world can do, and yet it will not be laudable. It will be grotesque. The reason is that the undertaking is very poorly calculated to achieve what is analytically the aim of playing the game in question; but the point of immediate interest is that, however particular cases may be assessed, we cannot take it as a general and unqualified proposition that it is good when something difficult is done. And we cannot make use of such a proposition in assessing art. Buddy Rich could do things when playing jazz drums that are beyond the technical capacity of all but a handful of drummers, and yet some of Rich's performances are at best stunning oddities that add nothing and may well detract from the musical value of the pieces in which they occur.

It is not always easy to identify a case in which the difficulty is irrelevant. Sometimes overcoming the difficulty is irrelevant to the point of the exercise, as when an athlete undertakes something that need not have been attempted at all. I will describe such examples presently, but first let me describe a kind of case we might call "mixed." In a mixed case an athlete bumbles initially and thus winds up with a much greater difficulty than he would have faced if he had performed well at the start, and yet he overcomes this self-imposed obstacle.[3] One can find and imagine comparable examples in the arts—photography and literature, for instance—in which the artist has created for himself an unnecessarily complex problem in composition or lighting or narration but then proceeded to solve it.

I want to observe a few more things about the appreciation of difficult doings. But first let me gather together the two very general points that are emerging about some circumstances in which, in both sports and art, we seem to appreciate the accomplishment of a task.[4]

First, we appreciate the accomplishment of a task when it is difficult, meaning that an average sort of performer probably couldn't do it. I do not pretend that this notion, the idea of "what someone could do," is unproblematic. One line of complexity leads to cases in which the "thing that is done" is clearly easy, yet it is not easy—in a particular place at a particular time—to *think* of doing it. It is not difficult to drop a soft liner in the infield on purpose in order to make a double play, and it is not so difficult to serve neither wide to the forehand nor steeply to the backhand but directly into the center of the receiver's body, but not every baseball infielder or tennis server thinks to do these things. Sometimes a maneuver of this kind is so rare that it is virtually unique, and its first occurrences constitute a permanent innovation. The "Fosbury flop" style of high-jumping is an example.

These cases have some similarity to cases in art in which it is quite clear that what has been done "could have been done by almost anyone," and yet it is just one artist who thought to do it. Much of Warhol, Christo, Cage, and Oldenburg is like this.

I am simply ignoring this complication in this essay, and I will not go into a refined conception of "being able to do it" that separates being able to think it up from being able to execute it.

Second, we appreciate the accomplishment of a task when there is some point in having the task done. The point is supplied typically by the context—the game or the work of art—in which the task is set. Within a game the point is typically given in terms of winning; within a work of art, things are not so clear. I am assuming that a desire to win is an analytical component in playing a game. Of course this doesn't deny that you are playing baseball when you really don't care whether you win, or even when, as with me in a weekly game I play with children, you actually want the other team to win. It does mean that spectators and players *understand* the efforts of the players in terms of a presumed wish all round that the players win. In the degenerate case a player deliberately loses, or tries to, and a corruption that is not merely moral is brought to the game. If you swing without trying to hit the ball or take what you know to be a third strike without swinging, it is difficult to say just what you are doing in terms of the idiom of playing baseball.

Do not, however, confuse individual units of play with the whole game. Sandy Koufax reports that in some games in which the Dodgers had built a substantial lead he would try a pitch he was unsure of just in order to determine whether the batter in question could handle it. Sometimes this resulted in a home run, but Koufax then knew better how to deal with this batter in difficult circumstances, should they arise. A case like this is not an example of someone's trying not to win, but to see this one must notice that the relevant context is broader than that consisting of only this pitch to this batter. I am a tennis player of markedly limited abilities. Early in matches, especially during games whose outcomes seem to me nearly independent of the point at hand, I sometimes go to the net, inviting a passing shot, and then deliberately fail to cover the ensuing ground stroke. My hope is that at some later, critical time I will come to the net, my opponent will go for the same passing shot, and I will confound him with greater speed and net coverage than he expected. Such cases are common, and they can be very complex when what is at stake is not one pitch or one batter or even one game but an entire series of games or perhaps a whole season.

The context supplied by a game or a work of art can rationalize one of its constituents, but if this rationalization is to be profound then the game or work itself must be significant. Why is it that some sports become entrenched objects of complex appreciation and others do not? Why baseball and not tug-of-war? Why tennis and not human-pyramid building? Why sprint racing and not speed typing? In some cases it seems to be because one activity has intrinsic possibilities that exceed those of another. But many apparently simple activities yield virtually endless refinements, and there are certainly examples of complex athletic activities that never become canonical sports. Some cases can be explained by the fact that one sport retains a connection with some natural endeavor while the other is utterly artificial. Can all cases be explained in these ways? Are these the explanations of why some productive enterprises become art and others do not?

Which athletic activities (can) become real sports? Which productive activities (can) become artistic: which made things (can) become works of art? In some cases—perhaps most—an after-the-fact explanation is available in terms of the natural coherence and significance of these activities. But not in all cases, and in general there is no possible a priori determination of the possibilities. What kinds of things will be art? What will be a medium? What will be a sport? There is no way to say in advance. Sports, like the genera of art, discover and create their own possibilities.

Virtuosity is obviously a significant idea in the appreciation of art, and it is almost as obvious that we do not yet have any reliable analysis of just what virtuosity is.[5] It is equally important and obscure in the appreciation of sports. In neither art nor sports is virtuosity of an unqualified determinate value. The phrase "mere virtuosity" makes that clear, for it acknowledges something remarkable but simultaneously depreciates it. If virtuosity is at least in part a matter of doing something difficult, then what remains to be said?

First there is the question of how it is that *mere* virtuosity becomes *serious*, how the flair and facility with which something is done become themselves the logical subjects of attention. What seems to happen is that what was at best a means to an end becomes itself an end. This is one way to think of the development of certain sports, and it is surely how art forms and media evolve (although it is not the only way). Think of the skills exhibited in master paintings: the portrayal of light and shadow, the modeling of shapes, the suggestion of motion, the creation and arrangement of color. It is natural to think of those abilities marshaled originally in the service of the depiction of recognizable objects, and in that capacity they are used to achieve a kind of generic end. But painters and audiences have long since appeared who are able to regard the exhibition of those skills as an end. Similarly in sports, an instrumental skill begins to be cultivated, as we say, in a useless but irresistible phrase, "for its own sake." Running fast, over short and long distances, jumping with and without the aid of a pole,[6] throwing objects, lifting weights—all these things make perfectly good sense, first as means to obvious natural ends like killing one's enemies, securing food, etc., and then as means to sporting ends, in particular, winning athletic games.

But entirely independent of those considerations we are able to appreciate skill in these activities, and we can take an interest in competitions in simply running or jumping. This is what makes possible one sense (never mind the truth) in saying that one competitor is better than another but the other is better than the one. One boxer may hit harder than another and also take punches better and even have more stamina, and yet the latter may always beat the former, say in the kind of boxing match staged in the Olympics. (If the weaker man can survive the stronger's punches and do this for the duration of a short fight, while landing more blows than he receives, he will win.) It is a frequent observation about pairs of tennis players that A is a better tennis player than B although B beats A more often than A beats B. We are able to separate the idea of good tennis play from the idea of winning at tennis, at least up to a point, and we can recognize and appreciate the former.

It is obviously possible to prefer A's play to B's for any of a variety of reasons that are not strictly sportive. For instance, A's play might be "aesthetically" more pleasing, or it might be more classical, or it might be in some style that the viewer just happens to prefer or to prefer looking at. The problem is to make sense of a preference for A's play on grounds intrinsic to the sport A and B are playing. The solution, I think, is to relate A's play to something like success at the game *in general*. A's play is generally superior to B's in being a kind of play more likely than B's to prevail in the sport in question, although perhaps not specifically against B. It is easiest to imagine this in a sport whose skills are complex and interrelated. Think of tennis. I (A) am able to beat some players who are better than I. It happens this way. I have rather weak ground strokes, but I have a fairly good net game and I possess a genuinely reliable overhead. And I am quick. When my opponent, B, has good ground strokes but neither particularly good passing shots nor an effective lob, he cannot keep me from the net often enough to win. Typically in such a situation, although not necessarily, it happens that there is a third player, C, who customarily beats A but loses to B. In my case such a player has the lob or the speed or the passing shots to neutralize my advantage at the net, but these skills are of little use against B, who does not rely on getting position at the net, and then B's superior ground game usually gets the better of C.

A striking feature of virtuosity is that one of its most characteristic expressions is a concealment of itself. The mark of this kind of virtuosity is that the virtuoso makes the difficult appear easy. This disguised effort, as we might call it, is as well marked in sports as it is in art. Julius Erving is unquestionably a virtuoso, and he has recorded the following estimate of virtuosity in the play of his fellow basketball players: "[Bernard King] will never get up to the level of the real all-timers like, say, Kareem, or myself, because he looks like he's working too hard. When you reach a level of greatness there's a certain added element that goes into making it look easy."[7]

Sometimes the act in question is so obviously difficult that even a novice spectator realizes that considerable skill is being deployed by whoever does it, but sometimes it is not at all obvious. In these subtle cases, how do we come to apprehend the virtuosity? How do we realize that it is there? Neither a description of the act nor the sight of its being done is sure to reveal the difficulty. This fact seems to me connected with a point articulated by J. O. Urmson thirty years ago in his preliminary descriptions of what he called "simple cases of aesthetic evaluation":

But there are some slightly more sophisticated cases which need closer inspection. I have in mind occasions when we admire a building not only for its colour and shape but because it looks strong or spacious, or admire a horse because it looks swift as well as for its gleaming coat. These looks are not sensible qualities in the simple way in which colour and shape are. . . .

We are now considering the facts which, exclusively emphasized, lead to the functional view of aesthetics. The element of truth in that view I take to be that if a thing looks to have a characteristic which is a desirable one from another point of view, its looking so is a proper ground of aesthetic appreciation. What makes the appreciation aesthetic is that it is concerned with a thing's looking somehow without concern for whether it really is like that; beauty, we may say, to emphasize the point, is not even skin-deep.[8]

Swiftness is a desirable quality in a horse, but it is incompatible with other desirable qualities. The kind of horse called a "thoroughbred," which runs in races like the Kentucky Derby, is swift—and it looks swift. Belgian draft horses, and Clydesdales, are not swift. And they certainly do not look swift. The very characteristics desirable in strong, hard-working horses of this kind are plainly incompatible with the characteristics that are the concomitants of swiftness in a horse. So far this is no problem for Urmson. There is a "point of view" from which one prizes the speed of a horse, and there is another point of view from which one prizes the strength of a horse. The slender-looking legs of a horse will strike one differently depending upon which of the two points of view one is taking. Neither is what Urmson thinks of as "aesthetic." Urmson thinks of aesthetic evaluation as involving a "point of view" itself, an aesthetic point of view, and I would not myself care to put things that way; but that is not the point here. The point is Urmson's interest in the swift look of a horse. This is not such a simple look, as he notes. It is not like a color or a shape. My question is, How do we know what a swift horse looks like? Surely there is a connection between looking like a swift horse and being a swift horse, although the connection is not so inflexible as to ensure that all swift horses look swift, or that all swift-looking horses are swift. It is possible, no doubt, to learn the use of an adjective like "swift-looking" on the strength of exposure to a number of cases of swift-looking horses, but in the central case one will need to know something about swift horses—and not just about the appearance of swift-looking horses—in order to have an idea of what a swift-looking horse would look like.

I wish very much not to open the general topic of "expression," and in particular I do not want to take up the question of what acquaintance, if any, we need with properties in order to be aware of their expression. I want only to note the point that not all the properties of a thing are open to casual, immediate inspection, whether these are expressive properties or any other kind. Compare the look of a horse with the look of a person. Federico Fellini has this to say about the look of Donald Sutherland, the actor he chose to play Casanova: "I like Sutherland because he has a wonderfully stupid look. He looks unborn."[9]

Although I do not know just what Urmson means by "aesthetic appreciation," I daresay that there could be as much aesthetic appreciation of a stupid look wrought in a picture as of a wise or compassionate look. But there may be no other "point of view" (other than the "aesthetic point of view") from which stupidity is a desirable characteristic in a person. Thus when Urmson identifies desirability as part of "a proper ground of aesthetic appreciation," he is led away from the remarkable (aesthetic?) phenomenon of one thing's being made to look like another. It may not matter so much whether that thing is a desirable thing.

How do we learn what a stupid person looks like? If something as evidently transparent as the look of a stupid person, or of a swift horse, is discernible only by those who are somehow acquainted with stupid people or swift horses, then the appearance of *difficulty* promises to be even less overtly detectable.

Ask yourself which is harder to do, to hit a pitched baseball with a bat, or to return a ping-pong ball. Do you know? Does it help to be told that you will have approximately three-fourths of a second to watch the baseball come toward you at the plate, and that you will have approximately one-tenth of a second to focus on the ping-pong ball before it bounces in front of you? I doubt that anyone who has not attempted these things can begin to answer, unless he has seen the attempts of others or knows the statistics concerning those who do attempt to do these things.

The proximate requirement is that one be able to imagine doing something oneself, or trying to, with enough vividness to achieve an estimate of the difficulty in doing it. It may be that this act of imagination, sometimes for some people, requires an actual attempt. There is a connection here with R. G. Collingwood's fine idea that all genuine appreciation of art, where appreciation entails understanding, is built upon an auditor's act of imagination in which he achieves the virtual creation of the work.

Are there, perhaps, difficulties that can be measured only by someone who has encountered them? If so, then whatever virtuosity is exhibited in overcoming them necessarily will be unappreciated by all who have no firsthand experience of these tasks. If that were true, then we might have to reconsider a chronic complaint of artists and athletes. Artists replying to critics, and athletes responding to sports reporters, sometimes voice peculiarly accusatory complaints, more or less on the order of "How dare you judge my work, you who have never painted or composed or concertized or tried to guard Julius Erving or return Ivan Lendl's serve?" The force of this charge seems moralistic. It seems to question the legitimacy of the critic's position, denying that he has the right to hold his opinion. It is like questioning the competence of a court on the grounds that it has no jurisdiction in the matter at hand, or, better, on the grounds that its jury is not composed of true peers of the defendant. It is as if only members of the relevant community were entitled to assess members of the community, and the relevant community consisted of actual practicing painters or tennis players.

This is an interesting idea, worth more attention than it will get if we treat these performers' complaints as (what they may well be, much of the time) the testy outbursts of people who have been pricked by negative remarks about their work.

There is another reason not to dismiss this kind of rebuttal too easily. It is the idea that the difficulty itself—or the overcoming of it—is part of what is being done. The difficulty is in the very substance of the thing. This is a difficult idea. It has been expressed forcefully by Claudio Arrau:

> Take the beginning of the Beethoven Opus 111. People play it with two hands because they don't want to risk dirty octaves. Well, first of all, it sounds different played with one hand, as written. And then technical difficulty has itself an expressive value.[10]
>
> The way it's [Brahms's F-sharp Minor Sonata] written is almost impossible—to make the big skips fortissimo. Actually, *without exception* people redistribute the notes. Here, for instance, they take the bottom notes in the right hand—F-sharp, C-sharp, A, F-sharp—with the left hand. . . . And then, of course, it's very easy. Again, I must say that such facilitation is wrong. Physical difficulty has itself an expressive value. When something sounds easy, its meaning changes completely.[11]

Arrau is saying that one can *hear* the difficulty, and I think that is right although, as I have been arguing, not every difficulty is identifiable as such to every spectator. One might need at least some experience, direct or indirect, with piano playing to hear the difficulty in a Brahms sonata. And this means that sometimes the challenge to the competence of critics may be not a denial of the critic's right but a claim of his factual incompetence. You are incompetent to appraise my work when, never having tried to do what I am trying to do, you cannot form any reliable opinion of how good my efforts are. With a little forcing we can say that you don't know what I am doing, and so you don't know what you are talking about when you talk about what I am doing. This construction seems attractive to me. Its plausibility depends on the truth of the proposition that at least some artistic and sportive tasks have a difficulty that can be measured only by those who attempt them.

Whether or not participation is requisite for one who would understand the efforts of those who do participate, non-participation is characteristic of a fan insofar as he is a fan. Whether or not he is a fan, when a spectator appreciates the difficulty of what is done, whether or not the difficulty is disguised, he has feelings whose dynamics are similar to those of a moral judge. We feel greater moral approbation for a person who does the right thing when it seems especially difficult for him to do that thing. And in ordinary life there are profound problems that escape the purview of many observers. For instance, there are difficulties in being a reliable spouse and parent that go unrecognized by many people, and these people are thus unable to appreciate—morally—the durability of married parents.

When the spectator is a fan, whether or not he can appreciate the difficulty of the players' efforts, he connects himself with the players in a very special way. Although he is not himself a player, which is to say that he does nothing *in the game*, his feelings are connected very directly to what is done by those who are playing. One of the best statements of this that I know of was given by the very fine baseball player Willie McCovey: "The fans sitting up there are *helpless*. They can't pick up a bat and come down and do something. Their only involvement is in how well you do. If you strike out or mess up out there, they feel they've done something wrong." McCovey goes on to offer this acute estimate: "You're all they've got. The professional athlete knows there's always another game or another year coming up. If he loses, he swallows the bitter pill and comes back. It's much harder for the fans."[12]

I think this is right, that it is often much harder for the fan. It is not just because the athlete knows that there will be another opportunity, as if the fan did not know that as well. It is because there is nothing the fan can *do* to make things better. Of course there is nothing the fan *did* that brought him his grief. And yet he feels it. I do not intend to attempt an explanation of this feeling, this feeling of being wrong, as Willie McCovey puts it, when in fact one has done nothing that could be right or wrong. Rather than take up questions in the psychology or sociology of sports fans, and rather than open a discussion of "identification,"[13] I will stick with this fact, the feelings engendered in fans by what the players do. It is a simple and beautiful phenomenon. And it is deep enough. It is located in what I think of as a moral dimension of sports appreciation.

Ethics

The relation of morality to sport is a marvelously rich topic, with a vast range of questions concerning the morality of cultivating an enjoyment of and a proficiency in activities that damage and destroy people, of taking pleasure in the emotional and physical pain of others, and so on; but I will be brief and develop only one extremely abstract point. I want to persuade you that our ability to become *fans* is an amazing fact about human beings. I am not recommending that you become a fan, nor am I lauding the condition in anyone who is a fan. I want only to note that the possibility of becoming a fan is a possibility predicated on the same fact that—if indeed it is a fact—makes morality possible.

For now I will characterize a fan (of some team or of a single competitor) as someone who *cares* how that team does in its competitions. It pleases a fan when his team wins, pains the fan when his team loses. A fan *hopes* that his team will win. The salient fact is that the team is *his*.

How do you get into this relation with a team? There are a number of possibilities, some of which will be mentioned in order to be excluded. First, let us not confuse the simple state of being a fan with thinking or predicting that the team will win. If you predict that the team will win, then you may hope that it will win, and if it does, then you will derive the pleasure that comes from being right. If you have enough confidence in your prediction, or someone else's, to make a bet, then certainly you will hope that the team wins, and you will be pleased and rich if it does. A bettor is a kind of fan, I suppose, but not the pure kind—unless he is the kind of romantic who bets on his team because he is already a fan, which is to say that it is already his team, and he has no reason to think he will win. In this case it is not the betting that makes him a fan; it is being a fan that makes him a bettor. We want, then, to characterize some way in which you can become attached to a team and care about its fortune independently of any expectations that the team will do well. There are a number of routes to this condition. Your friend or relative may play on the team. An enemy or relative may play on the opposing team. You or someone close to you may be the coach or owner of the team. The team may have members of your race, religion, sex, or age. (Or size. One of the reasons why I have tended to root for John McEnroe and Jimmy Connors over Bjorn Borg and Ivan Lendl, I think, while I don't seem to have cared how Roscoe Tanner does against them, is that they are more like me in size.)

In many cases a fan is connected with his team by a complex act of imagination, and the freedom of this act is not entirely unlimited. Besides the problem of estimating difficulty, which may seem like a problem in aesthetic appreciation, there may be the problem of thinking of oneself as sufficiently like the members of the team, which may be *like* a problem in moral appreciation. It may be easier to take pleasure in the success of someone relatively like oneself. It is thought by some that the popularity of the Boston Celtics is due in part to their having a relatively large number of capable white players in comparison with other American basketball teams. If this is true, then although this is a kind of racist phenomenon, it is not simple, generic racism, for it may be that some white fans have been unable to achieve an adequate "identification" with the Philadelphia 76ers or the Los Angeles Lakers, comparably successful basketball teams almost all of whose significant players are black. One of the finest baseball teams of the 1970's was the Pittsburgh Pirates. Sometimes when Dock Ellis was pitching, the entire team was "non-white," all nine players being either black or Hispanic. Some think that this explains the failure of Pittsburgh fans to fill their stadium consistently during those years.

This is *connected*, surely, with the affective component we see in social and moral racism when, say, a white person does not "feel" the pleasure and pain of a black person as keenly as he feels the pleasure and pain of another white person.

Why else might you become a team's fan? It might be your country's team, or your college's. It may be the team from your city or from the city in which you grew up or from the city in which you were living when you first became interested. Any of these connections can explain—and justify—your interest in the team. Your interest is predicated upon the interest of someone close to you, and that person has the interest of direct involvement. Such cases are different from the predicting and betting cases: in those you stake your reputation or your self-image or your money, and your interest in your reputation or your image or your money leads directly to an interest in the team's winning. In the former cases your interest is not by this kind of indirection, but it is indirect nonetheless, being predicated upon the direct interest of someone in whom you take an interest.[14]

There is a fascinating case that is none of these. It is the one in which your interest is engaged directly and is not predicated upon any anterior concern. This is what it is to be purely a fan, and just as in discussions of morality, some will say that such a thing does not happen, that it cannot happen. That is exactly like objecting to Kant that all imperatives are hypothetical. This is not the same as observing that whenever an act is obligatory there will be a hypothetical imperative in force, for this observation is no objection if there are still cases in which a categorical obligation obtains along with hypothetical ones. A persistent misreading has led to the widespread attribution to Kant of the conviction that no agent has moral worth when he does something he already wants to do. It would follow that an unqualifiedly good will can be exhibited only in the commission of acts that have no other, non-moral motive, and in fact Kant does suggest that it becomes increasingly easier to espy a good will as the non-categorical imperatives to the action become fewer. One might think, analogously, that the pure condition of a fan is to be found only in a fan who could have no rational reason for expecting his team to do well, nor any other wish to see the team do well. But this is a distortion of Kant's idea. As I understand him, a good will can show itself in any actions (except those that contravene one's duty), including trivial ones of no apparent moral consequence, and including those for which one has strong self-interested motives.

It is the same for fans. One's attachment to a team, just like one's obligation to do a deed, can be multiply grounded. You may have the stance of a pure fan of team T and also be linked to T by being a member of T yourself or by having predicted that T will win, for instance, or by any number of other contingent connections. Some contingent connection may have grounded your concern initially but have since lapsed, that is, ceased to be the ground of your connection. This is just how it is with Kantian categorical obligations: they may be commanded hypothetically as well, as when it is in your material interest to keep a promise, or when it is good business to develop a reputation for giving accurate change. A pure fan of Jimmy Connors would also once have had good, rational reasons for expecting him to beat Ivan Lendl at Wimbledon or in the U.S. Open.

When the pure condition happens—if ever it does, in morality or in sports appreciation—a person succeeds in attaching himself to a team in such a way that its success brings him pleasure and its failure is a source of pain, and these feelings are not mediated by any vested interest. This is a marvelous achievement. Think of what it means that a person is able to do this. It means that one of us can be moved by good or bad fortune that is not our own. (You may prefer to say that we can make some other fortune our own, but it is the same point, and I do not care which way it is formulated.)

This seems to me a wonderful thing. And it is wonderful yet again because this capacity, which makes it possible to be a fan, surely has its source in the capacity that makes morality possible. What this is, is the capacity for altruism. A straightforward form of moral skepticism is the denial that altruism is actual, or even possible. I am not a moral skeptic. For those who are and for those who are undecided I recommend some time pondering the lot of the true fan. It may not change your mind, but it will give you a chance to think freely about the phenomenon of fellow-feeling, unencumbered by whatever moral theories you already subscribe to, and without the pressure that comes with the consideration of official cases of moral gravity. It is very refreshing.

Reference Matter

Philosophical Writings of J. O. Urmson

This bibliography was compiled by C. C. W. Taylor, with the assistance of D. C. Cooper, H. R. D. Hardy, and J. O. Urmson.

Books Written

1956. *Philosophical Analysis: Its Development Between the Two World Wars.* Oxford.
——. Italian trans.: *L'analisi filosofica: Origini e sviluppo della filosofia analitica.* Trans. L. M. Leone. Milan, 1966.
——. Spanish trans.: *El análisis filosófico: Su desarrollo durante el período de entra guerra.* Trans. J. L. García Molina. Barcelona, 1978.
1968. *The Emotive Theory of Ethics.* London.
1982. *Berkeley.* Oxford.
——. Spanish trans.: *Berkeley.* Trans. J. M. Cordero. Madrid, 1984.

Books Edited

1960. *The Concise Encyclopedia of Western Philosophy and Philosophers.* New York, London. (2d, revised ed. 1975.) Contains numerous articles by the editor.
1961. J. L. Austin, *Philosophical Papers.* With G. J. Warnock. Oxford. (2d, enlarged ed. 1970; 3d, further enlarged ed. 1979.)
——. German trans.: *Wort und Bedeutung.* Trans. J. Schutte. Munich, 1975.
——. Spanish trans.: *Ensayos filosóficos.* Trans. A. García Suarez. Madrid, 1975.
——. Italian trans. by P. Stefani. Rovigo, forthcoming.
1962. J. L. Austin, *How to Do Things with Words.* Oxford. (2d, revised ed., with M. Sbisà, 1975.)

---. Spanish trans.: *Palabras y acciones. Como hacer cosas con palabras*. Trans. G. R. Carrió and E. A. Rabossi. Buenos Aires, 1971.
---. German trans.: *Zur Theorie der Sprechakte*. Trans. E. von Savigny. Stuttgart, 1972.
---. Italian trans.: *Quando dire è fare*. Trans. M. Gentile and M. Sbisà. Torino, 1974.
---. Japanese trans. by H. Sakamoto. Tokyo, 1978.

1975. *Aristotle, The Nicomachean Ethics*. Vol. 9 of *The Works of Aristotle Translated into English*. Trans. David Ross, revised by J. O. Urmson. Oxford. Reprinted in J. Barnes, ed., *The Complete Works of Aristotle* (Princeton, N.J., 1984).
1980. *Aristotle, The Nicomachean Ethics*. With J. L. Ackrill. Trans. David Ross, revised by J. L. Ackrill and J. O. Urmson. Oxford.

Articles and Reviews

1947. "Are Necessary Truths True by Convention?" *Proceedings of the Aristotelian Society*, supp. vol. 21: 104–17. (Symposium with Karl Britton and W. Kneale.)
"Two of the Senses of 'Probable.'" *Analysis*, 8 (1947–48): 9–16. Reprinted in M. Macdonald, ed., *Philosophy and Analysis* (Oxford, 1954).
1948. Review of J. O. Wisdom, *Causation and the Foundations of Science*. *Mind*, 57: 253–55.
1949. Review of W. H. Walsh, *Reason and Experience*. *Philosophy*, 24: 88–90.
1950. "On Grading." *Mind*, 59: 145–69. Reprinted in A. Flew, ed., *Logic and Language*, Second Series (Oxford, 1959), and (in German trans.) in G. Grewendorf and G. Meggle, eds., *Sprache und Ethik* (Frankfurt am Main, 1974).
Review of W. Carington, *Matter, Mind and Meaning*. *Mind*, 59: 406–7.
1951. Review of H. Reichenbach, *The Theory of Probability*. *Mind*, 60: 290–91.
1952. "Motives and Causes." *Proceedings of the Aristotelian Society*, supp. vol. 26: 179–94. (Symposium with R. S. Peters and D. J. McCracken.) Reprinted in A. R. White, ed., *The Philosophy of Action* (Oxford, 1968).
"Parenthetical Verbs." *Mind*, 61: 480–96. Reprinted in A. Flew, ed., *Essays in Conceptual Analysis* (London, New York, 1956).
1953. "Bibliography of Analytic Philosophy." *Revue Internationale de Philosophie*, 7: 384–86.
"The Interpretation of the Moral Philosophy of J. S. Mill." *Philosophical Quarterly*, 3: 33–39. Reprinted in Philippa Foot, ed., *Theories of Ethics* (London, 1967); in J. B. Schneewind, ed., *Mill* (London, 1968); in M. D. Bayles, ed., *Contemporary Utilitarianism* (New York, 1968); in S. Gorovitz, ed., *Mill: Utilitarianism*

(New York, 1971); in Thomas K. Hearn, Jr., ed., *Studies in Utilitarianism* (New York, 1971); and (in German trans.) in O. Höffe, ed., *Einführung in die utilitaristische Ethik* (Munich, 1975).

"Some Questions Concerning Validity." *Revue Internationale de Philosophie*, 7: 217–29. Reprinted in A. Flew, ed., *Essays in Conceptual Analysis* (London, New York, 1956), and in R. Swinburne, ed., *The Justification of Induction* (London, 1974).

Review of A. J. Ayer and R. Winch, eds., *British Empirical Philosophers*. *Mind*, 62: 281–82.

Review of J. Wisdom, *Other Minds* and *Philosophy and Psychoanalysis*. *Mind*, 62: 425–26.

Review of J. O. Wisdom, *Foundations of Inference in Natural Science*. *Philosophy*, 28: 84–86.

1954. Review of C. A. Fritz, *Bertrand Russell's Construction of the External World*. *Mind*, 63: 108–9.

1955. Review of J. Hospers, *An Introduction to Philosophical Analysis*. *Mind*, 64: 572.

1956. "Recognition." *Proceedings of the Aristotelian Society*, 56: 259–80.
Review of R. I. Aaron, *John Locke*. *Philosophy*, 31: 93.

1957. "What Makes a Situation Aesthetic?" *Proceedings of the Aristotelian Society*, supp. vol. 31: 75–92. (Symposium with D. L. Pole.) Reprinted in J. Margolis, ed., *Philosophy Looks at the Arts: Contemporary Readings in Aesthetics* (New York, 1962).
Review of Stephan Körner, *Conceptual Thinking*. *Philosophy*, 33: 267–69.
Review of H. D. Lewis, ed., *Contemporary British Philosophy*, Third Series. *Philosophical Quarterly*, 7: 267–75.

1958. "Saints and Heroes." In A. I. Melden, ed., *Essays in Moral Philosophy*, pp. 198–216. Seattle, Wash. Reprinted in J. Feinberg, ed., *Moral Concepts* (London, 1969).
Review of *International Encyclopedia of Unified Science*, vol. 1, pts. 1 and 2. *Mind*, 67: 571–73.

1960. "John Langshaw Austin (1911–1960)." *Analysis*, 20: 121–22.

1961. "J. L. Austin." With G. J. Warnock. *Mind*, 70: 256–57. Reprinted in K. T. Fann, ed., *Symposium on J. L. Austin* (London, New York, 1969).
Review of A. R. White, *G. E. Moore*. *Philosophical Quarterly*, 11: 190–91.

1962. "Histoire de l'analyse." In *La philosophie analytique*, pp. 11–39. Paris.
Review of N. Abbagnano, *Dizionario di filosofia*. *Mind*, 71: 425.

1963. Review of L. Wittgenstein, *Tractatus Logico-Philosophicus*, trans. D. F. Pears and B. F. McGuinness. *Mind*, 72: 298–300.

1965. "J. L. Austin." *Journal of Philosophy*, 62: 499–508. (The essay is a part of "Symposium: The Philosophy of John Austin," with Norman Malcolm, W. V. O. Quine, and Stuart Hampshire.)

Reprinted in K. T. Fann, ed., *Symposium on J. L. Austin* (London, New York, 1969).
1967. "Aristotle on Pleasure." In J. M. E. Moravcsik, ed., *Aristotle: A Collection of Critical Essays*, pp. 323–33. Garden City, N.Y. Reprinted London, 1968.
"Austin, John Langshaw." In Paul Edwards, ed., *The Encyclopedia of Philosophy*, vol. 1, pp. 211–15. New York, London. Revised version, "Austin's Philosophy," reprinted in K. T. Fann, ed., *Symposium on J. L. Austin* (London, New York, 1969).
"Ideas." In Paul Edwards, ed., *The Encyclopedia of Philosophy*, vol. 4, pp. 118–21. New York, London.
"Memory and Imagination." *Mind*, 76: 83–91.
"Ryle, Gilbert." In Paul Edwards, ed., *The Encyclopedia of Philosophy*, vol. 7, pp. 269–71. New York, London.
Review of F. Copleston, *A History of Philosophy*, vol. 8. *Philosophical Quarterly*, 17: 360–62.
Review of R. J. Hollingdale, *Nietzsche, the Man and His Philosophy*. *Mind*, 76: 144.
1968. "Criteria of Intensionality." *Proceedings of the Aristotelian Society*, supp. vol. 42: 107–22. (Symposium with L. J. Cohen.)
Introduction to H. A. Prichard, *Moral Obligation and Duty and Interest*. London, Oxford, and New York.
"The Objects of the Five Senses." *Proceedings of the British Academy*, 54: 117–31. (Annual philosophical lecture of the British Academy.)
"Utilitarianism: 1. The Philosophy." In D. L. Sills, ed., *International Encyclopedia of the Social Sciences*, vol. 16, pp. 224–29. New York.
1969. "Russell on Acquaintance with the Past." *Philosophical Review*, 78: 510–15. (Review of D. F. Pears, *Bertrand Russell and the British Tradition in Philosophy*.)
Review of R. J. Fogelin, *Evidence and Meaning*. *Mind*, 78: 623–26.
"Utilitarianism." In *The Isenberg Memorial Lecture Series 1965–1966*, pp. 63–79. East Lansing, Mich.
1970. "Moore's Utilitarianism." In A. Ambrose and M. Lazerowitz, eds., *G. E. Moore: Essays in Retrospect*, pp. 343–49. London.
"Polymorphous Concepts." In O. P. Wood and G. Pitcher, eds., *Ryle*, pp. 249–66. Garden City, N.Y. Reprinted London and Basingstoke, 1971.
1971. "Memory and Imagination." *Mind*, 80: 607.
Review of A. Ryan, *The Philosophy of John Stuart Mill*. *Philosophical Quarterly*, 21: 373–74.
1972. "Dramatic Representation." *Philosophical Quarterly*, 22: 333–43. Reprinted (in German trans.) in D. Henrich and W. Iser, eds., *Theorien der Kunst* (Frankfurt am Main, 1982).
Review of Gilbert Ryle, *Collected Papers*. *The Thomist*, 36: 346–48.
1973. "Aristotle's Doctrine of the Mean." *American Philosophical Quarterly*, 10: 223–30. Reprinted in A. O. Rorty, ed., *Essays on Aristotle's Ethics* (Berkeley, Los Angeles, and London, 1980).

"Representation in Music." In *Philosophy and the Arts*, Royal Institute of Philosophy Lectures (1971–72), vol. 6, pp. 132–46. London.
"Russell's Incomplete Symbols." *Analysis*, 33: 111–12.
1975. "A Defence of Intuitionism." *Proceedings of the Aristotelian Society*, 75: 111–19.
1976. "Fiction." *American Philosophical Quarterly*, 13: 153–57.
"The Performing Arts." In H. D. Lewis, ed., *Contemporary British Philosophy*, Fourth Series, pp. 239–52. London.
1977. "Filosofia Analitica." In *Enciclopedia del novecento*, Istituto dell'Enciclopedia Italiana, vol. 2, pp. 1005–15.
"Literature." In G. Dickie and R. J. Sclafani, eds., *Aesthetics: A Critical Anthology*, pp. 334–41. New York.
"Performative Utterances." *Midwest Studies in Philosophy*, 2: 120–27. Reprinted in P. A. French, T. E. Uehling, Jr., and H. K. Wettstein, eds., *Contemporary Perspectives in the Philosophy of Language* (Minneapolis, 1979).
1978. "The Goals of Action." In A. I. Goldman and J. Kim, eds., *Values and Morals*, pp. 131–41. Dordrecht.
1981. Review of W. F. R. Hardie, *Aristotle's Ethical Theory*, 2d ed. *The Pelican*, pp. 64–66.
1982. "Plato and the Poets." In J. Moravcsik and P. Temko, eds., *Plato on Beauty, Wisdom and the Arts*, pp. 125–36. American Philosophical Quarterly Monographs. Totowa, N.J.
1984. "Pleasure and Distress." *Oxford Studies in Ancient Philosophy*, 2: 209–21. (Review of J. C. B. Gosling and C. C. W. Taylor, *The Greeks on Pleasure*.)
Review of T. W. Adorno, *Aesthetic Theory*. *New Blackfriars*, 65: 290–91.
1985. "Berkeley on Beauty." In John Foster and Howard Robinson, eds., *Essays on Berkeley*, pp. 227–32. Oxford.
Review of N. J. H. Dent, *The Moral Psychology of the Virtues*. *New Blackfriars*, 66: 151–52.
Review of Peter Kivy, *Sound and Semblance*. *Music and Letters*, 66: 287–89.
Review of Lewis Rowell, *Thinking about Music*. *Music and Letters*, 66: 249–50.
1986. "Berkeley's Philosophy of Science in the *Siris*." *History of European Ideas*, Special Berkeley Issue, 7: 563–66.
"Russell on Universals." In Godfrey Vesey, ed., *Philosophers Ancient and Modern*, pp. 245–58. Cambridge, Eng.
1988. "Prichard and Knowledge." In Jonathan Dancy, J. M. E. Moravcsik, and C. C. W. Taylor, eds., *Human Agency: Language, Duty, and Value*, pp. 11–24. Stanford, Calif.
Forthcoming. *Aristotle's Ethics*. Oxford.
"Hare on Intuitive Moral Thinking." In D. Seanor and N. Fotion, eds., *Hare and Critics*. Oxford.
"The Methods of Aesthetics." In R. Shusterman, ed., *Analytic Aesthetics: Retrospect and Prospect*. Oxford.

Notes

Hornsby: Things Done with Words

It is for me a great pleasure to write for a volume in Jim Urmson's honor, and to write in an area to which he has contributed so much. I thank Christopher Taylor for comments on a previous draft.

1. J. O. Urmson, "Performative Utterances," in P. A. French, T. E. Uehling, Jr., and H. K. Wettstein, eds., *Contemporary Perspectives in the Philosophy of Language* (Minneapolis, 1979), pp. 260–67; the quoted conclusion is on p. 267. Page references to Urmson in the notes below are to this reprinting. The paper was originally published in *Midwest Studies in Philosophy*, 2 (1977): 120–27.
2. J. L. Austin, *How to Do Things with Words*, 2d ed. (Oxford, 1975).
3. I am influenced particularly by the work of Donald Davidson and John McDowell in philosophy of language. Essays by Davidson cited below are reprinted in his collection *Inquiries into Truth and Interpretation* (Oxford, 1984); all page references are to this collection.
4. Austin, pp. 4–7.
5. Ibid., p. 17.
6. See J. O. Urmson, "The Interpretation of the Moral Philosophy of J. S. Mill," *Philosophical Quarterly*, 3 (1953): 33–39.
7. Even when this is accepted, disagreements can surface about how speech acts are related to the doings of them. Can someone's doing one speech act be (the same as) her doing another? Or, asking more generally, can a single action be of different types? I answer yes, of course. For an argument especially pertinent to the present essay, see my "A Thesis Refutable by a Sentence Verifiable by Its Use," *Analysis*, 42 (1982): 177–78. To see our way through this controversy, we must be careful not to use terms that equivocate between particulars (Urmson's tokens) and universals (types). I use "doings," "actions," and "performances" only as denoting particulars; "things done" and "acts" only as denoting universals. I italicize phrases that mention acts. (If what I say about Urmson in nn. 12 and 13 below and about Searle in my main discussion of him

in the text seems correct, then my insistence here won't seem like mere pedantry: difficulties of interpretation [Urmson] or confusion [Searle] result from not employing any consistent policy.)

8. I take it that "with words" can be glossed "by using words"; and that the problem of understanding what is done with the words "with words" would be solved if we had a good account of the "by" to which philosophers of action have devoted much attention. My own view is that "by" does not express a relation either between actions or between acts, so that "with words" does not express a property either of actions or of acts. See my *Actions* (London, 1980), pp. 6–9.

9. It seems to be most people's view that, whatever the occasion, *vibrating the vocal cords* is not to count as a speech act. This view may be explained by pointing out that we know that we don't vibrate our vocal cords *intentionally*. If this is the correct explanation, then something like the conjunct I introduce with "perhaps" will be needed, and in what follows I assume that it is needed. But other explanations can be offered. And it would surely be wrong to suppose that any pre-theoretical notion of a speech act is a very definite notion.

10. Phrases like "Mary's speech act of . . ." may best be construed as implicitly relational: they are meant to convey an act (the thing [. . .] that Mary did) relative to an action (of Mary's doing it). Notice that "being intentional" and "being more basic than" likewise need to be understood in relation to acts *and* actions. (See my *Actions*, pp. 67–69.)

11. G. J. Warnock, see n. 13.

12. These things are what I referred to as "acts specifically associated with uses of performative sentences." There remains a difficulty about accommodating Urmson's terminology to the distinction between actions (tokens) and acts (types). When Urmson says that "every speech act has both a locutionary and an illocutionary aspect" (p. 262), he appears to put "act" to the work to which I put "action." However, if Urmson did mean particulars by "acts," then the thesis that performatives are not speech acts would be hard to take seriously: it could now only mean that an action such as someone's uttering her piece in a wedding ceremony is not a piece of speech.

13. Urmson, p. 265. It is true that at one point Urmson appears to deny that the term "performative" is appropriately used in connection with (so-called) explicit performatives at all. At p. 265 he writes, "An expression attached to an utterance to make its force clear . . . does not turn that utterance into a performative, which is essentially the doing of something." (It doesn't seem likely that Urmson is here merely asserting the categorial distinctness of linguistic items [to which expressions are attached] and items that are essentially doings.) In "Some Types of Performative Utterance" (pp. 69–89 of I. Berlin et al., *Essays on J. L. Austin* [Oxford, 1973]), G. J. Warnock distinguishes a class of Mark I performatives, with which Austin began his discussion, and another class made up of (roughly speaking) the explicit ones. Although Urmson puts the matter differently, his main contention represents concurrence with Warnock's view that Austin erred in assimilating the Mark II's to the

Mark I's. And it may be that the sentence I have quoted is used by Urmson to state this contention.

14. On the phonetic/phatic distinction, see Austin, p. 92; on the locutionary act, p. 109; on the rhetic act, p. 93; on the illocutionary act, p. 99.

15. Austin, p. 95.

16. John Searle, "Austin on Locutionary and Illocutionary Acts," in Berlin et al., pp. 141–59. Page references to Searle are to this reprinting. The paper was originally published in *Philosophical Review*, 77 (1968): 405–24.

17. I think that "locutionary" served two purposes in Austin, and that "rhetic" served the purposes to which Searle, following one of Austin's uses, puts "locutionary." As we have seen, Austin says of the locutionary act (a) that it is the sum of the phonetic, phatic, and rhetic, but also (b) that it is reported with *oratio obliqua* reports. Yet he uses the distinction between *oratio recta* and *oratio obliqua* to distinguish phatic from rhetic acts. If Austin did use "locutionary" ambiguously, then there is an explanation why at one stage (p. 102, as Searle notes at his p. 146) Austin should have given *oratio recta* characterizations of *locutionary* acts: Austin must at that stage have been using "locutionary" in sense (a), in which the locutionary is conceived as having the phonetic and the phatic, as well as the rhetic, as parts. I stick to "rhetic" where Austin and Searle might (ambiguously) have said "locutionary"; and I have replaced "locutionary" with "rhetic" in the quotations from Searle and Austin in the text.

18. Austin, p. 147.

19. Searle, p. 149.

20. Austin, p. 98.

21. "PERFORM an act" must be construed on a par with "DO something": acts are the things that performances (or doings or actions) are of; and we don't perform (or do) our actions (cf. n. 7 above). (A book called *How to Do Things with Words* might [with foresight] have been called *How to Perform Speech Acts*.)

22. Searle, p. 143.

23. When I speak of a *particular* act, I mean one having a particular content. So, for example, *warning* is a determinate act, and *warning that Kate has measles* a particular determinate act, subsumed by the determinable *illocutionary*. (I use "rhetic" and "illocutionary" also as predicates true of the determinate acts subsumed by the respective determinables.)

24. The argument was suggested to me by Julie Jack's "Stating and Otherwise Subscribing," *Philosophia*, 10 (1981): 283–313. It is notable that the main verb in explicit performatives—the so-called simple present—seems (from a semantic point of view) to be dynamic (i.e., non-stative) and both genuinely present in tense and genuinely perfective in aspect; whereas the same tense (from a syntactic point of view) seems everywhere else to be understood so that either it is stative, or the tense is future or past, or the aspect is imperfective (e.g., habitual). (Consider,

e.g., the possible uses of the third-person "He promises . . ." And see, e.g., Anthony Galton, *The Logic of Aspect* [Oxford, 1984], pp. 13–16.) In order to explain the usual absence in dynamic verb uses of a genuine present tense with perfective aspect, one might say that it is impossible to report a present event except as an ongoing event (where the idea of an event's being ongoing is conveyed with imperfective verb aspect). If this is right, then explicit performatives are not used to *report* events. This of course is connected with their not being usable to make statements, as may be apparent in the use of temporal perspective in the argument just given in the text.

25. See J. L. Austin, "Truth," in his *Philosophical Papers* (Oxford, 1961), pp. 117–33.

26. See E. J. Lemmon, "On Sentences Verifiable by Their Use," *Analysis*, 22 (1961–62): 86–89; Warnock; and Davidson, "On Saying That," *Inquiries*, p. 107, and "Moods and Performances," *Truth*, p. 117.

27. This is roughly put. When I say that an explicit performative is not used for stating, I mean that someone who uses the entire sentence "I V that q" (or "I V to X") does not state that she V's that q (or that she V's to X). If the argument in the text above is applied in the case of someone who comes out with the words "I state that it is raining" (say), it will have no tendency to show that she does not thereby state that it is raining, but could only show that she does not state that she states that it is raining.

28. See Davidson, essays 1–5.

29. I allude to work taking off from H. P. Grice's 1969 William James Lectures, "Logic and Conversation," given at Harvard.

30. For a theory of truth to be suitably constrained is for it to be such as to do the interpretative job to which it is put when it subserves a theory of locution, considered as a part of an account of the use of some language (an account considered in its turn as something that enables one to make sense of the people who speak it).

31. For instance, we must not think that there are large classes of indicative sentences that do not have truth values. (Here I can only suggest that such thoughts may depend on acceptance of a correspondence view of truth.)

32. This may explain why Austin said "With the constative utterance, we abstract from the illocutionary . . . aspects of the speech act, and we concentrate on the locutionary" (*How to*, pp. 145–46). But my point is not (as this remark of Austin's may suggest) that we can find an act of *stating* by abstracting from the illocutionary, but that the illocutionary act of *stating* is, so to speak, at no distance from the locutionary act of *saying*.

33. Searle's Principle of Expressibility (pp. 150–51) holds that "whatever can be meant can be said." Cases of *hinting, insinuating*, etc. have been said to give counterexamples. I suggest that these might be seen as counterexamples to the different principle that whatever can be meant can be *stated* (in the case of hinting, there is more to be said).

34. It follows (given the way in which theories of truth have been in-

troduced) that theories of truth will not treat non-indicatives. Some people have taken the evident fact that non-indicatives lack truth values to show that non-indicatives present a special problem for anyone who believes that theories of truth subserve theories of meaning. But I should prefer to say that the problem is not that theories of truth cannot treat non-indicatives: no theory could treat them if it did only what theories of truth can do. (In the account of non-indicatives that follows, theories of truth continue quite satisfactorily to play the role already assigned to them.)

35. There is such an assimilation, e.g., in the explicit performative account of non-indicatives given by David Lewis in "General Semantics," sec. 8 (in his *Philosophical Papers*, vol. 1 [Oxford, 1983], pp. 189–232) and in the mood-setter account given by Davidson in his "Moods and Performances," in *Inquiries*, pp. 109–21. Davidson criticizes the explicit performative account there; I criticize Davidson's in "A Note on Non-Indicatives," *Mind*, 95 (1986): 92–99 (see also n. 38 below).

36. No theory of meaning will speak at this schematic level; I am only trying to convey in a general way what we should imagine such theories as saying. Mood indicators have to figure in descriptions of sentences in rather the way that names of words figure there; but of course there are no words that they are names of. To obtain an instance of (P*) (which instance is itself a schema), write a mood indicator (e.g., a symbol I can name thus: "!") next to the name of a sentence. I take myself to be in essential agreement with P. F. Strawson in his "Austin and 'Locutionary Meaning,'" in Berlin et al., pp. 46–68. He suggests as a sort of canonical form for the description of an utterance:

X issues the _____ (that . . .) with the force of *xxxxx*,

where the name of a mood will fill the blank at "_____." I prefer to put the matter in such a way that it is an adverb (corresponding to a property of utterances) that we have to supply, because this serves to underline the fact that we are recounting what speakers *do*. And it will become clear why I should prefer to keep descriptions that reveal the mood of an utterance separate from descriptions that reveal its force.

37. A fuller defense of this view would require more acknowledgment than I have made of the point that, where there is a more interesting or informative report of what someone has done using words than is given in "She said that. . . ," it will often be inappropriate, and may be grossly misleading, to make the "She said that . . ." report. For example, it would be improper to report someone whose words were "I deny that *p*" as having said that *p*—unless one made it clear that this was something she said only in order that she could deny it. (Davidson supports the idea that in everyday *oratio obliqua* reports using "say," the reporter *says* the content he reports: "How am I to make [him whose speech I report] and me samesayers? Obviously by saying what he said" ["On Saying That," *Inquiries*, p. 104].)

38. Davidson emphasizes this point; see, e.g., "Moods and Performances," *Inquiries*, p. 110. On Davidson's own account of "Shut the

door," someone who utters this sentence can be taken to have said "My next utterance is imperative. You will shut the door." Now, given the point that nothing could guarantee any constancies between the use of a mood in uttered sentences and the force accruing to those utterances, we must take "My next utterance is imperative" to confer a mood-related, but not a force-related, property on the utterance that follows it. In that case Davidson's account and mine are related in the following way: that which on my account we have to see a speaker as doing is that which on Davidson's account we have to see a speaker as saying that she is doing.

39. Searle, p. 155.

40. What follows is provoked by some of Michael Dummett's writings. It is an indirect response to (e.g.) his "What Is a Theory of Meaning? (II)," in Gareth Evans and John McDowell, eds., *Truth and Meaning* (Oxford, 1976), pp. 67–137.

41. I rely on a formulation that McDowell and Davidson have used: a theory of meaning for L states something knowledge of which would suffice for interpreting L speakers' utterances. (See, e.g., Davidson's "Reply to Foster," in *Inquiries*, p. 171.)

42. "Basic" is used here in the sense in which it is used in philosophy of action; cf. n. 10 above.

Suppes and Crangle: Context-fixing Semantics

It is a pleasure to dedicate this paper to James Urmson, with whom we both enjoyed numerous philosophical discussions during the time he was at Stanford. We want to acknowledge the support of the Center for the Study of Language and Information at Stanford and the use of Lauri Karttunen's D-PATR grammar development system.

1. This view has been expressed earlier in Colleen Crangle, "A Computational Approach to Lexical Meaning" (Ph.D. diss., Stanford University, 1984), and in Colleen Crangle and Patrick Suppes, "Studies in Natural Semantics for Instructable Robots: Part 1," Technical Report No. 308, Institute for Mathematical Studies in the Social Sciences, Stanford University (Stanford, Calif., 1986), where it is integrated with the general semantic views of Suppes. (See his "Procedural Semantics," in R. Haller and W. Grassl, eds., *Language, Logic, and Philosophy*, Proceedings of the 4th International Wittgenstein Symposium, Kirchberg am Wechsel, Austria, 1979 [Vienna, 1980], pp. 27–35; "Variable-free Semantics with Remarks on Procedural Extensions," in T. W. Simon and R. J. Scholes, eds., *Language, Mind, and Brain* [Hillsdale, N.J., 1982], pp. 21–34; and "Congruency Theory of Propositions," in *Mérites et limites des méthodes logiques en philosophie*, Colloque international organisé par la Fondation Singer-Polignac en juin 1984 [Paris, 1986], pp. 279–99.)

2. David Kaplan, "On the Logic of Demonstratives," *Journal of Philosophical Logic*, 8 (1978): 81–98.

3. J. Barwise and J. Perry, *Situations and Attitudes* (Cambridge, Mass., 1983).

4. Patrick Suppes, "Semantics of Context-free Fragments of Natural

Languages," in K. J. J. Hintikka, J. M. E. Moravcsik, and Patrick Suppes, eds., *Approaches to Natural Language* (Dordrecht, 1973), pp. 370–94; "Elimination of Quantifiers in the Semantics of Natural Language by Use of Extended Relation Algebras," *Revue Internationale de Philosophie*, 117–18 (1976): 10243–59; and "Variable-free Semantics for Negations with Prosodic Variation," in E. Saarinen, R. Hilpinen, I. Niiniluoto, and M. P. Hintikka, eds., *Essays in Honour of Jaakko Hintikka* (Dordrecht, 1979), pp. 49–59.

5. See, for example, H. T. A. Whiting, ed., *Human Motor Actions: Bernstein Reassessed* (Amsterdam, 1984).

6. R. E. Maas and Patrick Suppes, "Natural-language Interface for an Instructable Robot," Technical Report No. 306, Institute for Mathematical Studies in the Social Sciences, Stanford University (Stanford, Calif., 1983); "A Note on Discourse with an Instructable Robot," *Theoretical Linguistics*, 11 (1984): 5–20; and "Natural-language Interface for an Instructable Robot," *International Journal of Man-Machine Studies*, 22 (1985): 215–40. See also Crangle and Suppes.

7. J. R. Hobbs, W. Croft, T. Davies, D. Edwards, and K. Laws, "Commonsense Metaphysics and Lexical Semantics," in *Proceedings of the 24th Annual Meeting of the Association for Computational Linguistics*, New York, June 10–13, 1986 (Morristown, N.J., 1986), pp. 231–40.

8. T. Winograd, *Understanding Natural Language* (New York, 1972); S. D. Isard, "What Would You Have Done If . . . ?" *Theoretical Linguistics*, 1 (1974): 233–55; G. A. Miller and P. N. Johnson-Laird, *Language and Perception* (Cambridge, Mass., 1976); Suppes, "Procedural Semantics"; and J. van Benthem, "Semantic Automata," Report No. CSLI-85-27, Center for the Study of Language and Information, Stanford University (Stanford, Calif., 1985).

9. J. McCarthy, "A Basis for a Mathematical Theory of Computation," in P. Braffort and D. Hirschberg, eds., *Computer Programming and Formal Systems* (Amsterdam, 1963), pp. 33–70; and R. Floyd, "Assigning Meanings to Programs," in *Mathematical Aspects of Computer Science*, Proceedings of the 19th Symposium in Applied Mathematics, American Mathematical Society, Providence, Rhode Island, 1966 (Providence, 1967), pp. 19–32. For a recent overview, see R. S. Boyer and J. S. Moore, "Proof-checking, Theorem-proving, and Program Verification," *Contemporary Mathematics*, 29 (1984): 119–32.

10. See, for instance, M. J. Cresswell, "Prepositions and Points of View," *Linguistics and Philosophy*, 2 (1978): 1–41, and the many references in that paper.

11. Patrick Suppes and E. Macken, "Steps Toward a Variable-free Semantics of Attributive Adjectives, Possessives, and Intensifying Adverbs," in K. E. Nelson, ed., *Children's Language*, vol. 1 (New York, 1978), pp. 81–115.

12. Suppes, "Semantics of Context-free Fragments," "Elimination of Quantifiers," and "Variable-free Semantics for Negations"; and Suppes and Macken.

13. S. M. Shieber, F. C. N. Pereira, L. Karttunen, and M. Kay, "A Compilation of Papers on Unification-based Grammar Formalisms: Parts

I and II," Report No. CSLI-86-48, Center for the Study of Language and Information, Stanford University (Stanford, Calif., 1986). On lexical-functional grammars, see R. Kaplan and Joan Bresnan, "Lexical-functional Grammar: A Formal System for Grammatical Representation," in J. Bresnan, ed., *The Mental Representation of Grammatical Relations* (Cambridge, Mass., 1982), pp. 173–281.
14. Suppes, "Semantics of Context-free Fragments."
15. Crangle and Suppes.
16. Barbara Partee, ed., *Montague Grammar* (New York, 1976).
17. More explicit details are to be found in Suppes, "Variable-free Semantics with Remarks."

Wilson and Sperber: Mood and Non-declarative Sentences

We are grateful to Christopher Taylor and Jonathan Dancy for comments on an earlier version.
1. For discussion of the notion of mood, see John Lyons, *Semantics* (Cambridge, Eng., 1977), vol. 2, secs. 16.2 and 16.3; Frank Palmer, *Mood and Modality* (Cambridge, Eng., 1986).
2. See Donald Davidson, "Moods and Performances," in A. Margalit, ed., *Meaning and Use* (Dordrecht, 1979), pp. 9–20, reprinted in Donald Davidson, *Inquiries into Truth and Interpretation* (Oxford, 1984), pp. 109–21, esp. p. 116.
3. See R. M. Hare, "Meaning and Speech Acts," *Philosophical Review*, 79 (1970): 3–24, reprinted in R. M. Hare, *Practical Inferences* (London, 1971), pp. 74–93, esp. p. 91.
4. For discussion of some non-literal, non-serious cases, see below; for arguments that force-based analyses of mood are inadequate to deal with embedded cases, see Michael Pendlebury, "Against the Power of Force: Reflections on the Meaning of Mood," *Mind*, 95 (1986): 361–72.
5. See Susan Schmerling, "How Imperatives Are Special, and How They Aren't," in *Chicago Linguistic Society: Parasession on Nondeclaratives* (Chicago, 1982), pp. 202–18.
6. See John Searle, "A Taxonomy of Illocutionary Acts," in Keith Gunderson, ed., *Language, Mind and Knowledge, Minnesota Studies in the Philosophy of Science*, vol. 7 (Minneapolis, 1975), pp. 344–69, reprinted in John Searle, *Expression and Meaning* (Cambridge, Eng., 1979), pp. 1–29.
7. See Colin McGinn, "Semantics for Non-indicative Sentences," *Philosophical Studies*, 32 (1977): 301–11, esp. 303–4. McGinn also argues convincingly against the claim that truth-conditional semantics can deal directly with non-declaratives. Though we will not consider this claim explicitly here, the notion of interpretive use developed in the following two sections of this essay lies well beyond the scope of truth-conditional semantics.
8. See Martin Huntley, "The Semantics of English Imperatives," *Linguistics and Philosophy*, 7 (1984): 103–33.
9. Ibid., p. 122.

10. See Dan Sperber and Deirdre Wilson, *Relevance: Communication and Cognition* (Oxford; Cambridge, Mass., 1986), chap. 4, sec. 7.
11. For discussion of the notions of analytic and contextual implication, see Sperber and Wilson, chap. 2, secs. 4–7.
12. See Dan Sperber and Deirdre Wilson, "Loose Talk," *Proceedings of the Aristotelian Society*, 86 (1985–86): 153–71. For summaries of relevance theory, see Deirdre Wilson and Dan Sperber, "Pragmatics and Modularity," in *Chicago Linguistic Society: Parasession on Grammar and Pragmatics* (Chicago, 1986), pp. 67–84; Dan Sperber and Deirdre Wilson, "A Précis of Relevance Theory," to appear in *Behavioral and Brain Sciences*.
13. For further discussion, see Sperber and Wilson, *Relevance*, chap. 4, secs. 7 and 8; see also references in n. 12 above.
14. See Sperber and Wilson, *Relevance*, chap. 4, sec. 9.
15. Kent Bach and R. M. Harnish, *Linguistic Communication and Speech Acts* (Cambridge, Mass., 1979), p. 40.
16. See Martin Bell, "Questioning," *Philosophical Quarterly*, 25 (1975): 193–212.
17. Lyons, p. 755.
18. See C. Hamblin, "Questions in Montague English," *Foundations of Language*, 10 (1973): 41–53; Lauri Karttunen, "The Syntax and Semantics of Questions," *Linguistics and Philosophy*, 1 (1977): 3–44, reprinted in Henry Hiz, ed., *Questions* (Dordrecht, 1978), pp. 165–210.
19. Lauri Karttunen and Stanley Peters attempt a non-truth-conditional account of these differences in "What Indirect Questions Conventionally Implicate," in *Chicago Linguistic Society: Papers from the Twelfth Regional Meeting* (Chicago, 1976), pp. 351–68.
20. Dwight Bolinger, "Yes-No Questions Are Not Alternative Questions," in Henry Hiz, pp. 87–105.
21. Bolinger, p. 102.
22. For the moment, we will ignore echoic questions, and make the simplifying assumption that interrogatives always reflect the speaker's estimations of desirability. In the next section, this simplifying assumption will be dropped.
23. This is not the only way to deal with exam questions and guess questions within our framework, but it is the simplest. When the full range of data is taken into account, a more complex treatment, involving triply interpretive use, may be needed.
24. Sperber and Wilson, *Relevance*, pp. 253–54.

Kenny: Aristotle on Moral Luck

1. Bernard Williams, "Moral Luck," *Proceedings of the Aristotelian Society*, supp. vol. 90 (1976): 115–35; Thomas Nagel, "Moral Luck," *Proceedings of the Aristotelian Society*, supp. vol. 90 (1976): 136–50. A revised version of Williams's paper appears in his collection *Mortal Luck* (Cambridge, Eng., 1981), pp. 20–39; and of Nagel's in his *Mortal Questions* (Cambridge, Eng., 1978), pp. 24–38. Subsequent references are to these revised versions.

2. Williams, p. 39.
3. Nagel, p. 27.
4. Immanuel Kant, *Groundwork of the Metaphysic of Morals*, trans. H. J. Paton (London, 1964), p. 3 (Prussian Academy edition, p. 394).
5. Nagel, p. 25.
6. Ibid., p. 28.
7. Henry Jackson, "Eudemian Ethics θ i, ii," *Journal of Philology*, 32 (1912): 170–221.

Taylor: Urmson on Aristotle on Pleasure

I am grateful to Jonathan Dancy, Justin Gosling, and, especially, Jennifer Hornsby for their comments on earlier drafts.
1. J. O. Urmson, "Aristotle on Pleasure," in J. M. E. Moravcsik, ed., *Aristotle: A Collection of Critical Essays* (Garden City, N.Y., 1967; London, 1968), pp. 323–33. For comments on Urmson's paper see G. E. L. Owen, "Aristotelian Pleasures," *Proceedings of the Aristotelian Society*, 72 (1971–72): 135–52; F. Lucash, "More Pleasure in Aristotle," *Rivista di Filosofia Neo-scolastica*, 66 (1974): 126–30; W. F. R. Hardie, *Aristotle's Ethical Theory*, 2d ed. (Oxford, 1980), p. 411; J. C. B. Gosling and C. C. W. Taylor, *The Greeks on Pleasure* (Oxford, 1982), pp. 273–76, 297–98.
2. Urmson, p. 326.
3. Aspasius, *Commentaria in Aristotelem Graeca*, vol. 19, p. 88, lines 11–13.
4. Urmson, pp. 329, 331.
5. The principle on which I rely, that in some cases one enjoys φ-ing by enjoying an immediate effect of φ-ing, has analogies elsewhere, e.g., one hears a car approaching by hearing the sound caused by a car approaching. The insistence that one does not enjoy φ-ing but only the effect of φ-ing is parallel to Berkeley's insistence that, *strictly speaking*, one does not hear the car, but only the sound (*First Dialogue*, in A. A. Luce and T. E. Jessop, eds., *The Works of George Berkeley* [London and New York, 1948–57], vol. 2, p. 204).
6. This abstract person is not to be identified with Urmson, who does not use the argument discussed in the paragraphs that follow.
7. Compare one version of the traditional argument from illusion. What one sees cannot be, e.g., a cat, because one could see *that very thing*, i.e., that irregular black shape, if no cat were present, e.g., if one were looking, not at a cat, but at a stuffed replica. The fallacy is the same.
8. Urmson, pp. 327–28.
9. Ibid., p. 329.
10. Touch is unique among the senses in that it can be exercised both actively and passively. One cannot exercise sight by being seen, hearing by being heard, smell or taste by being smelled or tasted, but one way of exercising the sense of touch is by being touched. Thus if someone strokes the back of my neck, I acquire tactile information, e.g., of the position of the stroker's hand, by being touched. The explanation seems to be twofold. Firstly, the verb "touch" has two principal uses. According to the first (let us call it "*A*-touching," i.e., "active touching"), touching

is a genus of activities of tactile exploration, including probing, stroking, and fondling among its species. This sort of touching requires intentional movement of parts of the body, normally the limbs. That is why it is appropriate to describe the example above as a case of Jane's touching the back of my neck with her hand, but inappropriate to describe it as a case of my touching her hand with the back of my neck. "*A*-touch" corresponds to "look at," "listen to," and perhaps "sniff," rather than to "see," "hear," and "smell." According to the second use ("*P*-touching," i.e., "passive touching"), to touch is simply to be in physical contact with; thus in the example the back of my neck *P*-touches Jane's hand and vice versa, though *I* do not *A*-touch her hand *with* the back of my neck. Secondly, the primary verb indicating the exercise of the sense of touch, answering to "see," "hear," "taste," and "smell," is not "touch" but "feel." Thus someone anesthetized might touch something, even intentionally, without feeling it, and hence without exercising the sense of touch. Not all feeling is tactile feeling: e.g., feeling a headache coming on or feeling giddy are not exercises of the sense of touch. Tactile feeling is feeling by *P*-touching, i.e., gaining information about the shape, size, position, movement, or texture of an object by direct physical contact between that object and one's body. Since x *P*-touches y either if x *A*-touches y or if y *A*-touches x, one way of exercising the sense of touch is by being *A*-touched. This does not hold for the other senses; e.g., "x is looked at by y" does not entail "x sees y." Hence there is no suggestion that x normally exercises the sense of sight in being looked at by y.

11. We do not distort Aristotle's thought by speaking of the activity of having sensations aroused in one. "Activity" renders *energeia*, which is strictly the actualization of a capacity or faculty; actually having a bodily sensation is the actualization of the capacity to have sensations of that kind.

12. Aristotle assigns to the process of swallowing the discrimination of certain properties of food—e.g., it is in swallowing, rather than tasting, that one perceives that what one is eating is warm or oily—and uses this to explain the fact that the same people are not greedy over food as are greedy over drink, which is discriminated by taste (*De Partibus Animalium* 690b29–691a4). This manifestly fails to explain discriminating greed over food; the only plausible explanation of the coexistence of lust for caviare with detestation of sago is the difference in taste.

13. E.g., *De Anima* 424a3–10, 432a16.

Moravcsik: Friendship and the Self

I wish to thank Michael Bratman, Dagfinn Føllesdal, Andrea Halliday, Stuart Hampshire, Edgar Morscher, Kayley Vernallis, Charles Young, and especially my co-editors for many helpful suggestions. They are not responsible for any shortcomings there may be in the final product.

1. For example, Aeschylus, *Prometheus Bound*, lines 270–73.
2. For example, Sophocles, *Philoctetes*, lines 169–90, 225–29, 691–705, and 950–60.
3. Aristotle, *Nicomachean Ethics* VIII.3–4.

4. For this interpretation see J. M. E. Moravcsik, "Reason and Eros in the 'Ascent'-Passage of the *Symposium*," in J. Anton and G. Kustas, eds., *Essays in Ancient Greek Philosophy* (Albany, N.Y., 1971), pp. 285–302.

5. This does not mean that a person might not have a variety of kinds of friends. Some of these may be good companions in sports, some in intellectual or political pursuits, and some in still other contexts. There are, however, some character traits that a person with a given ideal will expect to be present in all friends. One may share different activities with different persons, but it is expected that the same characteristic in the same context will be taken consistently as a reason for or against the forming or maintaining of specific friendships.

6. A very interesting modern account of this notion can be found in Josiah Royce, *The Philosophy of Loyalty* (New York, 1916), especially in chaps. 1 and 2.

7. Though within this essay we cannot describe exactly the kinds of changes that friendships are or are not supposed to survive, a brief sketch should give at least the outlines of such an account. We assume, of course, that the friend remains a person and that he or she remains the same person. We also assume that there will be a certain set of shared values and goals. A complete break in the latter is indeed a good ground for the discontinuation of a friendship.

8. This is not to deny that in the formation of a friendship contextually unique features, such as a certain smile or other facial expression, a characteristic gesture, or some striking verbal expression, may play a key role. But a genuine friendship will not founder solely because the friend loses some of these endearing features that attracted us to him or her in the first place.

9. For explanations of the different types of friendships see J. Cooper, "Aristotle on the Forms of Friendship," *Review of Metaphysics*, 30 (1977): 619–48.

10. For an illuminating account of supererogation see J. O. Urmson, "Saints and Heroes," in A. I. Melden, ed., *Essays in Moral Philosophy* (Seattle, Wash., 1958), pp. 198–216.

11. For an elaboration of the thesis that questions not amenable to deontic or utilitarian treatment were at the core of Greek ethics, see J. M. E. Moravcsik, *Plato and Platonism: Reflections on Being, Goodness, and Insight* (Oxford: Blackwell's, forthcoming), chap. 3.

12. See in this connection the notion of "loyalty to loyalty" in Royce, pp. 118–21.

13. Sophocles, lines 1452–68; my translation.

Heyd: Moral Subjects, Freedom, and Idiosyncrasy

1. J. O. Urmson, "Saints and Heroes," in A. I. Melden, ed., *Essays in Moral Philosophy* (Seattle, Wash., 1958), pp. 198–216. See pp. 203–4.

2. This may also explain the shift from the discussion of supererogation in terms of act-morality (as actions beyond the call of duty or beyond the requirement of moral rules) to that in terms of agent-morality

(as the adoption of a richer model by the agent). The two levels of analysis are compatible and complementary, as are the respective analyses offered in my *Supererogation* (Cambridge, Eng., 1982) and here.

3. Rawls treats his own model of a moral subject in the original position as a "construction," just a theoretical device meant to establish a moral consensus. Rawls believes that no lasting consensus can ever be achieved through a metaphysical model aiming at truth (moral realism), since its validity would always remain controversial. See "Justice as Fairness: Political Not Metaphysical," *Philosophy and Public Affairs*, 14 (1985): 223–51.

4. It is therefore hard to imagine how extreme rationalism or utilitarianism is at all possible. For it is inconceivable that the theory, or model, can determine every possible mode of the realization of the moral "ought." Some room for non-moral (idiosyncratic) reasons must always be granted, at least in our world of non-holy wills.

5. My view does not tally with that of philosophers such as John McDowell, who holds that the very perception of the moral features of the situation makes them the only relevant ones in the eyes of the agent, and thus completely silences all other, non-moral reasons for action. McDowell's view is also at variance with the common experience of dilemmas in which people find themselves caught between powerful (and perceptually lucid) moral reasons on the one hand and pressing non-moral reasons on the other. I shall not pursue here the discussion of the possibility of acting morally for non-moral reasons, which has been a controversial issue since Plato. See John McDowell, "Are Moral Requirements Hypothetical Imperatives?" *Proceedings of the Aristotelian Society*, supp. vol. 52 (1978): 13–29, and "Virtue and Reason," *Monist*, 62 (1979): 331–50.

6. For the non-universalizability of certain moral choices, including that of supererogation, see Alasdair MacIntyre, "What Morality Is Not," *Philosophy*, 32 (1957): 325–35.

7. Aristotle, *Nicomachean Ethics* 1137b22–24.

8. Maimonides recognizes this logically unavoidable incompleteness even of the ideal, God-devised system of the Law of the Torah, which recognition implies that the role of interpreting and applying the Law in particular contingencies should be left to the living human sages of every generation. Maimonides explicitly claims that if the Law depended on human contingencies it would be imperfect and its precepts would be undetermined. See *Guide to the Perplexed*, pt. 3, chap. 34.

9. Aristotle says of the relation between equity and justice that "they appear to be neither absolutely identical nor generically different." The same can be said of the relation between supererogation and justice (or duty). See *Nicomachean Ethics* 1137a33–34.

10. Cf. Ronald Dworkin, "The Model of Rules I," in *Taking Rights Seriously* (Cambridge, Mass., 1977), pp. 31–39. Dworkin, who has written extensively on the concept of legal discretion, also regards discretion as relative to a "standard" under which it is exercised. His distinction between strong and weak discretion, which partially corresponds to my distinction between idiosyncrasy of the second type and that of the first

type, consists in discretion in *rejecting* (or accepting) rules of law (on the basis of extralegal principles) vs. discretion in applying these rules. It is hard to tell whether discretion in the legal context is corrective or ameliorative, since it involves the dispute between legal positivists and nonpositivists.

11. Urmson, pp. 212–13.
12. Heyd, *Supererogation*, pp. 166–67.
13. Urmson, p. 214.
14. Immanuel Kant, *Critique of Practical Reason*, pp. 101–2, in the Prussian Royal Academy edition; p. 104 in L. W. Beck's translation (Indianapolis, 1956).
15. Immanuel Kant, *Metaphysical Principles of Virtue*, pp. 213–14 in the Prussian Royal Academy edition; p. 12 in J. W. Ellington's translation (Indianapolis, 1964).
16. Immanuel Kant, *Religion Within the Limits of Reason Alone*, p. 7 in the Prussian Royal Academy edition; p. 17 in T. M. Greene and H. H. Hudson's translation (New York, 1960).
17. For Kant's attempt to solve the problem of supererogation in a strictly deontological theory, see my *Supererogation*, chap. 3.
18. Heyd, *Supererogation*, chap. 8.
19. The justification of the essential role of idiosyncrasy in morality is similar to that provided by Bernard Williams for considering personal plans and preferences as the underlying basis for any moral theory (e.g., in "Persons, Character and Morality," in *Moral Luck* [Cambridge, Eng., 1981], pp. 1–19).
20. R. M. Hare, *Moral Thinking* (Oxford, 1981), p. 202.
21. Ibid., p. 211.
22. Ibid., pp. 199–201.

Dancy: Supererogation and Moral Realism

I am particularly grateful to Christopher Taylor, David Backhurst, and David McNaughton; I also owe thanks generally to colleagues at Keele, for their efforts to improve this paper.

1. The contrast between thick and thin properties comes from David Wiggins, "Truth, Invention and the Meaning of Life," *Proceedings of the British Academy*, 62 (1976): 331–78, and is elaborated in Bernard Williams, *Ethics and the Limits of Philosophy* (London and Cambridge, Mass., 1985), esp. chaps. 8–9. Thick properties are so called because they have more empirical content than the thin ones. If you know that an action is generous, you know more about what it is like than if you merely know that it is good.
2. The notion of salience is first found in David Wiggins, "Deliberation and Practical Reasoning," in J. Raz, ed., *Practical Reasoning* (Oxford, 1978), pp. 144–52.
3. Cf. J. O. Urmson, "A Defence of Intuitionism," *Proceedings of the Aristotelian Society*, 75 (1974–75): 111–19.
4. Paradigm cases here are J. O. Urmson, "Saints and Heroes," in A. I. Melden, ed., *Essays in Moral Philosophy* (Seattle, Wash., 1958), pp.

198–216; David Heyd, *Supererogation* (Cambridge, Eng., 1982); M. Clark, "The Meritorious and the Mandatory," *Proceedings of the Aristotelian Society*, 79 (1978–79): 23–33.
  5. The notion of "resulting" used here is intuitive. Later on the notion acquires some theoretical substance.
  6. Clark, p. 29.
  7. J. Raz, "Permissions and Supererogation," *American Philosophical Quarterly*, 12 (1975): 161–68.
  8. Heyd, pp. 170–71.
  9. Ibid., p. 171.
  10. Ibid., pp. 171–72.
  11. H. A. Prichard, *Moral Obligation* (Oxford, 1949), p. 153.
  12. Heyd, p. 172.
  13. Ibid., p. 175.
  14. For this relation and its difference from those of supervenience and universalizability, see my "On Moral Properties," *Mind*, 90 (1981): 367–85. Moral properties result from (exist in virtue of) non-moral properties; actions are right or wrong, good or bad in virtue of other properties they have, and those other properties themselves result from others, until the resultance tree takes us down to natural properties. But the moral properties are neither entailed by the natural ones nor simply co-present with them. To say this is not of course to offer an analysis of resultance; I know of none such.

Williams: What Does Intuitionism Imply?

  1. John Rawls, *A Theory of Justice* (Oxford, 1971), p. 34.
  2. For instance, see Stephen Toulmin, *The Place of Reason in Ethics* (Cambridge, Eng., 1950); R. M. Hare, *The Language of Morals* (Oxford, 1952); P. H. Nowell-Smith, *Ethics* (Harmondsworth, Eng., 1954).
  3. J. O. Urmson, "A Defence of Intuitionism," *Proceedings of the Aristotelian Society*, 75 (1974–75): 111–19.
  4. C. D. Parsons, "Mathematical Intuition," *Proceedings of the Aristotelian Society*, 80 (1979–80): 145–68.
  5. John Locke, *Essay on Human Understanding* IV.iii.18.
  6. Susan Hurley, "Objectivity and Disagreement," in Ted Honderich, ed., *Morality and Objectivity: A Tribute to J. L. Mackie* (London, 1985), pp. 54–97, in particular p. 56: "I shall refer to accounts that take the general concepts in some category to be logically prior to and independent of the specific as *centralist*. Non-centralism about reasons for action rejects the view that the general concepts *right* and *ought* are logically prior to and independent of specific reason-giving concepts such as *just* and *unkind*." I take it that in this formulation "independent of" introduces a non-symmetrical relation. For comment on Hurley's own non-centralism, see below.
  7. I have used this term for this purpose in *Ethics and the Limits of Philosophy* (London and Cambridge, Mass., 1985); see in particular chap. 8. If centralism is taken as a doctrine about the analysis or explication of such thick concepts as we have, I agree with Hurley—and, in this re-

spect, with John McDowell—in rejecting it. However, I do not think, as they do, that the degree of autonomy enjoyed by non-specific terms such as "right" is simply something to be determined by philosophical inquiry; the extent to which a society uses such terms as opposed to thick concepts is partly a historical question, and has important social implications. In this I agree with Alasdair MacIntyre; see *After Virtue* (London, 1981).

8. The statement to which the present discussion relates most closely is John McDowell, "Values and Secondary Qualities," in Honderich, pp. 110–29.

9. McDowell, p. 114.
10. Ibid., p. 117.
11. Ibid., p. 119; McDowell's emphasis.
12. Cf. "Wittgenstein and Idealism," in my *Moral Luck* (Cambridge, Eng., 1981), pp. 144–63.
13. McDowell, p. 122; his emphasis.
14. Hurley, p. 57; my emphasis.

Vermazen: Aesthetic Satisfaction

1. J. O. Urmson, "What Makes a Situation Aesthetic?" *Proceedings of the Aristotelian Society*, supp. vol. 31 (1957): 75–92.

2. W. E. Kennick notes that "Urmson's title contains a misnomer" in the introduction to sec. 4 of W. E. Kennick, ed., *Art and Philosophy: Readings in Aesthetics*, 2d ed. (New York, 1979), p. 396.

3. Urmson, pp. 76, 78, 82, 86, 87.

4. I am grateful to the editors of this volume for pointing out a serious problem in an earlier formulation of the thesis that satisfaction is a logical state. They suggested further that Urmson's topic was not satisfaction in my sense, but an emotional reaction one of whose components is a belief (true or false) that some want (etc.) of one's own has been satisfied. But in a case of that sort in which the subject's belief was false, I think it would be wrong to say that the subject was satisfied, though he might think he was. And in a case in which the belief was true, we would have satisfaction of my sort, so that the other components needed to make the "reaction" appear emotional would seem to be a sideshow. I suggest that "feelings of satisfaction" are just bodily sensations and further thoughts of the sort that typically accompany personal satisfaction in my sense, but that they do not *constitute* the satisfaction. The mistake I allege in Urmson's essay lies in his speaking as if those sensations and thoughts constituted the satisfaction.

5. Urmson, p. 78.
6. Ibid., p. 80.
7. Ibid., p. 83.
8. Ibid. Cf. "On Grading," *Mind*, 59 (1950): 145–69.
9. Urmson, "On Grading," p. 155.
10. Urmson, "What Makes," p. 85.
11. I am passing over the following problem: perhaps the truth about

something non-natural is itself natural. That is, perhaps the moral loftiness of the poetry is a natural property (since it is just that property the poetry has in virtue of containing a certain kind of truth) even though what the truth is a truth about is non-natural. It is completely obscure whether Moore would count truth as a natural or a non-natural property or whether perhaps the truth would be natural or non-natural according to the natural or non-natural character of what it was the truth *about*.

12. Urmson, "What Makes," pp. 85–86.
13. Ibid., pp. 88, 90.
14. Ibid., p. 86.
15. Ibid., pp. 82, 85.
16. Paul Oskar Kristeller, "The Modern System of the Arts," *Journal of the History of Ideas*, 12 (1951): 465–527 (first part) and 13 (1952): 17–46 (second part).
17. Morris Weitz, "The Role of Theory in Aesthetics," *Journal of Aesthetics and Art Criticism*, 15 (1956): 27–35.
18. Immanuel Kant, *Critique of Judgment* (Berlin, 1790), sec. 61.
19. Clive Bell, *Art* (London, 1914), pp. 36n and 161.
20. Roger Fry, *Transformations: Critical and Speculative Essays on Art* (London, 1926), p. 27.
21. Kant, sec. 49.
22. See Bell, and Fry.
23. Leo Tolstoy, *What Is Art?*, trans. Aylmer Maude (New York, 1960). Originally published in 1898.
24. Fry, pp. 8–9. Fry cites C. Mauron, "The Nature of Beauty in Art and Literature," in *Hogarth Essays* (London, 1926). He goes on to say, "And it became evident to me that the essential of great tragedy was not the emotional intensity of the events portrayed, but the vivid sense of the inevitability of their unfolding, the significance of the curve of crescendo and diminuendo which their sequence describes, together with all the myriad subsidiary evocations which, at each point, poetic language can bring in to give fullness and density to the whole organic unity" (p. 10).
25. Morris Weitz (see note 17 above); W. E. Kennick, "Does Traditional Aesthetics Rest on a Mistake?" *Mind*, 62 (1958): 317–34.
26. Monroe Beardsley, *Aesthetics: Problems in the Philosophy of Criticism* (New York, 1958), pp. 533–35.
27. Frances Hutcheson, *An Inquiry Concerning Beauty* (Glasgow, 1725), sec. 2, art. 3.

Kivy: Live Performances and Dead Composers

The first draft of this essay was presented as part of a symposium devoted to the aesthetics of Monroe Beardsley at the Pacific Division of the American Philosophical Association, Sacramento, California, March 26, 1982. I am grateful to my co-symposiasts, Margaret Battin and Guy Sircello, as well as to Henning Jensen, who was also present, for many helpful suggestions. Subsequent versions were presented at Swarthmore

College, Stevens Institute of Technology, Trenton State College, Arizona State University, and, most recently, at the University of Cincinnati, as one of my Taft Lectures. Many people in the audiences at these presentations gave me constructive criticism. I cannot name them; but I do thank them. And I wish to express my gratitude to Jonathan Dancy and Christopher Taylor for saving me from bloopers, great and small, in their reading of the revised manuscript.

1. Monroe C. Beardsley, *Aesthetics: Problems in the Philosophy of Criticism* (New York, 1958), p. 24.
2. Ibid., p. 22.
3. Ibid.
4. Alejandro Enrique Planchart, "The Performance of Early Music in America," *Journal of Musicology*, 1 (1982): 21.
5. Beardsley, p. 24.
6. Ibid., p. 23.
7. Randall R. Dipert, "The Composer's Intentions: An Examination of Their Relevance for Performance," *Musical Quarterly*, 66 (1980): 206, 207.
8. Ibid., p. 212.
9. One might, perhaps, argue after the manner of a rule utilitarian that although some pieces of music sound better in some respects if the composer's performing intentions are ignored, in general following the composer's intentions come what may will decrease the chance of ignoring them where observance would make the music sound better. Ignoring them on occasion, even when the occasion is propitious, will in the long run tend to encourage ignoring them when the occasion is wrong, thus making on the whole for more bad performances than good. Even here, however, where following the composer's intentions is made a hard and fast rule, it is the result, not the rule, that decides the issue after all.
10. I should point out that expressing my view in terms of possibly conflicting moral duties and obligations is not essential to the main argument of my paper. *Any* moral theory will do, *just so long as there is allowance made in it for duties and obligations to the dead.*
11. Dipert, p. 213.
12. Aristotle, *Nicomachean Ethics* 1101a22–b9, trans. Martin Ostwald (Indianapolis and New York, 1962), pp. 26–27.
13. Thomas Nagel, "Death," in James Rachels, ed., *Moral Problems*, 3d ed. (New York, 1979), p. 453.
14. Aristotle, 1100a18–21, trans. Ostwald, pp. 23–24.
15. G. W. Leibniz, *New Essays on Human Understanding*, trans. Peter Remnant and Jonathan Bennett (Cambridge, Eng., 1981), pp. 93–94.
16. Nagel, pp. 453–54, 455.
17. Joel Feinberg, "Harm and Self-Interest," in *Justice and the Bounds of Liberty* (Princeton, 1980), pp. 61, 62, 64.
18. Ibid., pp. 65, 68.
19. Dipert, p. 213.

20. Ruth Barcan Marcus, "Moral Dilemmas and Consistency," *Journal of Philosophy*, 77 (1980): 126.

Walton: Sound Patterns

This is a revised version of a paper with the same title, which appeared in *In Theory Only*, 2 (1977): pp. 3–16. The penultimate section has been considerably expanded; the final section, which is new, elaborates a suggestion made in a footnote in the earlier version.

1. I should emphasize that this question, as I construe it, is a question about our cultural institution of music. I am asking what roles pieces and performances have in our institution, how they are regarded and treated by participants in the institution: composers, performers, and appreciators. Neither works nor performances are *intrinsically* primary, apart from their place in some cultural institution.

2. A musical system may be understood as consisting, partly, of conventions concerning what performance features are to be notated in scores.

3. Many scores indicate not only what sorts of sounds are to be produced but also how they are to be produced. If the latter indications are regarded as contributing to the specification of patterns, the patterns specified are not pure sound patterns. I will ignore this complication for now but will return to it in the final section.

4. This amounts to a view of the nature of musical works that Nicholas Wolterstorff considers and rejects in "Towards an Ontology of Art Works," *Noûs*, 9 (1975): 130, namely, his formula (2). I would answer Wolterstorff's objection to (2) by denying that (in his terms) all performances of a work are necessarily examples of the kind with which the work is identical; i.e., I claim that a performance of a work need not fit perfectly the pattern that constitutes the work. Insofar as he endorses his formula (4), Wolterstorff and I agree, however, that the notion of a musical work is closely tied up with the notion of what constitutes a correct performance of it.

5. Cf. Wolterstorff, pp. 140–41.

6. This is essentially the view espoused by Nelson Goodman in *Languages of Art* (Indianapolis, Ind., 1968), pp. 117–18, 186–87.

7. J. O. Urmson has suggested that, in all of the performing arts (including music, cooking, ballet, etc.), what the creative artist does is to produce a recipe or set of performance instructions for the performer. This is only part of the story, in my opinion, at least with regard to music. Cf. J. O. Urmson, "The Performing Arts," in H. D. Lewis, ed., *Contemporary British Philosophy*, Fourth Series (London, 1976), pp. 239–52, and "Literature," in G. Dickie and R. J. Sclafani, eds., *Aesthetics: A Critical Anthology* (New York, 1977), pp. 334–41. It may seem obvious that "[m]usic is essentially sound; the performer produces sounds in accordance with the instructions of the composer" (Urmson, "Literature," p. 388). But I find this claim misleading, for reasons that will become clear shortly.

8. This helps to explain the appropriateness of saying that both performers and critics "interpret" works of art. Cf. Richard Wollheim, *Art and Its Objects* (New York, 1968), p. 73.

9. Stories can be construed as patterns, not of words, but of plot features, which are presented and portrayed by the specific words that the storyteller chooses.

10. For a fascinating collection of examples of permissible ways of elaborating various melodic formulas in an earlier age, see Diego Ortiz, *Tratado de glosas sobre clausulas y otros generos de puntos en la musica de violones* (Rome, 1553), ed. Max Schneider (Basel, 1936).

11. Not the same patterns; patterns of the same *kinds*.

12. Cf. Heinrich Schenker, *Neue Musikalische Theorien und Phantasien*, Universal Edition, vol. 1 (Vienna, 1906); vol. 2, pt. 1 (1910); vol. 2, pt. 2 (1922); and numerous secondary sources in recent music theory.

13. That suggestion would also have the counterintuitive consequence that different performances that have the job of presenting the same scored pattern—if that is the anointed one—but very different deeper-level patterns would count as performances of the same piece.

14. The considerations adduced in the final section of the essay will necessitate an additional requirement for performances to be of the same piece. Roughly, the performances must be such that they are to be heard in the same manner, or in the same "categories."

15. My discussion in this section is very sketchy. It relies heavily on more general considerations developed in my "Categories of Art," *Philosophical Review*, 79 (1970): 334–67; reprinted in W. E. Kennick, ed., *Art and Philosophy: Readings in Aesthetics*, 2d ed. (New York, 1979), pp. 287–315. Jerrold Levinson applied these considerations to music in ways that are similar in some respects to mine, in his "What a Musical Work Is," *Journal of Philosophy*, 77 (1980): 5–28. The most important differences between his conclusions and mine are, first, that he takes a single pattern rather than a set of them to be (partially) constitutive of a work and, second, that he takes the relevant pattern to be a sound/performing-means pattern; no pure sound pattern is involved.

16. This difference will be less pronounced if the performance is heard in the category of piano(-sounding) performances, as well as in that of electronic performances, and perhaps non-existent if it is not heard also in some such category as that of electronic performances. But the difference will be dramatic if it is heard as an electronic performance and not as a piano performance. (Depending on the circumstances, this could be the appropriate way to hear it.) Cf. Walton, sec. 3(d).

17. This is Levinson's suggestion, pp. 19–20.

18. They are to be heard in the "category" of eighteenth-century works, where this category is to be understood as a "perceptually distinguishable" one. Cf. Walton, sec. 2.

19. Alternatively, we might identify the piece with the set of patterns plus the appropriate way or ways of hearing its performances, or with the set of patterns plus the categories its performances are to be heard in.

Cohen: Sports and Art

1. It is important to imagine these cases as vividly as possible. It is not easy to give examples from sports that are equally familiar to all who might see this paper, and so here and later I will give a variety of examples, keeping these intrusions in footnotes in order to avoid making the text periodically arcane for various readers. The kind of gratuitous blunder I am thinking of here seems to be one that easily could have been avoided. For instance, getting picked off base when there was no reason to take a big lead; muffing a slow grounder by overrunning it when the batter is known to run so slowly that there was no need to rush the ball; missing a low, floating overhead two feet from the net; going up for a lay-up and having it blocked when a teammate is wide open on the other side of the basket; being run out after daring to cross the crease when one needn't have risked it because the bowler has been ineffective.

2. It is not so hard to conceive examples. I will give one. Suppose a basketball game is in its last few seconds with the score very close. A forward grabs a defensive rebound and heaves an outlet pass to a guard. The play works. The breaking teammate receives the pass and dribbles toward the other basket with no one within six feet of him. Instead of going straight in for a simple lay-up, he pulls up at the circle, leaps high and far, and executes a 360-degree turn in midair, culminating in a gargantuan slam-dunk. Suppose that he makes the shot, or nearly makes it, and, whether he makes it or not, if you like, that the force of his shot destroys the goal and backboard.

3. In recent years the Chicago White Sox—my baseball team—have turned up a number of outfielders who occasionally make this kind of play: running at great speed on a difficult angle to the ball, the fielder just manages to stab the ball in a one-hand catch over the shoulder. Good. But if the fielder had positioned himself properly and gotten even a decent jump on the ball, he could have made a standard two-hand catch above his head, standing still, facing the infield. What are we to make of the spectacular catch? On the one hand, many journeyman outfielders could have made the less dramatic putout; but on the other hand, only a few of all the outfielders in the game could have made the play in just the way that these White Sox outfielders did. How do we estimate what they did?

4. Both these points are implicated in one of the earliest appreciations of *difficulty* I have seen, Aristotle's. In *Poetics* VI, Aristotle presents a number of arguments to show that the plot is the most important of what he calls "the parts" of tragedy. It is difficult to make out just what he means by "most important." (Given various points he makes in his logical works, we may assume that he is not presenting any argument that is a mere truism. We must not assume, then, that by "most important part" he could mean the only necessary part, for then one of his arguments would be that the plot is the only necessary part because it is the only necessary part.) But it seems clear that when one part is more im-

portant than another, excellence in the more important part contributes more to the excellence of a tragedy than does excellence in the less important part. Aristotle's final argument in favor of the preeminence of the plot is his observation that beginning tragedians achieve success in constructing plots later than they achieve success in creating other parts of a tragedy. This sounds like an observation that it is relatively more difficult to construct a plot, and this is linked to the assertion that it is a more valuable thing to do.

5. It is possible to think of a work's taking virtuosity as its own subject. A sensitive, useful analysis of this idea is Thomas Carson Mark's "On Works of Virtuosity," *Journal of Philosophy*, 77 (1980): 28–45.

6. It is interesting to read of the development of pole-vaulting in the fen country of England, where it became the preferred method of moving about for those who did not care for the standard method, slodging. I owe my acquaintance with this fact as well as what little biology I know of the fen country to my wife, Julie, and both of us owe our introduction to the lore of that country and the country itself to our good friend Jeremy Butterfield of Jesus College, Cambridge.

7. Quoted by Mark Jacobson in "Doctor One and Only," *Esquire*, February 1985, p. 116.

8. J. O. Urmson, "What Makes a Situation Aesthetic?" *Proceedings of the Aristotelian Society*, supp. vol. 31 (1957): 88–89.

9. This quotation is said to appear in Hollis Alpert's recent book *Fellini: A Life* (New York, 1986). I have not located the book. The quotation is given by Cheryl Lavin in *Sunday, The Chicago Tribune Magazine*, February 15, 1987, p. 3.

10. Quoted in Joseph Horowitz, *Conversations with Arrau* (New York, 1982), p. 121. For this reference I am grateful to Larry Kart, who gave it to me during a conversation about his valuable essay "Taking a Look at the History of Jazz: The Bass Steps out of the Shadows," *Chicago Tribune*, March 11, 1984.

11. Horowitz, pp. 152–53.

12. Quoted by Roger Angell in *Late Innings* (New York, 1982), p. 105.

13. The word "identification" seems exactly the right word—and I will use it later—but I distrust it. Instead of explaining the phenomenon, it may just name it. And it is tempting to use it for a number of different phenomena. With regard to books I read, plays and movies I see, and sports I watch, for instance, it would not be remarkable for me to say I "identify with" King Lear, King Saul, Roy Hobbs, Cary Grant, Dustin Hoffman, Sandy Koufax, and Willie McCovey. But my relations to these figures are very different from one another, and it may cover more than it reveals to call them all cases of identification.

14. This kind of fellow-feeling ought to be a central topic in serious discussions of morality. The logic of the thing has been taken up by Thomas Nagel in *The Possibility of Altruism* (Princeton, 1979) and in a number of essays by Nagel and others that have followed that book. For an excellent introduction to the phenomenology of feelings on behalf of others, as well as many other matters in this paper, I am indebted to Stephen Cohen and his essay "Vicarious Pride" (unpublished).

Index of Names

In this index an "f" after a number indicates a separate reference on the next page, and an "ff" indicates separate references on the next two pages. A continuous discussion over two or more pages is indicated by a span of page numbers, e.g., "pp. 57–58." *Passim* is used for a cluster of references in close but not consecutive sequence.

Aeschylus, 293
Alpert, H., 304
Angell, R., 304
Aristotle, 2, 6ff, 11, 154f, 161–63, 229–31, 293ff, 300, 303f; on knowledge, 12–14; on moral luck, 108–19; on pleasure, 120–32; on friendship, 133, 136, 144, 150
Arrau, C., 268
Aspasius, 121, 292
Austin, J. L., 4f, 12, 27–40 *passim*, 44f, 283–86
Ayer, A. J., 12

Bach, J. S., 220–26 *passim*, 236, 251–53
Bach, K., 91, 291
Barwise, J., 48, 288
Beardsley, M., 216–17, 219–25, 299f
Beethoven, L., 223–25, 233–34, 238–39, 243, 248–50, 268
Bell, C., 212–15, 299
Bell, M., 93, 291

Bentham, J., 154
Benthem, J. van, 55, 289
Berkeley, G., 292
Berlin, I., 163, 166
Berlioz, H., 222, 239
Bolinger, D., 94–95, 291
Borg, B., 270
Boyer, R. S., 289
Bradley, F. H., 12
Brahms, J., 240, 252–53, 268
Bresnan, J., 290

Cage, J., 261
Cartwright, N., 19
Chopin, F., 255–57
Christo, 213, 261
Clark, M., 176–79, 182–85, 297
Cohen, S., 304
Collingwood, R. G., 267
Connors, J., 270, 272
Cook Wilson, J., 12–15
Cooper, J., 294
Crangle, C., 288. *See also* Suppes, P., and C. Crangle
Cresswell, M. J., 289

Index of Names

Croft, W., 289

Dancy, J., 297
Davidson, D., 78, 139, 283–90 passim
Davies, T., 289
Descartes, R., 1
Dipert, R. R., 225–27, 232–33, 300
Dummett, M. A. E., 288
Dworkin, R., 295–96

Edwards, D., 289
Erving, J., 265ff
Evert, C., 259

Feinberg, J., 231–32, 300
Fellini, F., 266
Floyd, R., 55, 289
Frege, G., 32
Fry, R., 213–15, 299

Galton, A., 286
Gauguin, P., 106–7, 110
Gettier, E. L., 15
Goodman, N., 301
Gosling, J. C. B., 292
Grice, H. P., 286

Hamblin, C., 94, 291
Hampshire, S., 7
Handel, G., 227, 233ff
Hardie, W. F. R., 292
Hare, R. M., 79, 168–69, 290, 296f
Harnish, R. M., 91, 291
Haydn, J., 232–33
Hegel, G. W. F., 215
Heyd, D., 176–86 passim, 297
Hobbes, T., 154
Hobbs, J. R., 289
Hornsby, J., 82, 283f
Horowitz, J., 304
Housman, A. E., 207ff
Hume, D., 14
Huntley, M., 83–84, 87, 290
Hurley, S., 192, 196, 297–98
Hutcheson, F., 217, 299

Isard, S. D., 55, 289

Jack, J., 285–86
Jackson, H., 292
Jacobson, M., 304
James, W., 11
Joachim, H. H., 12
Joan of Arc, 115
Johnson-Laird, P. N., 55, 289
Joseph, H. W. B., 11f
Josquin Des Prés, 239

Kandinsky, F., 213
Kant, I., 4, 106–8, 116ff, 154–67 passim, 212, 213–15, 272, 292, 296, 299
Kaplan, D., 48, 288
Kaplan, R., 290
Kart, L., 304
Karttunen, L., 70, 94, 289, 291
Kay, M., 70, 289
Kennick, W. E., 215, 298f
Kneale, W., 11
Kohlberg, L., 154
Koufax, S., 262
Kraft, W., 242
Kristeller, P., 211, 299

Lavin, C., 304
Laws, K., 289
Leibniz, G. W., 230, 300
Lemmon, E. J., 286
Lendl, I., 267, 270, 272
Levinson, J., 302
Lewis, D., 287
Ligeti, G., 242
Locke, J., 191, 297
Lucash, F., 292
Lyons, J., 93–94, 290f

Maas, R. E., 53, 60, 289
McCarthy, J., 55, 289
McCovey, W., 269
McDowell, J., 192–96, 283, 288, 295, 298
McEnroe, J., 270
McGinn, C., 82–83, 290
MacIntyre, A., 295, 298
Macken, E., 59, 289
Maimonides, 295

Index of Names

Marcus, R. B., 234, 301
Mark, T. C., 304
Mauron, C., 214, 299
Mendelssohn, F., 233
Meyer, L., 220
Mill, J. S., 11, 28, 154
Miller, G. A., 55, 289
Moore, G. E., 11, 189, 207, 299
Moore, J. S., 289
Moravcsik, J. M. E., 294
Mozart, W., 239, 243, 250, 255ff, 259
Musil, R., 136

Nagel, T., 106–8, 229–31, 291–92, 300, 304
Nietzsche, F., 160
Nowell-Smith, P. H., 297

Ockeghem, J., 221
Ortiz, D., 302
Owen, G. E. L., 292

Palmer, F., 290
Parsons, C. D., 191, 297
Pasternak, B., 146
Pendlebury, M., 290
Pereira, F. C. N., 70, 289
Perry, J., 48, 288
Peters, S., 291
Philoctetes and Neoptolemus, 133, 143–46, 148–51
Piaget, J., 154
Picasso, P., 259
Planchart, A. E., 300
Plato, 133–36, 154, 295
Poincaré, H., 51
Priam, 109–10, 115
Price, H. H., 11
Prichard, H. A., 4, 12–15, 24, 180–89 *passim*, 297

Raphael, 212–13
Rawls, J., 154f, 163, 189–90, 295, 297
Raz, J., 179–80, 297
Rich, B., 260
Ross, W. D., 189

Royce, J., 294
Russell, B., 11
Ryle, G., 20–23, 120–26 *passim*

Schenker, H., 253, 302
Schmerling, S., 82, 290
Searle, J. R., 33–35, 44–45, 82, 283–90 *passim*
Serkin, R., 255
Shieber, S. M., 70, 289
Sidgwick, H., 190–91
Socrates, 115
Solon, 109
Sophocles, 144–46, 293f
Sperber, D., and D. Wilson, 87–90 *passim*, 95–96, 101, 291
Spinoza, B., 163–64
Stamitz, J., 232–33
Strawson, P. F., 287
Suppes, P., 48, 53, 55, 59f, 288f
Suppes, P., and C. Crangle, 73, 288ff
Sutherland, D., 266

Tanner, R., 270
Taylor, C. C. W., 292
Tolstoy, L., 213–14, 299
Toulmin, S., 297

Urmson, J. O., 1–2, 4, 10; on speech acts, 4–5, 27–33, 37, 283–84; on pleasure, 6, 120–29, 132, 292; on supererogation, 7, 152, 162, 173–74, 177, 186, 294, 296; on the aesthetic, 9, 201–11, 217–18, 265–66, 298f, 301, 304; on the interpretation of utilitarianism, 28, 283; on intuitionism, 189–90, 206, 296f; on grading, 206, 298

Varèse, E., 216
Virgil, 233
Vreeland, D., 212

Walton, K., 302

Index of Names

Warhol, A., 261
Warnock, G. J., 284–85, 286
Weitz, M., 211, 215, 299
Whiting, H. T. A., 289
Wiggins, D., 170, 296
Williams, B. A. O., 106–11 *passim*, 291–92, 296, 297f

Wilson, D., *see* Sperber, D., and D. Wilson
Wimsatt, W. K., 220
Winograd, T., 55, 289
Wittgenstein, L., 13, 19
Wollheim, R., 302
Wolterstorff, N., 301

Library of Congress Cataloging-in-Publication Data

Human agency: language, duty, and value: philosophical essays in honor of J. O. Urmson; edited by Jonathan Dancy, J. M. E. Moravcsik, and C. C. W. Taylor.
    p.   cm.
Bibliography: p.
Includes index.
ISBN 0-8047-1474-6 (alk. paper)
    1. Knowledge, Theory of.   2. Languages—Philosophy.   3. Ethics.
4. Aesthetics.   5. Urmson, J. O.   I. Urmson, J. O.   II. Dancy, Jonathan.   III. Moravcsik, J. M. E.   IV. Taylor, C. C. W. (Christopher Charles Whiston), 1936–
B29.H85 1988   88-12306
100—dc 19   CIP